BRIDGEPORT

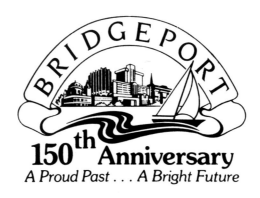

BRIDGEPORT

150th Anniversary

A Proud Past . . . A Bright Future

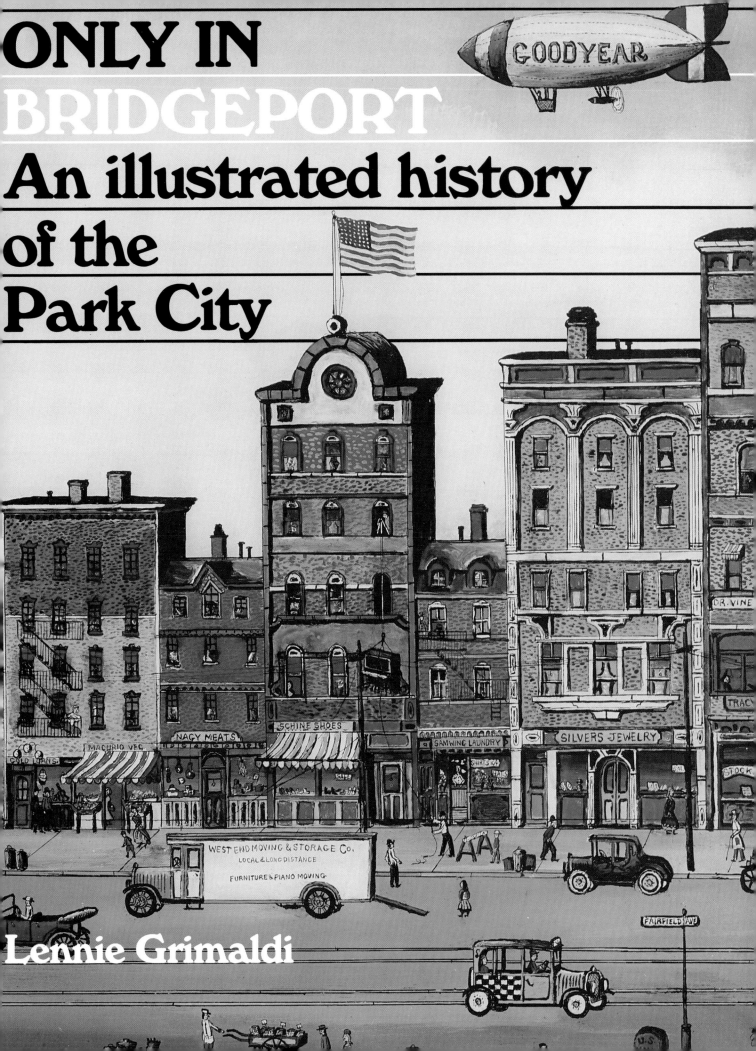

ONLY IN BRIDGEPORT

An illustrated history of the Park City

Lennie Grimaldi

Harbor Communications, Inc.
Redding, CT

Only in Bridgeport 2000: An Illustrated History of the Park City

Graphic Design Consultation: Graziano Associates, LLC, Fairfield, CT

Library of Congress Cataloging in Publication Data

Grimaldi, Lennie, 1958-
          Only in Bridgeport 2000
Copyright 2000 by Lennie Grimaldi
All Rights Reserved

Only in Bridgeport
First Edition, 1986
Second Edition, 1993

Bibliography
Includes Index
ISBN 0-9632522-2-4

Published 2000
Printed in the United States of America

Harbor Communications, Inc.
Email: harbcom@aol.com

Contents

This postcard of Pleasure Beach Park (circa 1900) best describes the once-great amusement park. The park featured a carousel, miniature train ride, Ferris wheel, roller coaster, and pool. Courtesy, Robert Clifford Collection

Foreword

My father was born in Black Rock in a house on Ellsworth Street. His uncle was a Bridgeport cop and his father worked at the Gas Company. My mother worked at Remington Arms and her father was chief custodian of Bridgeport Hospital, where I was born Easter Sunday morning in 1947.

If souls had tattoos, mine would say "made in Bridgeport." I grew up in Black Rock and went to Bassick High. After four years at Sacred Heart University I stepped out into the world to spread my wings (which, incidentally, were also made in Bridgeport).

The wings seemed to work O.K. As I write this, I'm sitting in my office at Warner Brothers Studio in Los Angeles where I am Executive Producer and Creator of a T.V. show called *Locals*. The show, as it happens, is based on characters and memories of Bridgeport. There is a guy who sits at the dump and fishes for rats. A barber who can give you any haircut you want as long as it's a crewcut. An Irish-Italian couple who run a pancake house and provide entertainment with their endless loud arguments. All true, all Bridgeport.

When I was growing up in the Park City I thought it was all normal. I was a kid, why would I think otherwise? It wasn't until I left home and started my wanderings that it hit me...hey Bridgeport is different. I'll never be able to say exactly how or reduce it to a measurable theorem, but it is. Believe me, it is.

P.T. Barnum was mayor once. Harry Houdini almost drowned in our harbor after one of Bridgeport's finest rigged a trick so it would backfire on him, (sometimes I get this nagging feeling that cop was a relative of mine). Speaking of cops, where else could a local police chief, under investigation by the F.B.I., turn a sting operation around and arrest the F.B.I. informant on bribery charges? Only in Bridgeport.

Over the years I've drawn from Bridgeport quite a bit. In 1971 I went to London, England to visit for what I thought would be 3 weeks; 10 years later I was still there.

The first two years were the toughest. I lived in an abandoned building and had to improvise such necessities as a stove for heat and cooking, and part of a roof for shelter. The skills and tenacity that got me through came from an inherited Polish-Hungarian immigrant resolve mixed liberally with a certain Bridgeport attitude that, most gently, can be described as "Don't *mess* with me." I've always felt that if I'd grown up anywhere else, like Westport for instance, I would have come whining home after a couple of months because the English don't serve water in a restaurant unless you ask for it.

My return to the U.S. landed me in Los Angeles where, shortly after, I auditioned for a television series called *Cheers*. I failed the audition miserably and was being escorted to the door by the casting director when I sidestepped his helpful out-the-door arm and asked the producers if they had a bar know-it-all. Their furrowed brows told me they had no idea what I was talking about so I launched into a short improvised version of the bar side windbag so common in the gin mills of Bridgeport. In fact I had a certain windbag in mind but can never tell who it is because he thinks it's based on someone else. The producers laughed, I got the job and Cliff Clavin was born to annoy the folks at *Cheers* for eleven glorious years.

Whatever the next 10 years has in store is anybody's guess. But whatever or wherever I'll always raise my glass to a rough hewn jewel on the Connecticut coast. Thank you Bridgeport, I couldn't have done it without you.

John Ratzenberger

Bassick Class of '65

For
Dad, Mom, Julie
and
The Captain

Isaac Sherman, Jr., Bridgeport's first mayor, symbolizes the city's birth and the period that launched Bridgeport's rise as a major city. Sherman owned a lucrative saddlery business during his days as mayor, but twelve years after he left office he died bankrupt. Courtesy, Historical Collections, Bridgeport Public Library

CHAPTER I

The Birth of Bridgeport

"We do most solemnly protest against this resolve (the formation of the town of Bridgeport)."

—Enoch Foote, town moderator, June 11, 1821

Isaac Sherman, Jr., had a lot to think about on October 3, 1836. Five months earlier the Connecticut Legislature had designated Bridgeport to become a city on this day, and now, under the new charter, voters had a job to do. Bridgeporters, and Sherman—who that day would be elected the city's first mayor—were looking toward the future: toward the day when the ferocious fires that had been destroying their livelihoods would die out, and when streets would be free of garbage, carts, and animal droppings. Sidewalks would be repaired and the city's harbor would be dredged to make way for larger vessels sailing to and from the West Indies and nearer East coast ports. The improvements, though needed, would be costly. It was an earlier time of taxpayer grumbling. Sherman was determined that he would be the one to keep the city going in the right direction.

The city's first day was biting cold, much too cold for Sherman to be out walking. But he was a politician and he wasn't about to miss the chance to be seen by the voters in his best top hat and black satin bow tie. He stepped outside his frame house at the corner of Division and Beaver streets—now one of the city's busiest intersections at Park and Fairfield avenues—and brooded.

Sherman broke off from his thoughts. Standing on his front steps while the city went out to vote wasn't going to get him elected. As he approached the schoolhouse to cast his vote, he waved to well-wishers and went inside. It wouldn't be until ten o'clock that night that he would make Bridgeport history as the city's first mayor.

But within a year—at the end of his first and only term—Sherman was back in his saddlery business. He left Bridgeport politics, disillusioned by the bureaucratic red tape that kept him from achieving the great things he had in mind on that cold October day. Twelve years later, bankrupt and debt-ridden, he died of cholera in Freeport, Illinois.

Though Sherman's precedent-setting position leaves him known only to present-day trivia buffs, never to be included among prominent Bridgeporters like P.T. Barnum and Jasper McLevy, he became a symbol of the city's birth and of the period that catapulted Bridgeport's rise as a big city—the period of the harbor and the railroad.

*   *   *

Years before even a settlement existed at what would later become Bridgeport, the land was a fertile plain of loamy soil bounded by vast bodies of water, which would later serve to transport Indian-chasing settlers.

Over 200 years before Isaac Sherman, Jr., died, his colonial descendants discovered a village of 500 Pequonnock Indians, who took their name from the "clear fields" where they had settled and farmed years earlier. The area's reservoir of resources—thick forests, abundant fish and wildlife, a mild climate, and waterways such as the Pequonnock River—had drawn the Pequonnock tribe from their northern locations.

The Pequonnock was one of five tribes of the Paugussett nation—a group of blood-related tribes that once controlled much of the southwestern part of Connecticut. In 1637 English colonists met the Pequonnock tribe for the first time in the Pequot War, a conflict caused by the Indians' trading problems with the English and Dutch. The war, fought near the Mystic River along the state's eastern shore, killed hundreds in the tribe and brought a bloody end to the Pequot's power, forcing the tribe to flee westward. A group of Pequot refugees reached what later would become Stratford and were joined by a number of Pequonnock Indians who aided them against the colonists in a later battle. It was while the colonists were pursuing the tribes that the colonists became aware of the excellent areas for settlement along the Connecticut coast.

The tribes flourished in the warmer southern New England climate. Roasted, boiled, and fresh corn dominated the Indian diet. They braided the husks into mats for sleeping or covering houses, and used cobs for scrubbing. The Indians ate a wide range of animals killed by bow and arrow, and trapped, snared, and hunted in communal drives.

Skins and feathers were used for clothing and decoration, and as tools. They ate fresh and saltwater fish caught in weirs strung across streams or speared from shore or from canoes. For the winter months, corn was dried and buried in pits in woven sacks or baskets. Even fish and shellfish caught in times of abundance were dried for use in other seasons. Indians drank only water until the colonists introduced them to corn whiskey.

Indian settlements were always near cornfields or fishing, hunting, and gathering areas. A typical home was a dome-shaped wigwam made by planting a circle of flexible poles into the ground and bending the tops together to form a dome-like frame. It was then covered with bark, hides, or woven mats, leaving a doorway and rooftop smoke hole. Simple furniture, mats, skins, woven items, and a few wooden bowls and spoons filled the wigwam.

Not everything went smoothly for the Indians during this relatively quiet period. The

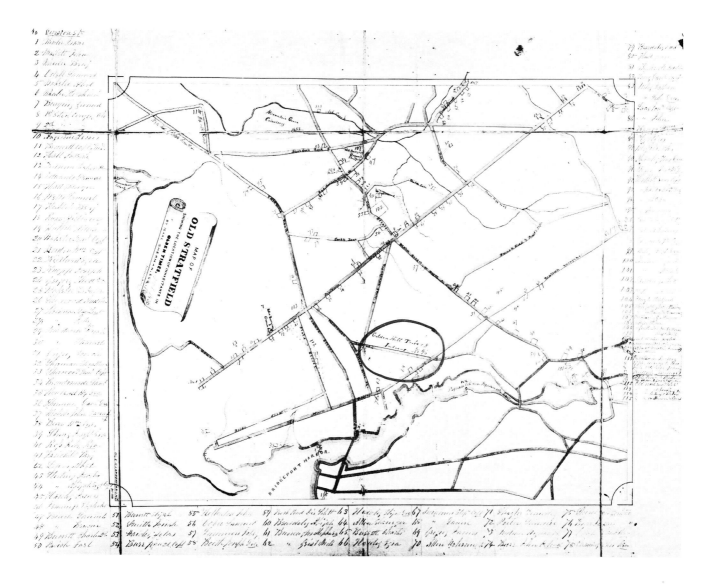

This map of Stratfield highlights the eighty-acre reservation of the Golden Hill Indians, which sprawled along present-day Washington Avenue. The first such reservation established in Connecticut, the General Assembly ordered the Indians to the land in 1659. Courtesy, Historical Collections, Bridgeport Public Library

The main attraction at Captain's Cove Seaport is the
H.M.S. Rose. *The original* Rose *was built in England in
1756 for the seven-year war with France and Spain.*
Photo by Neil Swanson

lack of a common language between the tribes made it difficult for them to form solid bonds, and left room for a great deal of animosity. The strong tribes dominated the weak and entered into loose alliances to strengthen themselves against enemies.

The arrival of white men from Massachusetts settlements reinforced the inter-tribal rivalry rather than promoting mutual support. In fact, the Indians greatly outnumbered the colonists for a few years, and, had they joined forces, they could have driven them out of the area. But the colonists exploited the rivalries, playing tribes off against each other, weakening the Indian power and halting the threat to white settlement in Connecticut. This "divide and conquer" policy throughout the years drove the Indians farther westward.

In the meantime, upstate colonists were watching the southwestern part of the state with great interest. In 1639, the General Assembly commissioned Connecticut's Deputy Governor Roger Ludlowe to establish the settlement of Pequonnock, to include the lands east of the Uncoway River (what is now Ash Creek), and extend as far north as King's Highway and as far south as Long Island Sound.

But Ludlowe, an enterprising colonist, never made it. As he and four other pioneers headed south with their livestock, they heard that some competing settlers were planning a plantation west of the Pequonnock area. Ludlowe took claim to the land before they did and promptly settled the village of Uncoway, which would be known as Fairfield by the following year.

"Some others intended to take up said place who had not acquainted the court with their purpose," Ludlowe told the General Court in October 1639 by way of explanation—or apology. The court reprimanded Ludlowe, and a committee headed by Governor John Haynes traveled to Pequonnock and Uncoway to investigate.

Pequonnock was settled by other colonists after Ludlowe's diversion to Uncoway, and the governor administered an oath of fidelity to the Pequonnock planters. He ordered them to send one or two deputies to the next General Court for instruction in the formation of their own local court. Haynes and Ludlowe were ordered by the General Court to determine the boundaries between Pequonnock and Uncoway.

* * *

Ludlowe enjoyed Uncoway so much that he stayed around as part of a four-man team "to execute justice there as cause shall require," which sometimes meant hanging anyone he deemed a witch. Witch hangings were by no means a daily occurrence, but they did happen from time to time when superstitious townspeople found a woman bearing "witch signs," sometimes nothing more than a birthmark, mole, freckle, or scar. To avoid suspicion, many women covered anything that might invite a noose fitting.

In 1653, settlers came from miles around to attend the hanging of Fairfield's Goody Knapp, a suspected witch whom one historian described as nothing more than a simple-minded woman. (*Goody* and *Goodwife* were terms indicating a rank of social stature granted to the common woman of the time.) The testimony of Goody Odell, a midwife who examined Knapp and reportedly spotted "witch marks," sealed the poor woman's fate. The beginning of the end was a "confession" by convicted Stratford witch Goody Basset who, before her death, suggested "others who hold their heads full high" were no different than she. This confirmed colonists' belief that other witches abounded.

The hysterical Knapp refused to confess but was given a speedy trial and declared guilty by Ludlowe. She was executed just northwest of an Indian field, now the site of the Burroughs Home at 2470 Fairfield Avenue. Many women crowded around her body when it was cut

In 1653, settlers came from miles around to witness the hanging of Goody Knapp. Settler Roger Ludlowe declared Knapp a witch based on the testimony of another woman who was declared a witch. Illustration by Don Almquist. Courtesy, Historical Collections, Bridgeport Public Library

down from the gallows, anxious to peek at the witch signs. A friend of the deceased, Goodwife Staples, shook her head and said, "They were naught but such as she herself or any woman had." At that remark, another woman countered, "Aye, and be hanged for them, and deserve it too."

Goodwife Staples' tongue nearly dug her own grave as Ludlowe accused her of being a witch. But her infuriated husband sued Ludlowe on behalf of his wife for defamation of character. Staples won the suit, his wife won acquittal, and Ludlowe left the colonies forever.

* * *

Ludlowe's departure caused him to miss much of the newlywed period between the Indians and the white settlers—a time when both realized they were stuck with each other and resolved to make the best of it. Nevertheless, curiosity and distrust remained between the two groups.

Country Road and King's Highway, the same North and Boston avenues now traveled by thousands every day, were Indian trails that joined Fairfield and Stratford. The first house built between those towns was owned by Thomas Wheeler at Black Rock Harbor in 1644. Wheeler was so concerned about the possibility of an Indian uprising that he built a small fort by his house and equipped it with two guns aimed at the harbor and the Indians.

But forts such as Wheeler's didn't always keep the Indians at a respectful distance. They were being caught in a squeeze between the expanding settlements of Fairfield, to the west, and Stratford, to the east. Because many Indians had an intense desire to learn more about the white man, it wasn't uncommon for a settler to look up from his chores and find an Indian peering right back at him. But before any major disruptions between the two groups occurred, the General Assembly in 1659 ruled that Stratford's parcel of land known as Golden Hill (that lay within the Pequonnock area) should be given to the Indians. The eighty-acre parcel today lies within Bridgeport on Washington Avenue, and was the first such reservation established in Connecticut.

Since Stratford was ordered to hand over

property to the Indians, the court also ruled that Fairfield should compensate its neighbor with $100 worth of beef, pork, wheat, and peas. In return for the reservation, the Indians promised never to steal any cattle, corn, or peas, and to maintain their fences so cattle wouldn't break through to destroy settlers' crops.

To keep the peace, settlers were forbidden to sell arms, ammunition, liquor, horses, or boats to Indians. Indians were forbidden to enter the settlers' houses or handle their firearms. Any Indians prowling near settlers' homes after dark could be shot.

Regardless of the new rules, by the early 1700s all of the tribes in the Paugussett nation had been disturbed enough by contact with white men to move west. The remaining Golden Hill Indians complained to the General Assembly about losing parts of their reservation through white encroachment and illegal land sales. To compensate, the court granted the Indians a supplemental land parcel on Corum Hill, in Huntington, Connecticut. But white settlers continued to move into the Golden Hill area, driving out the Indians. In 1769, with but a few wigwams remaining, settlers invaded the reservation, claimed all but six acres, and forced out every Indian by tearing apart their wigwams. Town authorities took no action.

In 1854 the tribe bought a twenty-acre reservation in Trumbull and for the next 100-plus years battled in court to retain their land. In June 1979 the tribe purchased a sixty-nine-acre strip in upstate Colchester—an effort to maintain a natural environment incorporating riding trails, timber management efforts, and wildlife habitats as federal and state authorities stepped up protection to the Indians and their property. The present-day history buff would be hard-pressed to find concrete remains of the Indians' life in Bridgeport. But while few Indian relics may be unearthed between the high-rise buildings and paved roads, the Indians' legacy survives in names such as the Housatonic and Pequonnock rivers, Golden Hill Street, and Chopsy Hill, named after an Indian whose wigwam stood in that North End area.

* * *

From the mid-1600s to the pre-Revolutionary War period, the Bridgeport area became a prosperous farming community, resplendent with cornfields and occasionally visited by foreign vessels carrying cargoes of livestock and wheat. The settlers lived in unpainted oak clapboard houses with sloping roofs. Many of the men engaged in agriculture or seafaring trades; others were millers, blacksmiths, and tanners. Besides churches and a schoolhouse, the only other public building was a tavern on the site of present-day 2354 North Avenue. Legend alleges that General George Washington stopped off at the tavern in 1775 while on his way to Boston to take charge of the Continental Army.

Pequonnock underwent several name changes between 1694 and its designation as Bridgeport borough in 1800. In 1694 it became Fairfield Village; in 1701, Stratfield; and in 1798, Newfield. The first was prompted by the formation of a school. In 1694, while part of the settlement was still owned by Fairfield, many citizens complained to the General Court that the four miles their children had to travel to attend school in the center of Fairfield was much too far. In response, the court allowed the citizens to establish a school and the settlement became known as Fairfield Village. Residents took on all educational expenses for the forty-seven students and separated themselves from the Fairfield educational system. At the same time, the settlers also engaged their own minister and were allowed to set up their own local government. Seven years later, in 1701, the village became Stratfield, and a road, now State Street, was built through Stratfield to the Pequonnock Harbor, opening up a route between Fairfield and Stratford along the shore.

The residents of Stratfield during the American Revolution were far removed from the battles. Stratfield was still a quiet farming community considered too small for plunder. A few local settlers fought in the war, such as Captain Thaddeus Bennett, a shoemaker and farmer, and Nathaniel Fayerweather, also a farmer. One resident, Dr. Lyman Hall, a minister ordained in Stratfield in 1749, went on to become one of the signers of the Declaration of Independence. But the majority stayed close to home to tend their families and properties.

The Revolutionary War period brought growth for the village of Stratfield. From the close of the war, a whole new community sprouted—including a public ferry, the first bridge, and a newspaper. Stratfield became Newfield, and was formally recognized in 1798 by the Connecticut General Assembly upon maintaining a fire engine company. Nevertheless the village of Newfield still belonged to Stratford.

Two years later, the General Assembly incorporated Newfield as a separate borough, making it the state's first borough, and giving residents their first degree of independence from the larger community of Stratford. The area was declared the Borough of Bridgeport—taking its name from the old Lottery Bridge that connected it to Stratford. The borough was given the responsibility of caring for its own streets, and was granted most of the privileges extended to towns, except representation in the General Assembly and the right to vote in their own borough. To vote, residents still had to travel the five miles to Stratford.

Bridgeport borough, with its wealth of foreign and coastal sea trade, began a period of remarkable growth. A census of the borough in 1810 counted 1,089 residents, two churches, 123 houses, and eighteen sailing vessels engaged in trade with the West Indies. Exports included livestock, wheat and rye flour, Indian meal, corn, oats, pork, butter, and cider. Manufactured articles included beaver hats, rope, saddles, boots and shoes, cabinetwork, and

Isaac Sherman, Sr., uncle to Bridgeport's first mayor, invested money in a saltworks that pumped saltwater from the Pequonnock River into vats using a windmill near the bank. Courtesy, Historical Collections, Bridgeport Public Library

carriages. There were two tanneries, three printing offices, two weekly newspapers, one pottery, and forty-three stores.

But the War of 1812 brought all that economic activity and progress to a halt. Few ships left the relative safety of the Pequonnock River for fear of being seized by the British. Blockades by British ships made necessities, such as flour, a luxury. But several townspeople—who saw the war as an inconvenience because it interfered with shipping—rowed a small boat to New York City to get a fresh supply of flour. The British fired on them but missed, and became so infuriated that they fired on Grover's Hill, a military detachment in Black Rock.

On February 22, 1815, news of the peace between Great Britain and America launched a parade of events in Bridgeport that included cannon firing, bell ringing, and a ball at Knapp's Hotel at Wall and Water streets.

The war's aftermath left a massive salt shortage and many communities learned to make their own. Isaac Sherman, Sr., uncle to Bridgeport's first mayor, invested money in a saltworks located north of Gold Street and west of the present Congress and Water streets. At the works, saltwater was pumped from the harbor into vats by a windmill near the bank. Bridgeporters used homemade salt for many years, but the undertaking was unprofitable and dried up due to one major fault: the salt works was located near the river and the harbor water was too diluted with fresh water from the river's tributaries.

Soon, Bridgeport became financially sound again, perhaps too sound for some. The borough's saddlery and carriage industry and West Indies trade had started to boom, and Stratford's influential citizens feared that Bridgeport's economic strength would some day give it the balance of power. So Stratford unceremoniously dumped Bridgeport from under its control, and despite violent protests from its residents, Bridgeport borough became a town in 1821.

* * *

"We do most solemnly protest against this resolve," said town moderator Enoch Foote in

Bridgeport's transportation in the late 1800s included horse-drawn trolleys such as the one shown here on Main Street heading toward Seaside Park. Courtesy, Historical Collections, Bridgeport Public Library

1821 during the first official town meeting. Renegade Bridgeporters complained bitterly to the General Assembly that they were "deprived of their lawful name as town (Stratford) and have another imposed upon them all without their consent."

They claimed the lines of division were unjust as they were getting but one-fourth of the actual territory of Stratford. Bridgeport now had a seacoast of less than 1,000 feet, while Stratford had five miles on the coast and ten miles on the Housatonic River. And Stratford received half of Bridgeport's harbor while it unjustly divided the lands so three-fourths of the bridges (and their upkeep expenses) were in Bridgeport. Park Avenue remained the western boundary of the city until 1870 when the state legislature extended it to include the portion of Fairfield lying east of Ash Creek.

Meanwhile, as Bridgeport carried on in its cramped surroundings, its citizens soured on the town's form of government and decided that it needed all the privileges of an incorporated city, including the power to borrow money to build a railroad. A petition of incorporation was approved in May 1836 to take effect the following October, and the city's boundaries were enlarged so that the eastern line was extended to Yellow Mill Creek to include what would later become East Bridgeport.

Though Bridgeporters were still harboring bad memories of Stratford cutting them loose, the city was considered a thriving community and showed potential as an industrial center, confirming Stratford's earlier fears. Some waterfront businessmen owned their own wharves and small boats, and sailed between Bridgeport and New York and sometimes Boston. Stores of every kind filled downtown, including shops advertising women's shawls from Paris, and specialty shops dealing exclusively in hats, clothes, and hand-sewn boots.

But one thing was missing: a railroad. The world's newest and fastest way to travel had so far eluded the residents and merchants of

The first trains of the Housatonic Railroad Company steamed into Bridgeport Harbor in 1840 and were of great importance to the busy commercial area. These trains handled freight arriving by ship from the West Indies and more local ports such as New York, Boston, and Baltimore. Oyster and whaling boats used the harbor as well. Courtesy, Historical Collections, Bridgeport Public Library

Bridgeport and luring it to the area became the chief reason for the city's incorporation. Progressive Bridgeporters were anxious for a rail line into Bridgeport to carry on trade that had never before been possible, and knew that incorporation would give them the authority to borrow money to build a line.

In March 1837, just five months after its incorporation, Bridgeport passed a resolution pledging aid to the Housatonic Railroad Company. The state legislature had earlier granted incorporation papers to Enoch Foote, William Peete, and W.C. Sterling of Bridgeport, allowing them to form the railroad company and grant a charter with permission to build a line into Bridgeport. The railroad had been connected from Boston to Albany with a Connecticut line to New Milford. Alfred Bishop, a Danbury native who tired of farming in New Jersey, settled in Bridgeport and became president of the Housatonic, and the most persistent figure in the drive to locate a terminal of the Housatonic Railroad in the city. Bishop and company built the line from the Massachusetts border, just south of Sheffield, to New Milford, Connecticut, and south into Bridgeport.

Work on the railroad began in July 1837, and in less than three years, chiming church bells and thundering cannons ushered in the first railroad steam engine.

Train travelers suffered many inconveniences in the early days of the railroad. Sometimes the weight of a passing train would force track spikes to pop up and poke through the train floor. Railroad employees wielding sledge hammers would watch the track for stray spikes, and would drive them back into the rail if they spotted one sticking up. The wood-burning engines sprayed sparks over the passengers, and fires were frequent. The traveling coaches were hard and uncomfortable and springs were scarce.

Stopping, with the use of a hand or foot brake, was not easy. Sometimes when the train reached the station, several strong porters

Alfred Bishop settled in Bridgeport and became a major force in attracting the Housatonic Railroad to the city. Courtesy, Historical Collections, Bridgeport Public Library

seized the end of the train and heaved while the station agent thrust sticks of wood through the wheel spokes. Locomotives often broke down and horses and oxen were hired to drag the cars to the nearest station and repair shop. Accidents were frequent. Bridgeport had street-level tracks, and several pedestrian fatalities occurred until the tracks were elevated onto the present viaduct system around 1900.

The railroad and the harbor transformed the city into a great industrial center. Though much hullabaloo was made of the railroad, the harbor and seafaring trades were of equal importance to Bridgeport's evolution. In 1836, numerous vessels sailed between Bridgeport and New York, Boston, Baltimore, and the West Indies. Several whaling companies were formed, including the Bridgeport Whaling Company, which had four boats proclaiming the "prosecution of whale and other fisheries in the Atlantic and Pacific Oceans." Whaling expeditions sometimes lasted two years with a net capture of thirty to forty whales. Spectacular crowds assembled at the water's edge to welcome mariners home from their voyages—voyages that sometimes left many men at sea.

During the port's early days, a store and wharf were built by Philip Nichols at one end of Pembroke Street, and just before the American Revolution, sea-going cargo was handled on the west side of the harbor at the mouth of the Newfield Harbor.

It wasn't until the work of harbormaster Captain John McNeil, years later, that Bridgeport's harbors became revered throughout the East Coast. In 1846 Captain John Brooks, Charles Middlebrooks, and Charles Rockwell, officers of the steamboat *Nimrod,* asked if their steamer could enter the harbor over the outer bar at night, something that was not normally done. Since the channel was sixty feet in width at low tide, determining the exact location of the channel during darkness was crucial and delays would inconvenience passengers who had to connect with the Housatonic train for Albany. Abraham A. McNeil (the future harbormaster's father) had the idea to position a small rowboat with a mast bearing a signal light off the outer bar. The steamer advancing to port followed the light for direction, and Bridgeport's first lighthouse became operational. But many crucial improvements still had to be completed before large crafts could enter the harbor.

In 1888 John McNeil asked the Army Corps of Engineers for money to widen the harbor channel as far as Black Rock and Cedar Creek so manufacturers could bring their freight to within a few yards of their factories instead of carting it the two to three miles from Bridgeport's East Side. The request was approved, and the work was done at the expense of the Beardsley Dredging Company, which reim-

bursed itself by selling the dredged gravel to owners of oyster grounds. About 100,000 cubic yards of gravel were excavated.

McNeil then planned construction of a breakwater to extend from near the point of Welles Tongue (near the current United Illuminating Company plant) to the inner beacon, with as large an area of the north dredged as needed to supply protection for all crafts against storms. It would also afford crafts of all classes a harbor out of the way of incoming and outgoing vessels.

The plan fostered a large oyster industry, yielding $350,000 to $400,000 per year, of which $60,000 reached the coffers of local merchants. Construction of the breakwater also saved many shoreside property owners from damaging winds and crashing waves. Steamers moored safely at docks in the mouth of the lower bay.

Bridgeport's old railroad depot on Water Street, circa 1890. Elevation of the tracks in 1900 onto the present viaduct system brought an end to the many pedestrian fatalities and injuries. Courtesy, Historical Collections, Bridgeport Public Library

Above: *In January 1893, hundreds of Bridgeporters journeyed on ice to the Bridgeport lighthouse when the harbor froze solid. This lighthouse, built in 1871, replaced an earlier effort—a small rowboat with a mast bearing a signal light. Courtesy, Historical Collections, Bridgeport Public Library*

Above right: *This view of East Bridgeport and the harbor, from the roof of the Security Building in 1905, shows the industrial growth during the early 1900s. The many smokestacks and ships in the harbor are evidence of this period of rapid growth. Courtesy, Historical Collections, Bridgeport Public Library*

McNeil widened and deepened the harbor, raised beacons, and installed lighthouses regarded as some of the best equipped and maintained in Long Island Sound. The lighthouse at Penfield Reef was described by McNeil as the "key" to navigating Bridgeport harbor for vessels bound from New York. Bridgeport harbor became one of the finest on the Atlantic coast—annual water-borne commerce reached more than one million tons by the 1890s.

*　　*　　*

While Bridgeporters adjusted to the beginning of the city's industrial revolution, some farsighted entrepreneurs—such as Phineas Taylor Barnum and General William H. Noble—began to take advantage of its potential for growth. Most of the eastern side of Bridgeport (actually still within Stratford's boundaries at the time) was owned by General Noble, a wealthy land developer who bought the land from Stratford and planned to subdivide it and build streets. Barnum bought 700 acres at $200 each from Noble and together they laid out Washington Park and presented it to the city. The park is still located on Washington Avenue.

Barnum went on to create an innovative financing plan for residents who could not afford to buy outright their own homes. His project encouraged people to make payments on a house and lot and secure ownership at the expiration of the payments. The plan helped develop the city, and brought new residents and the first industrial establishments to the area.

One company Barnum's plan attracted was owned by Elias Howe, the inventor of the first working sewing machine which he manufactured in a factory built at Howe and Kossuth streets in 1863. Factories joining Howe's included the Wheeler and Wilson Sewing Machine Company, The Bridgeport Brass Company, the Warner Brothers Company, the Bullard Company, the Bridgeport Machine Tool Company, and the Southern New England Telephone Company.

Bridgeport banking, begun in 1806, flourished from the economic expansion and Bridgeport's status attracted some big-name politicians. In 1860 Abraham Lincoln addressed a large crowd in Washington Hall during a campaign visit and reportedly tasted his first fried oyster dinner at the Bridgeport home of Frederick Wood. In 1864 President Lincoln's call to arms during the Civil War effort drew an overwhelming re-

sponse as seven regiment companies were organized in Bridgeport.

In the mid-to-late-1800s fires destroyed numerous buildings and upset years of planning. On December 12, 1845, a midnight blaze in George Well's oyster saloon on Bank Street changed the course of the city's business section, forcing an overnight move from Water Street to the present downtown district on Main Street. The fire engulfed Bridgeport at a vulnerable time—low tide—when pipes from fire engines filled with mud as fire fighters tried to pump water from the river.

When it was over, half the downtown area was burnt to the ground, including 800 barrels

The work of Bridgeport harbormaster Captain John McNeil initiated harbor development, including a breakwater to supply protection for all crafts, such as the steamer Doris, *shown here in 1893. Courtesy, Historical Collections, Bridgeport Public Library*

Left: *Elias Howe, Jr., the inventor of the first working sewing machine, made his machines in a factory at Howe and Kossuth streets. P.T. Barnum lured Howe to the city during Barnum's development of East Bridgeport. Courtesy, Historical Collections, Bridgeport Public Library*

Right: *Sewing machine partners Nathaniel Wheeler and Allen Wilson left Middletown, Connecticut, to occupy a building (shown here in 1890) on East Washington Avenue in 1856. Wheeler and Wilson earned credit for making the sewing machine a commercial success by reducing the cost of its manufacture. Courtesy, Historical Collections, Bridgeport Public Library*

Below: *Elias Howe, Jr., successfully defended his 1845 sewing machine design against patent infringers, and twenty years later began production in this large building at Howe and Kossuth streets, which had a dock for shipping the machines to New York buyers. Courtesy, Historical Collections, Bridgeport Public Library*

Above: *The Fairfield County Courthouse (as seen from the roof of the Security Building in 1905) was built in 1888, to replace the original courthouse, now McLevy Hall, built in 1853-54. Courtesy, Historical Collections, Bridgeport Public Library*

Below: *On December 12, 1845, a midnight blaze in a saloon on Bank Street destroyed half of the Water Street downtown area, as this outline shows. The business district was forced to be moved to the present downtown district on Main Street. Courtesy, Historical Collections, Bridgeport Public Library*

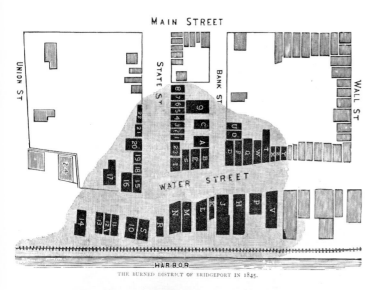

of flour, 100 barrels of mackerel, and great quantities of leather goods, groceries, meats, carpets, and clothing. Forty-nine buildings were destroyed and forty families were left penniless. After losses were totaled, Water Street merchants moved to Main Street for a new start.

One of the city's most gruesome blazes began in a hat factory on Crescent Avenue on June 8, 1877. Eleven people died in the fire, and editorials in the *New Haven Palladium,* the *New York Tribune,* and the *New York World* denounced Bridgeport's negligence in not providing an adequate water supply for fire emergencies. Another fire, six years later, gutted Elias Howe's sewing machine factory, crippling the company financially although production continued for many more years.

Despite fires, deaths, and crushed businesses, Bridgeport again rebuilt itself into a bustling city with the aid of Irish residents who had first begun immigrating following the potato famines of the 1840s. By 1850 about one out of seven Bridgeport residents had been born in Ireland.

Bridgeport's industrial growth during this period was followed by geographic growth as well. With a population nearing 20,000 in 1870, the West End and Black Rock were annexed from Fairfield. In 1889 Bridgeport reached its present bounds when the East End and West Stratford were annexed. A railroad, a renewed harbor, and geographic extension came in handy for Bridgeport's next stage—the tide of immigration.

*Large stores such as Dorsen's "Modern Department Store" did
a booming business on Main Street in 1915. Courtesy, Historical Collections, Bridgeport Public Library*

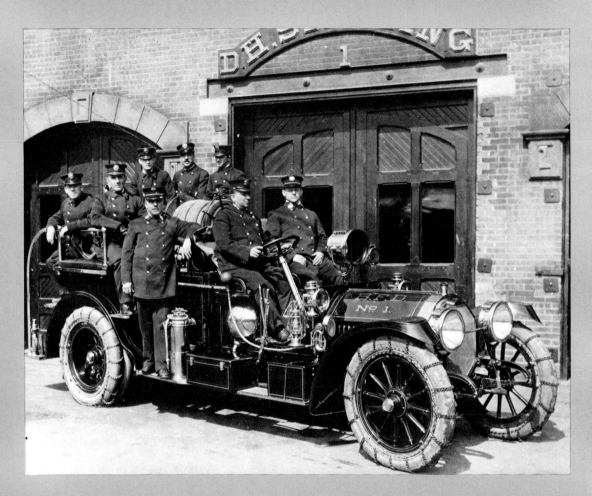

The administration of Clifford B. Wilson, lasting from 1911 to 1921, marked a progressive period in Bridgeport. Wilson motorized the fire and police departments and paved much of the city. His administration also established school dental programs and the city's recreation department. Pictured above is the Bridgeport Fire Department's Engine Company #1, circa 1920. Courtesy, Historical Collections, Bridgeport Public Library

CHAPTER II

The

People

"Bridgeport had so many ethnic groups that the joke in Boston was, 'They don't speak English there.'"

— Charles J. Stokes,
professor of economics,
University of Bridgeport

In 1978, Tom Quach thought he had as much a chance of escaping Communist-controlled Saigon for America as he had of "flying to the moon."

"Everybody was looking for a way to leave," the native Vietnamese said. "The Communists controlled you. Things were so bad that if a lamppost could walk it would escape."

Quach is one of Bridgeport's most recent immigrants. He had worked for the Exxon Corporation in South Vietnam, but after the Viet Cong takeover things got so bad that Quach and his wife were confined to their home, their food was rationed, and many of their possessions were confiscated.

The one concession the Communists granted was mailing Quach's letters, but generally only after they were censored. Fearful of being branded a spy and arrested, Quach could not petition the government for emigration papers. He instead successfully explored transfer options with his employer, the Exxon Corporation in Paris, which provided Quach with money and food and sent him through a training program. He stayed in France for about a year until his brother, who had arrived in Bridgeport many years before, contacted Deacon Joseph Farley, director of Ethnic and Cultural Services

In the early 1900s the city's population grew by thousands. Organized labor cut the workday from twelve to eight hours, and in 1915 the city was subjected to roughly 100 strikes. These workers for the T.J. Pardy Construction Company built the famous twin theatres of Sylvester Z. Poli in 1921. Courtesy, Historical Collections, Bridgeport Public Library

for the Diocese of Bridgeport, which had recently begun a program to resettle refugees. Quach and his wife Kim arrived in Bridgeport in August 1979. His first job was as a store manager for Cumberland Farms in Bridgeport. Athough he spoke little English he swayed the store owners to hire his wife, brother, and nephew so they could operate the store as a family. He and his wife took some courses at the University of Bridgeport, saved their pennies, and with his brother chipped in to buy a house on Iranistan Avenue. They have twin girls born in Bridgeport.

Today Tom Quach works for Deacon Joseph Farley, the man who helped bring him to Bridgeport. Together they have relocated hundreds of refugees in the Bridgeport area through the Catholic Center, supplying clothes, food, and housing, and guiding them through educational programs and monitoring their progress.

"I'm an American citizen now," says Quach. "You could not understand the feeling I have, knowing a few years ago it was nothing but a dream. I want to kiss the ground when I think about it. It's a totally new life."

*   *   *

Tom Quach's story has a precedent in the tales told by thousands of immigrants and refugees who have come to Bridgeport since the 1840s to escape hunger, joblessness, or war in their home countries.

Bridgeport has undergone numerous changes in 150 years—it's been a Yankee farming community, the arms and munitions center of the country during wartime, a seaport and railway center, one of Connecticut's smallest towns, and the state's largest city. The changes were the result of the passage of time and the growth of technology, and mirrored progress in the rest of the country. Yet the one consistent factor steering these changes hasn't changed at all: Bridgeport's ethnic diversity.

"Bridgeport has had many nicknames bestowed on it throughout history," wrote Herb Geller, whose *Ethnic History* series appeared in the *Bridgeport Sunday Post* from October 1977 to February 1980. "It has been called the Park City, Industrial City, Harbor City, and even Circus City, but one name this community deserves above all is the Ethnic City."

Should a visitor be whisked around town, he or she would catch a glimpse of many of the world's cultures in eighteen square miles. As many as sixty ethnic groups have settled in Bridgeport during the past 150 years. Bridgeport today has a predominantly Italian and Irish North End, Portuguese in the Hollow, blacks on the East Side, and a Hispanic West

Patrick Coughlin, an early Irish settler in Bridgeport, set a new standard for immigrant groups arriving in Bridgeport by becoming the city's first Irish-born mayor. The new arrivals recognized that real power rested with the vote, and they were quick to register and exercise that right. Courtesy, City of Bridgeport

Side. There are Eastern Europeans, including Hungarians, Poles, Lithuanians, Ukrainians, Slovaks, Albanians, and Rumanians, recently joined by the new wave of immigrants and refugees from Cambodia, Laos, and Vietnam. The city's ethnic festivals include a St. Patrick's Day Parade, Columbus Day Parade, Puerto Rican Day Parade, and an international folk festival honoring all ethnic groups. It may be that if Bridgeport ever realized the great spirit of its cultural diversity, every day would be a Fourth of July celebration.

Bridgeport, as one of America's magnet cities, has attracted millions of starving, tired, and persecuted immigrants hopeful for a job and a new way of life. A look at Bridgeport's population trends shows the story of the foreign surge. But the statistics hardly tell the entire story behind Bridgeport's immigrants, as each face reflects deprivation, turmoil, war—and new hope.

Bridgeport Population Growth		
1830	2,800	
1840	4,570	
1850	7,560	
1860	13,299	
1870	19,835	
1880	29,148	
1890	48,868	
1900	70,996	
1910	102,054	
1920	143,555	
1930	146,716	—Immigration restrictions
1940	147,121	
1950	158,709	

*   *   *

The Irish were the first foreign group (after the English) to settle in Bridgeport, and were the most important contributors during the city's early years. Hundreds of thousands of Irish poured into the United States in the late 1840s after a blight fell upon their potato harvests. More than half the Irish people had become homeless wanderers, living on bark and berries while despair spread over their land. News of the disaster sparked a wave of sympathy, and Americans sent shiploads of food worth nearly one million dollars—a great sum in those days. But it wasn't nearly enough. Stricken Irish families fled their land in masses to the United States. Over one-and-a-half million immigrated by 1860, more than all the world had sent since 1776.

Until their great move to Bridgeport in the late 1840s, the Irish community numbered only 100 or so. But the colony was large enough

to have constructed St. James Cemetery (1829) and St. James Church (1843), the third Catholic church built in Connecticut. The Irish initially settled around Middle Street and in the South End, the two oldest parts of town. Later they filtered into the Hollow and the East Side, courtesy of the land made available by P.T. Barnum and General Noble.

The Irish influence couldn't have come at a better time for Bridgeport, a city with plans. The railroad had already been completed by the time the Irish arrived in Bridgeport, but the Irish helped to build Bridgeport's factories and aided railroad improvements, filling the industrial East's ever-mounting demand for labor.

The Irish, like many of the other ethnic groups that would follow, encountered a solid wall of prejudice and open hatred. They were given the lowest paying and most difficult jobs, and poverty was their common denominator. Nevertheless, they won admiration through their persistent hard work and warm-hearted humor. The Yankees were still—and would remain for many years to come—the financial establishment and held a solid grip on the city. Financial and business decision makers were almost always Yankees. But the Irish recognized that real power rested with the vote, something they were denied in their native land. They registered as quickly as possible. Because of their large families, they sought jobs with steady incomes, particularly in the public service areas. The Irish were cops, firemen, and teachers, and their jobs often were political appointments.

Patrick Coughlin, one of the first Irish settlers in Bridgeport, became the city's first Irish-born mayor in 1888. But it wasn't until the election of Denis Mulvihill in 1901 that the Irish gained serious political clout. Mulvihill, born in Tralee, Ireland, in 1838, personified the rise of the early immigrant. He labored as a stoker at the Wheeler and Wilson Sewing Machine Company and appealed to voters with such battle cries as, "Who made the world? Denny Mulvihill with his pick and shovel."

Such a gift of gab launched the Irish to positions of power. In the early 1900s the Irish brain of Bridgeport was Republican Town Chairman John T. King, who convinced members of the Ancient Order of Hibernains, newly ensconced on Washington Avenue, to elect Clifford B. Wilson, an English descendant, mayor. Wilson served from 1911 to 1921 and many credit him as Bridgeport's most progressive mayor of all time. Bridgeport then was a horse-and-carriage town dependent on trolley car transportation. Anticipating the arrival of the automobile, Wilson took Bridgeport out of the dirt by paving most of the city. He also motorized the police and fire departments, built the city's first emergency medical clinic,

Denis Mulvihill, known as the stoker mayor, was Bridgeport's first workingman's mayor, laboring at the Wheeler and Wilson Sewing Machine Company. "Who made the world? Denny Mulvihill with his pick and shovel," was his rallying cry. Courtesy, City of Bridgeport

instituted dental programs in schools, developed Seaside Park, and established the city's Recreation Department.

One of the great Irish contributions to Bridgeport is St. Vincent's Hospital, organized by the Irish clergy in 1905 and staffed mostly by Irish-American doctors and nurses. The Irish also made a major contribution to Bridgeport's nightlife district, what Richard Howell, a reporter at the long-gone *Bridgeport Herald*, called "Bohemia," because city residents would wander in and out of the piano and fiddler music halls. At the turn of the century these establishments lined Middle and Water streets. Bill Sheridan was noted for his Black and Tan saloon, in which both blacks and whites congregated. The Alhambra Music Hall was run by Jimmy McNally, where Bert Green, one of the first ragtime pianists, performed. Morris

Above: *By the turn of the century, Bridgeport's electric trolley system began replacing the city's horse-drawn variety, and personified growth and modernization. Bridgeport's greater work force and factories had created the need for newer transportation. Courtesy, Historical Collections, Bridgeport Public Library*

Facing page: *The trusty Bridgeport Department of Public Works, two of its workers shown here in 1917 at Clinton and Fairfield avenues, was prepared for practically all sanitation emergencies. Photo by Lew Corbit, Sr. Courtesy, Historical Collections, Bridgeport Public Library*

King and Tom Tobin owned the Star Cafe, and George "Needles" Downing ran the Tremont Hotel (for a time the home of ex-bare knuckles champion John L. Sullivan).

Howell wrote that Water Street watering hole faithfuls would sometimes walk across the street and drop off the dock. "Some were fished out and some drifted out with the tide into Long Island Sound, never to be heard of again."

The Irish maintained a numerical leadership among all immigrant groups in Bridgeport for six decades (until about 1920, when the Italians surpassed them). By World War I, Bridgeport had become home to numerous other ethnic groups, including Germans, Lithuanians, Hungarians, and Poles. The immigrants had nothing more than enough money to reach Bridgeport, where they found little in the way of family and social services.

But work was their salvation and work they did. The firearm, brass, electrical, valve, and machine tool industries which catapulted Bridgeport to economic prominence were dependent largely on the labor of these ethnic groups. But practically every new group was subjected to cruel treatment due to their naivete and ignorance of the English language (particularly the German population, one of the city's leading ethnic groups). Often Ital-

Above: "Bohemia" is how newspaperman Richard Howell described Bridgeport saloons because people would wander in and out of the watering holes along Middle and Water streets, Bridgeport's nightlife district at the turn of the century. Courtesy, Robert Clifford Collection

Below: The Remington Arms plant, Bridgeport's massive anchor of the Arsenal of Democracy, was the largest factory complex in the United States. This photo, shot from Boston Avenue, shows the complex under construction in 1915. Photo by Lew Corbit, Sr. Courtesy, Historical Collections, Bridgeport Public Library

ians were victimized by the *padrone and barracks* system. On the promise that they would receive jobs, they were offered cramped housing in old carriage shops, which featured deplorable sanitary conditions and provisions at exorbitant prices. Special agents from the Department of Labor closed down such an operation in January 1900 at an old shop on Railroad Avenue, adjoining the Barnum & Bailey Circus winter headquarters.

Economic prosperity came to Bridgeport during the war years, sparked by the 1915 construction of the Remington Arms Company, which was born out of the Union Metallic Cartridge Company plant established in Bridgeport in 1867. When war broke out, the U.S. government capitalized on the arms plant and Bridgeport's labor force, which in less than a year built thirteen interconnected, five-story buildings on Boston Avenue and Bond Street. It became the largest single factory in the country, occupying 77.6 acres and covering 1,680,000 square feet. The Browning machine gun and Colt automatic pistol were manufactured at Remington Arms, which produced seven million rounds of ammunition a week, two-thirds of all ammunition produced in the United States for the allied forces. More than 20,000 people worked in the plant and Bridge-

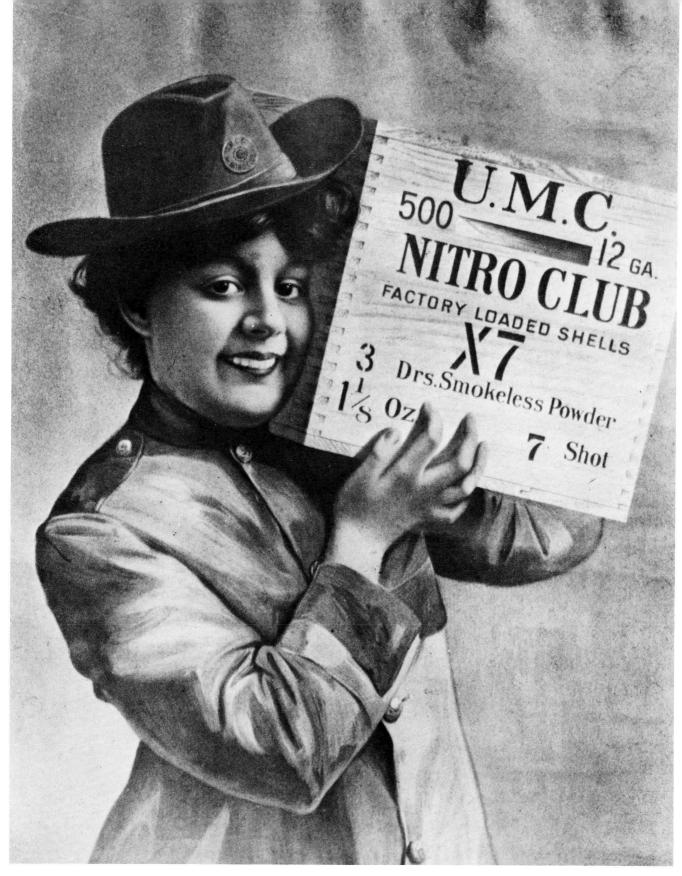

The Union Metallic Cartridge Company, established in 1867, packed quite a wallop. When World War I broke out, the United States government capitalized on Bridgeport's labor force and backed the construction of the Remington Arms Company, which was born out of Union Metallic. Courtesy, Robert Clifford Collection

The legendary, and kindly, Charles "Charlie the Bum" DiStasio was as much a part of the Bridgeport landscape as Seaside Park. Long before homelessness was highlighted as a national concern, Charlie the Bum, as he was affectionately known, was an accomplished violinist and mandolin player whose personal tragedies led him into a life in the streets. To those who knew him, this son of Neapolitan immigrants will always be in their hearts. Ed Brinsko, the brilliant photographer, captured the normally camera shy Charlie in 1963. Charlie died in 1965.

port became known as the Arsenal of Democracy of the industrial world.

Bridgeport's ethnic groups supported the war with an outburst of patriotism. But Bridgeport also suffered the pains of rapid growth. While tens of thousands flocked to Bridgeport for work, the city was the main target of labor's drive to go from a twelve- to an eight-hour work day. Roughly 100 strikes marred the city during the summer of 1915, with immigrant groups leading the revolt. The war boom caused a critical housing shortage, and the government pressed attics and basements into service. The Bridgeport Chamber of Commerce, established in 1915 from the Board of Trade (1876), organized the Bridgeport Housing Company, which built a series of war workers' housing projects. The U.S. Housing Corporation built 470 single- and multiple-family dwellings in Bridgeport, and created a local innovation: the one-family attached row house. Higher tax rates, increased property valuations, and growing bond issues were needed to finance additional schools, street lighting, police and fire protection, and expanded city services such as trolley lines to factories.

The great prosperity that propelled Bridgeport through the war years collapsed after the conflict ended. The loss of war orders sent the city into a slump. By 1920 the average hourly wage for unskilled labor—laborers, helpers, and handymen—had fallen to forty-six cents an hour. Toolmakers did better at eighty cents an hour, but female workers, whose positions in the manufacturing field included machine operators, inspectors, and assemblers, earned roughly thirty-seven cents an hour. For the first time in sixty years Bridgeport experienced a decline in immigration due to loss of available jobs and because of new government restrictions enacted in 1921 and 1924 limiting eastern and southern European immigration.

These restrictions left the Italians as the dominant population group in the city. Be-

tween 1890 and 1930, 80,000 Italians came to Connecticut. Like most of the immigrant groups, Italians, particularly those from southern Italy, came here primarily to escape homelessness and poor economic conditions. The arrival of the southern Italians triggered a rivalry which persists today among the various Italian groups, and in some parts of Bridgeport it still makes a big difference which province of Italy an Italian's mother or father came from. For instance, former Mayor Leonard Paoletta's family descends from Castelfranco, a mountain village about fifty miles northeast of Naples. The man Paoletta defeated in 1981, John Mandanici, was of Sicilian heritage. To this day there remains a competition between the two Italian provinces, and it was mirrored in the fire the two candidates breathed at each other during the 1981 mayoral campaign.

Italian-American Colonel Henry Mucci became Bridgeport's most honored World War II Army officer when he led 121 Rangers on a daring raid twenty-five miles into Japanese-occupied territory. Mucci and his men rescued 513 Allied troops from an enemy prison camp in the Philippines during the raid. In 1974 Bridgeport's section of Route 8 was named for him.

Bridgeport's population peaked at about 158,709 in 1950, but Mayor Jasper McLevy claimed a population of nearly 170,000 in the mid-1950s. The influx of blacks during and after World War II, and Hispanics in the fifties and sixties, accounted for the increase.

Bridgeport's immigrant groups organized many associations, such as the Ancient Order of Hibernians, The Bridgeport Deutsche Schulen, the Bridgeport Schwaben Veiren, The Germania Singing Society, St. Patrick's Society, the Danish Benevolent Society, The Trinacria Society, the Italian Community Center, and the Jewish Community Center. The ethnic groups also formed their own communities, in some respects preserving the ways of the

Fred Atwater, who defeated John T. King's machine in 1921, is something of a trivia question. He has the distinction of being Bridgeport's last one-term mayor. King received a measure of revenge in 1923 when William Behrens (facing page), a butcher by trade, defeated Atwater for the first of his three terms. Courtesy, City of Bridgeport

old country. In the early 1900s, for example, the Park City had seven different newspapers published in Italian, three in Hungarian, and one each in German, Yiddish, and Slovak.

Father Stephen J. Panik, born in Slovakia in 1893, came to Bridgeport in 1912 and be-

came a determined advocate for housing the poor and the working class. Father Panik, the pastor of Saints Cyril and Methodius Roman Catholic Church, was named chairman of the newly formed Bridgeport Housing Authority in 1936 and led the establishment of the Fa-

Stephen J. Panik was born in Slovakia in 1893. He came to Bridgeport in 1912 and took over for his cousin Gaspar at St. Cyril & Methodius Roman Catholic Church in 1933. Panik served the church for twenty years till his death on November 22, 1953. Father Panik was the man behind the Father Panik Village Housing Project for the poor. The project was completed in 1941. Photo by B. Brignolo, Brignolo Studios. Courtesy, Historical Collections, Bridgeport Public Library

ther Panik Village housing project in 1941. In the 1930s, the East Side neighborhood bounded by Hamilton Street and Crescent, Pembroke, and Waterview avenues—known as Hell's Kitchen—suffered from unacceptably high housing density and was noted as a high-risk fire hazard. Backed by federal money, several city blocks were cleared to immediately upgrade apartment housing and living conditions for thousands. The housing project opened as Yellow Mill Village, but years later Panik's success would deteriorate into a crime-ridden complex.

Other past examples of the city's wide-ranging ethnic flavor include the White Eagles, a Polish semipro baseball team; Syrian and Lebanese stores that featured Arabic food; and South End Greek candy stores and restaurants. The Hungarian community, the second largest in the country, played gypsy music in restaurants in the West End, the section of the city once called Hunk Town. Some of the foreign flavor dissolved as families moved to the suburbs and as ethnic groups adopted American lifestyles. But the city has managed to retain a large part of its ethnic flavor. The new wave of refugees is a result of the U.S. government's policy of granting political refugee status almost exclusively to people from Communist nations. Bridgeport now has six Vietnamese stores, a Korean food store, a Cuban bakery, and a Ukrainian arts and crafts shop.

These neighborhoods have sown a crop of unique foreign-born characters. A Bridgeport tradition of many years' standing finds foreign-born Italians, Portuguese, and Hungarians lined alongside the railroad tracks on Housatonic Avenue waiting for grape vendors during the fall wine-making season. These old-fashioned wine brewers with their caps and baggy pants drive out in their pickup trucks and station wagons to buy grapes to make wine, continuing a family tradition. They wait for Joseph Visconti, who's sold the California grapes for

seventeen years, to open his thirty-foot trailer so they can sample the grapes and slip him orders on pieces of paper, because many of them do not speak English.

The South End has the city's heralded smiling hot dog man Skirmantas Rastas, whose family left economically-ruined Lithuania for the United States in 1949. Rastas is renowned for selling thousands of hot dogs each year at Pleasure Beach, Seaside Park, Beardsley Park, and from his other concession stands in the city. Another side of Rastas shows his talent for turning depressed tenements into restored Victorian gingerbreads, helping to rejuvenate Bridgeport's South End.

Bridgeport's neighborhoods have remained a bargain bazaar. The Park City still offers fifty- to seventy-five-cent beers at neighborhood bars such as Dolan's Corner, the Shamrock Pub, the Bon Ton, and Sol's Cafe—and together they reflect the city's ethnic mix.

The city has had its share of ethnic tensions in various overcrowded neighborhoods, however. In 1981, as Laotians moved into an East Side Puerto Rican neighborhood, a fire set in an apartment building killed a Laotian woman. The Laotians blamed the Puerto Ricans, but differences were settled through the help of the International Institute of Connecticut. This social agency grew from the YWCA (formed circa 1900) with a mission to relocate foreign-born women. Today the Bridgeport agency aids hundreds of refugees and immigrants each year through counseling, resettlement, employment, job training, language education, and a wide variety of other social services.

The U.S. Immigration and Naturalization Service no longer keeps a breakdown on immigrants entering Connecticut, but Myra Oliver, executive director of the International Institute, says her agency serves populations from sixty different nationalities. "We in Bridgeport help the foreign-born," says Oliver. "Bridgeport is still a city of immigrants."

Cesar Batalla looked out his ninth-floor office of the Southern Connecticut Gas Co. toward the empty factories that were the very reason thousands of Latinos came to Bridgeport. Bullard's, Bryant Electric, Underwood. All gone. Even when the jobs were aplenty, life in Bridgeport was far from idyllic. For the toughest of the Latinos, perseverance, hard work and the determination to care for family inspired achievement and provided the lifestyle they had dreamed about in Puerto Rico, that made them risk that air trip those many years before. A job - at least they had a job.

Many of the factories that put food on the table, clothes on their backs and provided the little extras for a future college education are gone - squeezed by the global competition. So many jobs are gone, but Batalla's people are still here, and growing. During the middle and late 1980s, Bridgeport's historically rough inner streets had become war zones. Drug dealers, gunfire and killings tormented families trying to survive among the poverty.

Batalla, the "social alligator," was one of many Latinos inching the Latin community's agenda forward: greater representation on the City Council; control of the Board of Education; and creation of a political power base to carry a louder community voice - a voice now broadcast over the Bridgeport based-Spanish radio station WCUM, 1450 on the AM dial.

Batalla recognized that the city's children continued to suffer increasing poverty, violence and health problems. A 1992 report by the Bridgeport Child Advocacy Coalition showed that in Bridgeport almost one in three children lived in poverty, 30 percent of all African American children and nearly 45 percent of all Latino children.

Active in a number of programs targeting teen pregnancy, drug abuse and infant mortality, Batalla groomed a new generation of young people through a local chapter of Aspira, the Spanish word for aspire, a national group promoting leadership programs to at-risk youths.

"We are reaching out to a cadre of bright kids to season them governmentally, politically and socially," Batalla said in 1993. Batalla, the leader, fell to cancer just a few years later, but other Latino leaders represent the hopes and dreams for his city and people.

Leaders and role models in both the Latino and African American communities have emerged. In the Latino community Carmen Lopez and Eddie Rodriguez sit as respected state Superior Court judges; Rosa Correa oversees Gov. John Rowland's Bridgeport office. Town Clerk Hector Diaz, state representatives Edna Garcia and Hector Diaz Jr. and City Councilmen Lydia Martinez and Joel Gonzalez are involved in the governmental decision making on both a local and state level. Police Chief Hector Torres is the first minority to lead the police department.

In the African American community, State Senator Alvin Penn, City Clerk Fleeta Hudson, City Treasurer Sharon Lemdon, City Council representatives James Holloway, Shirley Bean and Sybil Allen and Board of Education members Nancy Geter and James Horne are among a growing network of leaders serving the community. Charles Smith, the Harding High School basketball star, hasn't forgotten his Bridgeport roots. Now retired from the National Basketball Association, where he played for the New York Knicks, Smith's foundation has helped hundreds of inner city kids blossom academically and athletically.

Latinos and African Americans now make up more than 50 percent of the city's population. The city's more than $100 million education budget now reflects these growing populations, offering cultural programs that emphasize ethnic history, identity and pride.

Just as today, schools at the turn of the century had school bands. The Lincoln School Band seen here circa 1900 wasn't a typical school band as known today, but was a Fife and Drum Corps. If you look carefully you'll see that the band members have fifes under their arms. Courtesy, Robert Clifford Collection

CHAPTER III
Spirit, Mind, and Voice

"No Fear—No Favor—We Do Our Part—The People's Paper"
—Bridgeport Herald *slogan*

The immigrant groups that settled in Bridgeport arrived with deep religious feelings that had accompanied them through their lives of poverty, war-born dislocation, and political unrest. Today, Bridgeport has some 150 churches, synagogues, and missions that link its people to their cultures and communities.

Bridgeport's early churches were Congregational, Episcopal, and Baptist. Methodism came to Bridgeport in 1789. The first Catholic Mass was said in 1830 and the first Catholic church dedicated in 1843. The first Universalist church was organized in 1845; the Presbyterian church was founded in 1853; the first Jewish congregation was established in 1859; and the first Lutheran church opened in 1887.

While Bridgeport's church activities are today generally confined to services, prayer, and an occasional evening of church-basement bingo, the church in the days of the Yankee settlers served an additional, quite different function. The church was the most important building in the community—a sort of all-purpose center. Prayers were said, psalms read, town meetings conducted, disputes settled. Basically, any and every problem that involved the community was aired in the church or meetinghouse. Church officers were appointed, including tax collectors, a treasurer, a school committee, a constable, a secretary, and selectmen, who set taxes which supported the church and school. The constable was the busiest town official. He chased after thieves, Sabbath breakers, and those who spent too much time drinking. But for many years this would be the spot where all local affairs were settled.

In 1695 the community, then called Fairfield Village, erected the First Church of Christ in Stratfield. The church's dedication came the year after the community had estab-

lished its first school, and the church was built for similar reasons. Since the settlers who lived in Fairfield Village, between Fairfield and Stratford, were troubled by the difficult trips to either town to attend church, the legislature granted approval for them to build their own house of worship. The new building was on Park Avenue, and the Reverend Charles Chauncey became the first pastor. He was a busy one at that, baptizing more than 400 children. In those days, the booming sound of a drum summoned people to church, until bells were installed in 1774. Church services during the winter months could get uncomfortable in the cold, drafty, and unheated meetinghouse, especially when the sermon ran three to five hours, as it did on occasion. This church was the predecessor of today's United Congregational at Park Avenue and State Street, making it the oldest church in Bridgeport.

In the 1800s Broad Street became known as Church Row. The churches shown in this circa 1836 woodcut are, from left to right: the First Congregational or North Church, built 1807; St. John's Episcopal, built 1801; and the Second Congregational Church, built in 1830. Woodcut by John Warner Barber. Courtesy, Historical Collections, Bridgeport Public Library

Below: *Founded in 1807, the First Congregational Church (First Church of Christ in Stratfield) is the oldest in the city. In 1830 the congregation split and a group formed the Second Congregational Church. By 1916, differences had been settled and the United Congregational was formed. The church above is the First Congregational or Old North Church as it appeared around 1910. The church was built in 1850. Courtesy, Historical Collections, Bridgeport Public Library*

Above: *Though the original church was built in 1748, this 1888 interior photo of St. John's Episcopal shows the structure built in 1873-75 on Fairfield Avenue. In early Bridgeport, churches were the most important building in town. Town meetings were held, town officials were appointed, and disputes were settled in those meeting places. Courtesy, Historical Collections, Bridgeport Public Library*

Walter W. Curtis has served as Bishop of the Diocese of Bridgeport since 1961. In 1963 Bishop Curtis led a drive to establish a commuter college now familiar to all as Sacred Heart University. Photo by Frank W. Decerbo. Courtesy, Post Publishing Company

The second church in the area, St. John's Episcopal, founded in 1748, now stands on Fairfield Avenue. The First Baptist Church was erected in 1837 on Broad Street and now is located on Washington Avenue. It has increased neighborhood minority attendance through a department which ministers to Spanish-speaking worshippers. The emergence of many churches by 1837 produced Bridgeport's "Church Row" on Broad Street. In succession came the Second Congregational, the First Baptist, the First Congregational, the Episcopal, and the Methodist churches.

Today Walter W. Curtis, Bishop of the Diocese of Bridgeport (which encompasses all of Fairfield County) is the spiritual leader of some 325,000 Catholics, the most populous of all Bridgeport denominations. The Diocese of Bridgeport was formed from the Diocese of Hartford by Pope Pius XII in September 1953. The Most Reverend Lawrence J. Shehan, auxiliary bishop of Baltimore, was named the first bishop.

Bridgeport's first Catholic mass was celebrated by Father James Fitton of Boston in the Middle Street home of James McCullough, a leader of the tiny Irish colony which dedicated St. James Church in 1843. St. James became the predecessor of St. Augustine Cathedral, the seat of the Diocese of Bridgeport, after the construction of the new church on Washington Avenue in 1868. The first members of Bridgeport's Irish community are buried in St. James Cemetery on Grove Street.

In 1874, three Roman Catholic churches served Bridgeport: St. Augustine's; St. Mary's on Pembroke Street, built in 1857; and St. Joseph's on Catherine Street, built in 1874. As the new century approached, the Catholic population surge resulted in the construction of several new churches, including St. Michael the Archangel on Pulaski Street and St. Patrick's on North Avenue, both built in 1889; St. John Nepomucene on Jane Street in 1891; and St. Anthony of Padua on Colorado Avenue in 1892.

By 1930, Bridgeport had more than 100 houses of worship, their congregations working and sacrificing for several years, dependent on local support and contributions from the numerous ethnic groups.

The Hungarians formed The Hungarian Reformed Church in 1894, and the Lithuanian St. George's Church on Park Avenue was chartered in 1859. But recent times have seen many churches renovated, dissolved, moved, or displaced because of industrial development. Many minority congregations have purchased vacated church buildings or erected their own. Messiah Baptist, a black-congregation church on Arch Street, was replaced by an $800,000 building a short distance from the Arch Street church that was razed during the Congress Street redevelopment program in the 1960s. The oldest black church in Bridgeport is Bethel African Methodist Episcopal Church on Grove Street, formed in 1826 by blacks who had escaped southern slavery and found refuge in Bridgeport before Abraham Lincoln's Emancipation Proclamation.

*   *   *

Founded in 1826, the Bethel African Methodist Episcopal Church is the oldest black-congregation church in Bridgeport. Now located on Grove Street, the church was formed by escaped slaves from southern states. Photo by Neil Swanson

The formation of the first school followed the same pattern as the first church's establishment. In 1650, the Connecticut Code of

Now a Park Avenue garage complete with a basketball hoop, this simple one-room building is thought to be the oldest existing schoolhouse in the United States. It was built in 1738 in Fairfield County and the last teacher there was Ellen M. Spear. Courtesy, Historical Collections, Bridgeport Public Library

Laws required that every township of fifty or more households must provide a school where children could learn to read and write. The Village of Pequonnock was far from either Fairfield or Stratford, so before 1678, the children of Pequonnock had to travel several miles to one of those towns to attend school. Parents, in particular, grew tired of the long trips, so the general court allowed them to organize their own school, which had forty-seven students the first year. The villagers were responsible for funding the institution, which had a curriculum and disciplinary standards that make today's standards seem lax.

Students not only had to haul their books to school, they had to supply wood for fuel. Failure to bring wood to school led to merciless teachers banishing pupils to the coldest, darkest corner of the schoolroom. School days, including Saturdays, were generally eight hours of long, constant work. No study halls, no

physical education, no nap periods. The children of the colonists were first required to learn the alphabet, syllables, and the Lord's Prayer from a "hornbook," a thin piece of wood about five inches long and two inches wide which had a cover sheet of printed letters. The printed page was covered with a thin sheet of yellowish horn which allowed the letters to be read. A strip of brass fastened the paper and the horn to the wood, which had a string hole so the hornbook could be carried around the pupil's neck or to the side.

Most students wouldn't dare cheat or talk out of place. Breaking those rules brought swift consequences, not easily forgotten. Schoolmasters were ruthless and had many a torture tool, including the birch rod, the walnut stick, and a stick with heavy leather straps. Perhaps the most feared was the flapper, a piece of heavy leather with a hole in the middle. When the flapper came down, a blister the size of the hole was raised on the flesh. Whipping the soles of students' feet, forcing them to sit on a unipod, or gagging them with a stick were other disciplinary methods.

Punishment became less severe as the school system progressed. By 1796, when the settlement was known as Stratfield, three schools had been erected, funded by money given to Connecticut from the sale of lands in Pennsylvania and Ohio to repay losses in the Revolutionary War. By 1876, Bridgeport's eleven school districts, which collected their own taxes, were consolidated under one governing body—the Board of Education. H.M. Harrington served the first of his fourteen years on the board as superintendent of schools.

The new management didn't waste any time upgrading the school system. New schools were needed during the school board's early days, but until it overcame a cash flow problem, stores and dwellings were rented as temporary classrooms. Within one year, a public high school opened on Prospect Street with Charles D. Peck serving as principal. Two

The Prospect School was built in 1877-88 on Prospect Street and by the turn of the century it held grades one through eight. In 1963 the school was demolished as part of Mayor Samuel Tedesco's downtown redevelopment project. Courtesy, Historical Collections, Bridgeport Public Library

The forty-three ninth grade students from room five in this photo (1898) are an indication of the overcrowding the city's schools experienced at the turn of the century. The huge increases by 1899 caused the Board of Apportionment to order a yearly tax of one mill to fund new schools. Courtesy, Historical Collections, Bridgeport Public Library

years later a training school for teachers was housed in the same building.

The Board of Apportionment in February 1899 passed a resolution ordering a tax of one mill to erect buildings for educational uses. By 1920, Bridgeport's school board had moved into its new quarters at 45 Lyon Terrace (the present site of City Hall). It instituted medical inspection and free kindergartens, built fire escapes in schools, and built a high school on Congress Street, known years later as Congress Junior High School. Still, Bridgeport schools were overcrowded during World War I from the mass of immigrant children. In the 1920s, married female teachers struggled against a school board ruling that married women whose husbands earned a decent living could not be kept in the system. Superintendent of Schools Carroll Reed suggested that married teachers were motivated by a desire for luxuries.

Classes in the thirties and forties, although cramped, offered some much-needed harmony from the discord of the Depression and World War II. Ukulele clubs, harmonica bands, and boys' glee clubs were formed. Students from Maplewood School aided the war effort by manning war bond booths and packing Christmas boxes for USO distribution to armed services hospitals. In the late 1950s, severe overcrowding in the three city high schools forced the school board to inform students from Trumbull and Monroe that Bridgeport could no longer accomodate them. Mayor Jasper McLevy was criticized for continued slashing of the educational budget, which left schools in disrepair and teacher salaries low. But, the 1960s saw more school construction resulting in four new facilities: the Read, Blackham, Roosevelt, and Columbus schools. The influx of blacks and Hispanics drastically changed the composition of the student population, and busing was implemented.

These events of the 1970s perhaps affected the school system more than any other municipal department. School officials found themselves explaining why city tests scores were among the worst in the state. A desegregation suit brought against the city by the NAACP, the Spanish-American Coalition, and many parents, forced U.S. District Court Judge Ellen Bree Burns to oversee ten years of sweeping changes to complete racial balance in the schools' population. In July 1976 Geraldine Johnson was named the first black superintendent of schools; two years later she came face to face with the longest teachers' strike in Connecticut history when Mayor John C. Mandanici couldn't make progress in negotiating a new contract. After repeated warnings to return to work, the Superior Court ordered 200 teachers to jail. They were incarcerated at

Camp Hartell, a National Guard facility in Windsor Locks, Connecticut, for thirteen days until they agreed to return to work.

"The strike was the saddest event in Bridgeport educational history," said James Connelly, the present superintendent of schools. "The school system hit rock bottom."

Fallout from the strike included the transfer of about 1,000 Bridgeport students from public to private schools. The strike was instrumental, however, in the passage of a binding arbitration law to prevent future teacher strikes.

Today the Bridgeport school system administers 20,000 students, thirty-one elementary schools, three high schools, three alternative schools, and one special education facility, all sharing a yearly budget of fifty million dollars.

Bridgeport's college days began in 1927, when Dr. E. Everett Cortright, Dr. Alfred C. Fones, and James H. Halsey pushed for the

Originally the Bridgeport High School built in 1882, this building served as the Congress Junior High School after the new Bridgeport High School was constructed on Lyon Terrace in 1916. Courtesy, Historical Collections, Bridgeport Public Library

formation of the Junior College of Connecticut. These men took the lead in raising money for the school, recruiting students and faculty, and developing educational opportunities. In 1947 with an enrollment of 3,000, the school was rechartered as the University of Bridgeport, and three years later all operations were moved to a twenty-two-acre campus at Seaside Park. Today the university boasts a law school and the Carlson Library, named after longtime benefactors William and Philip Carlson, founders of the Metropolitan Body Company.

In 1963, the Most Reverend Walter W. Curtis, Bishop of Bridgeport, led the drive to establish a commuter college for students who chose not to attend boarding schools. Sacred Heart University, on north Park Avenue near the Bridgeport line in Fairfield, has since served as an ideal opportunity for students outside Bridgeport to attend a university nearer their homes. In addition, Fairfield University, home of the Fairfield College Preparatory School started by the Society of Jesus in 1942, has become one of the finest institutions of higher learning in the country.

Mirroring the formation of community colleges around the country in the 1960s, the Stratford Board of Education and the State Commissioner of Higher Education established Housatonic Community College in 1966. It operated from Bunnell High School in Stratford before relocating to the former Singer Building on Barnum Avenue in Bridgeport. The college won immediate cultural acclaim through its founding of the Housatonic Museum of Art.

The one Bridgeport institution of learning that transcends all others is the Bridgeport Public Library at Broad and State streets. The library, headquartered in the Burroughs Building, is the largest library system in Connecticut, containing 500,000 volumes. About 40,000 people pass through the doors of the downtown building each month to visit the

reference and newspaper rooms, the children's department, the Popular Library, and the exhibition areas. The Klein Porcelain Room displays Chinese porcelain, paintings, etchings, and a Rembrandt, all donated by former library director Milton Klein. The library's Henry A. Bishop Room has been the home of the Historical Collections for fifty years, and the technology and business department is one of the finest in New England. The city's library system includes four neighborhood branches and a bookmobile.

The Bridgeport library system grew out of the urging of twelve-year-old Stiles Middlebrook, who wrote in 1830 "that some source of reading material should be at the disposal of the people of Bridgeport." Middlebrook would slip such letters under the office door of the *Weekly Farmer,* which published them. The immediate result was the formation of a library on Wall Street by a group of city leaders led by Alanson Hamlin, the foremost lawyer of the city. The Bridgeport Library Association was formed in 1850 and city leaders such as P.T. Barnum, Hanford Lyon, Philo C. Calhoun, and Frederick Wood regularly donated books and thousands of dollars to the library. Within twenty years, the library had 8,500 books and dozens of newspapers and magazines as it settled into its new quarters in the Wheeler Building at Main and Fairfield, built by Nathaniel Wheeler of the Wheeler and Wilson Sewing Machine Company. In 1883, Catharine Burroughs Pettengill, whose father had made a fortune through his fleet of vessels in foreign trade, willed $100,000 toward the construction of a new library. The current

Originally founded in 1880, the Bridgeport Public Library's first permanent home was in the Burroughs building (pictured here circa 1880) on the corner of Main and John Street. Now the largest public library in Connecticut, it is housed today at Broad Street in a building erected in 1927. Courtesy, Historical Collections, Bridgeport Public Library

Before occupying the top three floors of the Burroughs build-ing, the Bridgeport Public Library was located temporarily in the Wheeler building at Main and Fairfield. The circulation room seen here in the Burroughs building circa 1890 was one of the many specialty rooms. Courtesy, Historical Collections, Bridgeport Public Library

Facing page, top right and bottom: *What is today known as the Dinan Center was once called the Hillside Home Hospital. Founded in 1915, a survey by the National Civic Federation called it "an outstanding example of the trend toward scientific and humane care for the destitute poor." Half of the inmates were foreign born. The hospital, seen here circa 1917, was vir-tually fireproof and had it's own kitchen, laundry, bake shop, and barber shop. Superintendent of the Department of Public Welfare Anges P. Thorne was praised by Mayor Fred Atwater for the facility's operation. In 1930 the average patient popula-tion was 314. Courtesy, Historical Collections, Bridgeport Public Library*

federal-style building was completed in 1927.

Catharine Pettengill also co-founded Bridge-port Hospital along with two other women, Frances Pomeroy and Susan Hubbell. The women acted in response to an urgent call by Dr. George F. Lewis for an institution to han-dle accident cases and serious illnesses. City patients had been cared for in the basement of what later became police headquarters. The new hospital opened in November 1884, with P.T. Barnum as the first president and Dr. Lewis as the first physician in charge. That first year 148 patients were treated. Now the 650-bed facility annually treats some 23,000 patients. The hospital is acclaimed for its burn unit and its link with the Rehabilitation Cen-ter of Eastern Fairfield County formed in 1935.

St. Vincent's Medical Center formally opened on June 28, 1905, following a call for a new Catholic hospital. Ann Bohan, a par-

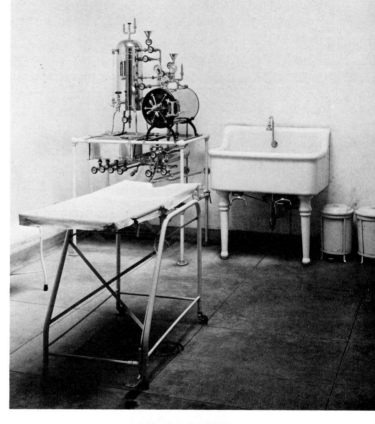

Above: *Catharine Burroughs Pettengill co-founded Bridgeport Hospital with Frances Pomeroy and Susan Hubbell in 1878. P.T. Barnum was its first president when it moved into its own building in 1884; it served 148 patients that year. Courtesy, Historical Collections, Bridgeport Public Library*

BRIDGEPORT HERALD.

VOL. 9. No. 581.   BRIDGEPORT, CONN. SUNDAY, NOV. 17, 1901.   PRICE FIVE CENTS.

THE LARGEST CIRCULATION IN THE STATE.

FLYING MACHINE FACTORY
THE LATEST OF
BRIDGEPORTS INDUSTRIES

Gustave Whitehead, Inventor of Only Practical Air Ship, Engaged in Building Soaring Carriages Which Will Be Placed on the Market in Spring and Sell For About the Same Price That a High Grade Automobile Brings. Night and Day Forces Working. Fifteen Mechanics and Two Engineers Employed at the Flying Machine Works.

ADMITTANCE TO SHOP REFUSED.

New York Men of Money Backing the Project and Already $10,000 Has Been Placed at the Disposal of the Inventor. A Good Family Machine With Seating Capacity For Six Will Cost About $2,000. Inventor Whitehead Will Fly From Bridgeport to New York

WILL USE NEW MOTIVE POWER.

IF THE PLANS OF his financial backers mature and the indications are that they will Gustave Whitehead, the flying machine inventor will shortly experience the pleasure of having his product manufactured on a large scale and Bridgeport will win the distinction of possessing the machine and modern industry in the whole civilized world.

[text continues]

RADICAL CHANGE IN BRIDGEPORT'S STREET CAR SERVICE PROPOSED

Connecticut Railway and Lighting Company May Inaugurate the Polo System of Making Stops. Belief That Better Time Can be Made With This System in Force.

FOR THE PUBLIC TO DECIDE.

THE CONNECticut Railway & Lighting Co. has under its consideration, a radical change in the operation of its cars...

[text continues]

FRIEND PROVES FALSE
AND HUSBAND SUES

Walter M. Conway Sues Arthur Gross for $25,000 Damages For Alienation of His Wife's Affections.

FAMOUS IRONMASTER
TWISTED IN ROMANCE

(Special to the Herald.)
NEW YORK, Nov. 16.

WALTER M. CONway, proprietor of the largest summer hotel in Belle Haven, Conn., and who is said to have inherited more than $1,000,000 from his father, who was one of the best known men in the wholesale dry goods district...

[text continues]

STORM BOUND VESSELS

[text continues]

DEATH OF MISS LEE.

[text continues]

INJURIES WERE FATAL.

[text continues]

VISITED THEATER,
SAW ELOPEMENT,
FOLLOWED SUIT

Miss Beulah Shelley and William V. Leary Were So Impressed With an Elopement They Saw at the Theater That They Went Straightway to a Minister and Were Made One.

BRIDE'S MOTHER WAS
FORGIVING BUT PAPA
WAS NOT AT FIRST

Wedding Had Been Set for Easter But the Young Couple Took Time by Both Forelocks and Stole a March on Well Laid Plans.

BRIDE RETURNS TO
FORMER POSITION

A WEEK AGO YESterday afternoon, while present in a New York theater, where a love romance with an elopement for a climax was being enacted, William V. Leary, an employee of a New York mercantile house...

[text continues]

DROPPED DEAD,
DELIRIUM TREMENS

Child Saw Her Father Fall to the Floor and Asked Ambulance Surgeon if He Would Soon be Well Again.

FRANK DARK A
HARD DRINKER

FRANK DARK, a Slavonian, died of delirium tremens at his home, 175 Church street, Bridgeport, shortly after 10 o'clock last night...

[text continues]

EMERGENCY CASES

[text continues]

CAT SCRATCHED MISTRESS

A pet cat, owned by Lillian Lamb of 67 Prospect street, lost its temper yesterday afternoon and scratched the hands of its benefactress...

DOG BIT QUINN'S LEG.

[text continues]

JOHNNY BROKE AN ARM

Johnnie Norton, thirteen years old, whose parents live at 1 Harrison court, has a record among his associates for his ability to climb high fences...

HOLE IN HER BOW

Lumber Lizzie D. Small Arrives With Logs For Railroad Improvements.

[text continues]

THE REPUBLICAN MACHINE
WAS HOT AFTER
DIRECTOR WILLIAMS' HEAD

They Had Him at the Atlantic Hotel Where They Tried to Force Him to Resign So That Marie Cowles Could Succeed Him.

He Turned Them Down

The Machine Men Pointed Out to Him That He Would Have to Go and That Marie Cowles, If Made Director By Mayor Stirling Might Hold the Office By Not Leaving Himself Liable For Charges of Any Kind. Mr. Williams Was Firm and Held On.

IF THERE IS A Republican politician in Bridgeport who has the least bit of sympathy for Director of Public Works Williams, Herald reporters were unable to find them the past week...

[text continues]

DIRECTOR WILLIAMS

[text continues]

Claiming the largest circulation in the state, the Bridgeport Herald (founded in 1890) was one of the city's four newspapers at the turn of the century. Sold to Leigh Danenberg in 1929, the paper gained a reputation as a scandal sheet. Its slogan—"No Fear—No Favor—We Do Our Part—The People's Paper." Courtesy, Historical Collections, Bridgeport Public Library

ishioner of St. Patrick's Church, willed $14,000 to the Reverend J.B. Nihill for the new hospital. The facility was the first in Bridgeport to adopt an eight-hour work schedule for nurses instead of the customary twelve-hour work day. The hospital today is a 391-bed facility. Park City Hospital, organized in 1926, has grown from a tiny 35-bed unit to a larger 200-bed facility. All three hospitals care for Bridgeport and the surrounding communities, including Fairfield, Westport, Easton, Trumbull, Monroe, and Stratford.

*   *   *

Bridgeport has been a newspaper town since Lazarus Beach, a local Stratfield printer, decided villagers needed a documented source to spread gossip about new bridges, stores, and streets. In 1795 he established the weekly *American Telegraph and Fairfield County Gazette* which was distributed by riders on horseback. Subscriptions sold for $1.50 a year and the circulation was about 800.

Bridgeport's first daily paper was the *Republican Farmer,* founded in 1810. Just about everything was recorded with a touch of Yankee humor. The front page was one gray mass of poetry and advertising, and daily events generally were reserved for pages two and three. Pictures and fancy layouts were light-years away—this paper didn't even have headlines. In a typical edition of the 1830s, residents saw an ad plugging "Dr. Bowen's remedy for the piles," and a few columns away appeared a story about rats as big as cats creating havoc. "No devices which human ingenuity can plan for their destruction have been left untried," proclaimed the paper. Numerous ads selling flour, cheeses, guns, boots, and saddles covered the rest of the front page. Page two might have covered a local fire, a shipwreck in Cape Cod, or a flight of locusts ravaging the East Indies.

Soon many papers sprouted in Bridgeport,

some for a brief time only, including the *Connecticut Courier* in 1810, the *Bridgeport Republican* in 1830, the *Spirit of the Times* in 1831 (later the *Bridgeport Standard*), and the *Bridgeport Chronicle* in 1848.

Bridgeport had many other dailies and weeklies that passed quickly. When the newsprint settled in the 1920s, four newspapers competed for supremacy: *The Farmer,* the *Times-Star* (consolidated from the *Times* and *Star* in 1926), the *Bridgeport Sunday Herald* (est. 1890), and the *Bridgeport Post* (est. 1883). News carriers were sure never to drop off the wrong paper on someone's doorstep, as each paper was easily distinguishable by its own distinctive style.

The Farmer retained much of the early-day flavor, the *Time-Star* was known for its diverse sports section, and *The Bridgeport Post* succeeded on its local coverage. But the paper everyone talked about, even if they hated it, was the *Herald.* Richard Howell, the paper's editor and publisher for more than twenty years, was noted for his intriguing sports writing and his reports on Bridgeport's nightlife. His 1928 book, *Tales from Bohemia Land,* chronicled Bridgeport's tavern characters as seen by their drinking partner, Richard Howell. In 1929, the paper was sold to Leigh Danenberg, whose daring news style, exposure of Bridgeport corruption, and campaigning for governmental change catapulted the *Herald*'s reputation as a scandal sheet. "No Fear—No Favor—We Do Our Part—The People's Paper," boasted the front page slogan.

Danenberg owned the paper, but Harry Neigher was "Mr. Herald." His column, "Bridgeport Night Life," appeared for forty-two years and jabbed at every gin mill, every celebrity, and every socialite divorce in town. When the legendary mobster Dutch Schultz took residence at the Stratfield Hotel, Neigher cracked, "Dutch Schultz has given the Bridgeport Police Department 24 hours to get out of town."

Such columns lured residents right from church to line up outside the Herald plant on Lafayette Street, listening for the pounding presses and smelling the wet ink while waiting for the day's edition. The newspaper did not maintain popularity with advertisers, however, and ceased publication in 1974, leaving The Connecticut Post (formerly the Bridgeport Post) as the dominant paper in the city. The Post flourishes as the city's family newspaper, reporting a heavy dose of local news ranging from city government and civic groups to birth and wedding announcements. Robert Laska assumed the community active role of a predecessor publisher Betty Pfriem, both of whom have served as ringmaster of the city's annual Barnum Festival activities and utilized their positions to better the city. Bridgeport is also served by the Bridgeport News, a community weekly newspaper that highlights neighborhood issues and activities.

The early sketches of Bridgeport's two most famous cartoonists appeared for many years in the Post. Al Capp, born Alfred C. Caplan, attended Bridgeport High School and ten years later, during a hitchhiking trip through the South, won inspiration for his "Li'l Abner," which was syndicated by hundreds of newspapers. Warren Harding High School graduate, Walt Kelly, employed by the Post as a cartoonist, later used many Bridgeporter names in his "Pogo" series, created while he drew for the New York Star in 1943. Kelly's P.T. Bridgeport, an arrogant swamp creature in a straw hat, caricatured Bridgeport's first citizen, P.T. Barnum. Kelly died in 1973 and "Pogo" was continued by his wife, Selby Kelly, until 1975. Another prominent city cartoonist is Ray Dirgo, creator of the Flintstones cartoon strip. Dirgo brings smiles to the faces of city school children with his sketches of Fred, Wilma, Barney, Dino and company.

Radio came to Bridgeport in 1926 with the founding of radio station WICC (call letters Industrial Center of Connecticut), which remains the most popular station in Bridgeport. Depression-era radio filled the airwaves with logs of local programming. A typical day would include Bridgeport Post-Telegram news flashes, record-request hours, live performances by local baritone Thomas Wall or pianist Patsy Stoccatore. Mayors Edward Buckingham and Jasper McLevy would highlight municipal affairs. One highly-acclaimed show, hosted by Sheriff Edward A. Platt, featured an all-talent show for inmates direct from the local jail which was heralded for improving inmate morale. Some listeners even responded with job offers to first offenders.

WICC and WNAB, founded in 1941, were fierce competitors on the early airwaves. An underground railroad seemingly connected the two, as many of the popular disk jockeys worked first for one station and then the other. Since New York radio played a big factor, Bridgeport had its share of radio successes due to the competition. Bob Crane, who later found stardom with television's Hogan's Heroes, was Bridgeport's most famous disk jockey of the 1950s. Crane added a new dimension to radio, interjecting one-liners between record-spinning. Crane also played the drums and often talked his way into performing with bands at the Pleasure Beach Ballroom. Crane left WICC for Los Angeles and Hogan's Heroes in the mid-1960s.

Bridgeport's most famous voice was Tiny Markle, whose orchestra played frequently at the Pleasure Beach Ballroom in the 1950s before he entered radio as a record spinner, later to become the long-time talk show host for WNAB and WICC in the 1980s.

WICC remains an AM powerhouse with its morning news and information featuring John LaBarca, also host of the popular Sunday morning Italian House Party program, and witty news director Tim Quinn. Jim Buchanan's week day Sound Off program provides a regional forum for talk radio junkies.

The 1450 AM spot occupied by WNAB is now the voice of the Latino community, Radio Cumbre, which provides a blend of music, news and public affairs programming.

Erwin "Tiny" Markle, the legendary radio voice. In 1926 WICC (Industrial Center of Connecticut) was founded to provide the city's listeners with news flashes, live broadcasts and music by request. Photo by Dennis Bradbury

Bridgeport's first adventure into television came in the mid-1950s. Radio station WICC operated a UHF television station, but since UHF television was almost nonexistent and an adaptor was needed for fine tuning, the station had few viewers. WICC's owner, Ken Cooper, appealed to the Federal Communications Commission to take the station off the air until a new buyer was found, because the station had no viewers. The FCC wasn't convinced. To prove his point, Cooper hired Bob Crane to go on the air and hold up a $100 bill. The first person to call the station, said Crane, would win the $100. No one called.

Within a few weeks a trade publication ad proclaimed: "Television station WICC has proven conclusively that it has no viewers." The station was taken off the air.

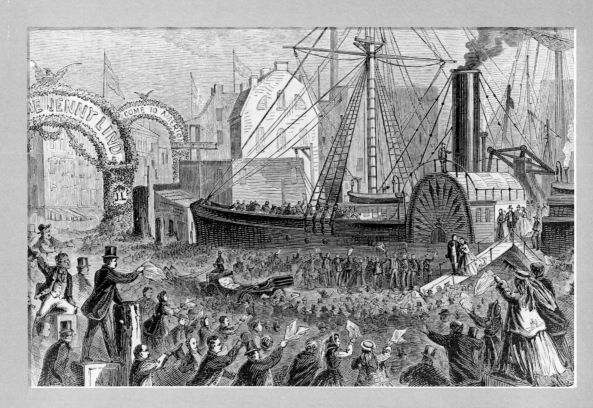

Jenny Lind, a great mid-nineteenth century soprano, was lured to America to tour for P.T. Barnum to establish him as a legitimate cultural empressario. Barnum's advance publicity turned out thousands to greet Lind when she arrived in New York in late 1850. Courtesy, Historical Collections, Bridgeport Public Library

CHAPTER IV

Barnum's
the Name

"There's a sucker born every minute"

—origin unknown

"The Prince of humbug," they called him. "The Shakespeare of advertising," "the king of adjectives." He was a man with a genius for inspiring lucrative curiosity, like a circus parade lures spectators to the paid admission of the big top. He could convince hundreds of thousands to step right up and inspect the 160-year-old nurse of George Washington, the bearded lady, the smallest man in the world. With whirlwind tours of circus freaks, exotic animals, and human feats, he cranked out humbug by the yard.

Phineas Taylor Barnum knew better than anyone else in creation that every crowd had a silver (dollar) lining. Barnum was the master myth maker, and he's still a favorite subject of playwrights and authors because he was so up-front and amiable about his humbuggery. "There's a sucker born every minute," is a Barnum quote entrenched in cliche history. Now nearly 100 years after his death it's in some ways fitting and in other ways sad that he is most esteemed and credited for that often-parroted apocryphal expression. If he ever said it, no historian has ever been able to document it. The statement may have found its place as a corruption of a Barnum suggestion or attributed to Barnum by one of his circus rivals.

The real legacy of Barnum—showman, circus innovator, author, philosopher, humanitarian, public servant, humorist, and even Bridgeport mayor—has been clouded over by the obfuscation of the man's many promotions. That old huckster impression lingering these many years overshadows his contributions to the entertainment profession and to Bridgeport. But as Barnum said, "I don't care what they say about me if they only say something."

Beneath the charm and extravagance of his circus persona is a man whose contributions to Bridgeport are unmatched. Barnum is quite simply the single most important contributor to the city's history. He developed thousands of acres of city property, converting farm and pasture land into choice building lots; enabled the working class to purchase land and houses through an innovative payment system; donated a large part of Seaside Park, one of the first waterfront parks in the country; attracted numerous manufacturing companies; served as the president of Bridgeport Hospital, the local water company, and the Pequonnock Bank (a predessesor of Connecticut National); donated the money to establish the Barnum Museum; established Mountain Grove Cemetery; and provided funding for Bridgeport schools, the library system, parks, and other civic ventures. Another side of Barnum was his drive to grant blacks the right to vote and his sympathy for the woman's rights movement.

Bridgeport's first citizen is best explained by his biographer A.H. Saxon: "P.T. Barnum has the paradoxical distinction of being one of America's best-known least-understood phenomena."

*   *   *

East Bridgeport was P.T. Barnum's "pet" project. He wanted to remind anyone who passed through the East Side that he had planned the district. There's Barnum Avenue; Hallett Street (the maiden name of his first wife, Charity); and Caroline, Helen, and Pauline streets, named for three of his daughters. Noble Avenue is named for Barnum's land developer partner, William Noble. In 1851, five years after Barnum took up residence in the city following his discovery of Charles Stratton (Tom Thumb), Barnum purchased a tract of farmland from Noble. Together they laid out streets, reserved several acres for a park (Washington Park), and initiated the sale of lots. For the next two decades Barnum urged people to invest in a new home and offered a unique incentive. "It is evident," Barnum commented in the *Bridgeport Standard,* "that if the money expended in rent can be paid towards the purchase of a house and lot, the person so paying will in a few years own the house he lives in, instead of always remaining a tenant."

Anyone who could furnish in cash, labor, or material, 20 percent of the amount needed for the construction of a home, would be loaned the rest of the money at 6 percent interest by Barnum, who would be repaid in small weekly, monthly, or quarterly sums. Upon completion of the payments, the residents owned the house. The average cost of a house was roughly $1,500.

Barnum wrote in his autobiography that "it is much better that every person should somehow manage to own the roof he sleeps under. Men are more independent and feel happier who live in their own houses; they keep the premises in neater order, and they make better citizens."

They also made P.T. Barnum richer—the entrepreneur reserved the sale of some lots until after the price of the real estate increased.

Phineas Taylor Barnum, the most important individual contributor to Bridgeport's history, is shown here in 1875 during his only term as the city's mayor. Barnum developed thousands of acres of city property, helped the working class to purchase land and homes through a unique payment system, and attracted numerous manufacturing companies, in addition to many other achievements. Courtesy, City of Bridgeport

Born July 5, 1810, in Bethel, Connecticut, P.T. Barnum was the oldest of five children in a family so poor that he attended his father's funeral in borrowed shoes. Courtesy, Historical Collections, Bridgeport Public Library

Land that Barnum purchased less than forty years earlier for $200 had increased in value to more than $3,000 by 1885. Nevertheless, the townspeople and the *Standard* were behind his admitted "profitable philanthropy" approach. "Barnum may make money by the operation," wrote the *Standard* in 1864, "Very well, perhaps he will, but if he does, it will be by making others richer, not poorer; by helping those who need assistance, not by hindering them, and we can only wish that every rich man would follow such a noble example, and thus, without injury to themselves, give a helping hand to those who need it. Success to the enterprise!"

Barnum's farsightedness also produced thousands of jobs in an industrial development led by the Wheeler and Wilson Sewing Machine Company and Elias Howe's sewing factory. Barnum was constantly planning new real estate deals. The *Standard* reported in 1886 that Barnum had made 1,637 real estate transfers since May 30, 1846, the year he purchased the tract of land to build his orientalstyle mansion, Iranistan.

But not every Barnum business decision proved timely. Though his East Bridgeport plan was ultimately successful, Barnum lost a bundle trying to resettle there the struggling Jerome Clock Factory. By the time the costly venture failed in 1856 he was $500,000 in debt and bankrupt.

Barnum always looked at "the bright side," however. Writing in 1869, by which time he was solvent again, he observed that "My pet city, East Bridgeport, was progressing with giant strides ... That piece of property, which, but eight years before, had been farmland, with scarcely six houses upon the whole tract, was now a beautiful new city, teeming with life, and looking as neat as a new pin."

*   *   *

Before Barnum ever gave much thought to such a place as Bridgeport, he was halfway through his life. Barnum was born July 5, 1810, in Bethel, Connecticut. He was the son of Philo Barnum, a tailor, farmer, and tavern keeper. His grandfather, Ephraim Barnum, was a captain in the Revolutionary War. P.T. was the eldest of five children in a family so poor that he attended his father's funeral in borrowed shoes. In 1826 his father died and Barnum accepted a job as a clerk in a Brooklyn, New York, store. Shortly after, he took a job as a clerk in a porterhouse before returning to Bethel in 1828 with $125 to his name. In

Bethel he established a retail fruit and confectionary store. The next year he married Charity Hallett and opened a lottery office.

Barnum's first great test as a promoter came when he turned his attention to the newspaper business and circulated on October 19, 1831, the first issue of *The Herald of Freedom,* a muckraking sheet which fought "bigotry, superstition, fanaticism and hypocrisy." Barnum was arrested for libel three times in three years; the third time sent him to jail for sixty days after he accused a Bethel deacon of being "guilty of taking usury of an orphan boy." Barnum's jailing won him praise and mushroomed the popularity of his paper, which continued to publish despite his incarceration.

Townspeople gave Barnum a parade upon his release. He sold his paper and a mercantile business in 1834 and moved to New York where he launched his showman career with the hiring of an old black woman, Joice Heth, who he claimed to be 161 years old and once George Washington's nurse.

Barnum exhibited Heth and several other attractions for several months, then joined Aaron Turner's traveling circus as ticket seller, secretary, and treasurer, which prepared Barnum for circus life. After a brief stint with his own traveling show he returned to New York, worked at various jobs, and went broke. Barnum had not a cent to his name, but he built up a reservoir of moxie and convinced some friends to

Page 72: *P.T. Barnum launched his showman career with the unveiling of an old black woman, Joice Heth, whom he claimed was 161 years old and once George Washington's nurse. Courtesy, Historical Collections, Bridgeport Public Library*

Page 73: *Late-nineteenth century trade cards often used a popular person or place to attract attention to a product. Bean's Dry Goods store used P.T. Barnum's face to sell dry and fancy goods. Hood's Sarsparilla used the circus to attract customers to the special qualities of that remedy. Photo by Neil Swanson. Courtesy, Robert Clifford Collection*

GREAT ATTRACTION
JUST ARRIVED AT HINGHAM.
☞ FOR A SHORT TIME ONLY. ☜

JOICE HETH,
NURSE TO
Gen. George Washington,

(The father of our country,) who has arrived at the astonishing age of **161** years! will be seen at HINGHAM for a SHORT TIME ONLY, as she is to fill other engagements very soon.

JOICE HETH is unquestionably the most astonishing and interesting curiosity in the World! She was the slave of Augustine Washington, (the father of Gen. Washington,) and was the first person who put clothes on the unconscious infant who in after days led our heroic fathers on to glory, to victory and freedom. To use her own language when speaking of the illustrious Father of his country, "she raised him." JOICE HETH was born in the Island of Madagascar, on the Coast of Africa, in the year 1674 and has consequently now arrived at the astonishing

Age of 161 Years!

She weighs but forty-six pounds, and yet is very cheerful and interesting. She retains her faculties in an unparalleled degree, converses freely, sings numerous hymns, relates many interesting anecdotes of *the boy* Washington, the red coats, &c. and often laughs heartily at her own remarks, or those of the spectators. Her health is perfectly good, and her appearance very neat. She was baptized in the Potomac river and received into the Baptist Church 116 years ago, and takes great pleasure in conversing with Ministers and religious persons. The appearance of this marvellous relic of antiquity strikes the beholder with amazement, and convinces him that his eyes are resting on the oldest specimen of mortality they ever before beheld. Original, authentic and indisputable documents prove however astonishing the fact may appear, JOICE HETH is in every respect the person she is represented.

The most eminent physicians and intelligent men in Cincinnati, Philadelphia, New-York, Boston and many other places have examined this *living skeleton* and the documents accompanying her, and all *invariably* pronounce her to be as represented 161 *years of age*! Indeed it is impossible for any person, however incredulous, to visit her without astonishment and the most perfect satisfaction that she is as old as represented.

☞ A female is in continual attendance, and will give every attention to the ladies who visit this relic of by gone ages.

She was visited at Niblo's Garden New York, by *ten thousand persons* in two weeks.——Hours of exhibition from 9 A. M to 1 P. M. and from 3 to 6 and from 7 to 9 P. M.—Admittance 25 cents—Children 12½ cents.

☞ For further particulars, see newspapers of the day. ☞ Over

EVERY MAN RIDES HIS OWN HOBBY.

P.T. BARNUM

THE GREAT EST SHOW ON EAR TH !!!

GO TO B E A N'S, FOR YOUR
DRY AND FANCY GOODS.
BEST STYLES and LOWEST PRICES.
Springfield, Vt.

Above: *Barnum's first mansion, Iranistan, was built in 1848 and cost about $150,000 to complete. It was a replica of the Oriental Pavilion of George IV. Painting by A.B. Guernsey. Courtesy, P.T. Barnum Museum*

Right: *Little was saved in the 1858 fire that destroyed Barnum's Iranistan mansion. However, this exhibit in the P.T. Barnum Museum contains some of the furniture from that home. Photo by Neil Swanson. Courtesy, P.T. Barnum Museum*

Facing page, top: *Bridgeport became the circus capital of the world when P.T. Barnum selected the city to be his winter headquarters. Courtesy, Robert Clifford Collection*

Facing page, bottom: *In 1842 P.T. Barnum opened his American Museum in New York City. The museum, on the corner of Anne and Fulton streets, contained animals, oddities of nature, and such attractions as the Fejee Mermaid and the Wild Men of Borneo. Courtesy, P.T. Barnum Museum*

COMPOSED BY

FRANCIS H. BROWN

Published by BERRY & GORDON 297 Broadway.
NEW YORK
PHILADELPHIA, JOHN E. GOULD.
50 Cts nett.

Left: *In 1880 Barnum joined with James A. Bailey to create the Barnum and Bailey Circus. Photo by Neil Swanson. Courtesy, P.T. Barnum Museum*

Facing page: *For a mere fifty cents in 1855 you could own the music to P.T. Barnum's "National Poultry Show Polka." Courtesy, Historical Collections, Bridgeport Public Library*

Above: *Thousands bought tickets to see the celebrated soprano, Jenny Lind. Lind gave ninety-five concerts in nineteen cities in less than one year. Courtesy, Historical Collections, Bridgeport Public Library*

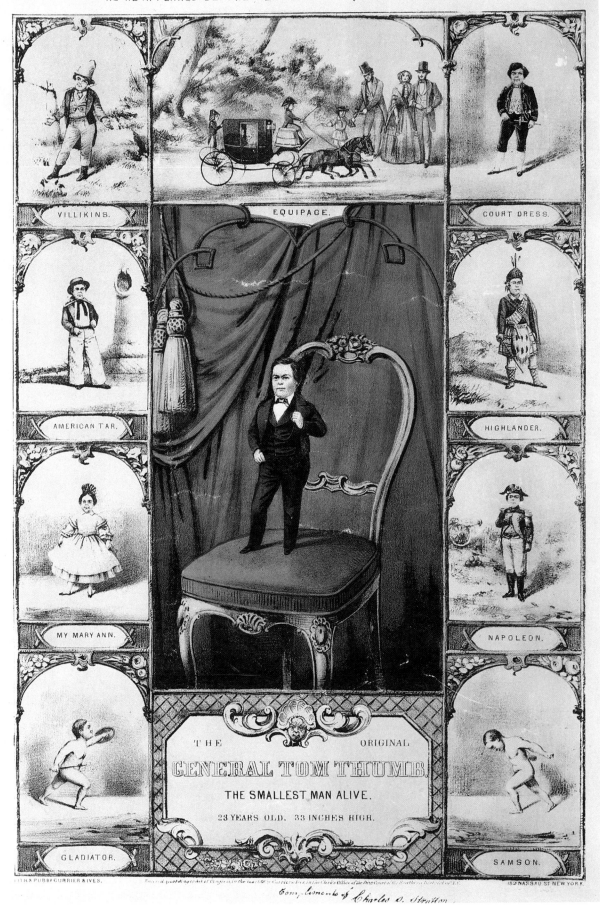

VILLIKINS.

EQUIPAGE.

COURT DRESS.

AMERICAN TAR.

HIGHLANDER.

MY MARY ANN.

NAPOLEON.

THE ORIGINAL

GENERAL TOM THUMB.

THE SMALLEST MAN ALIVE.

23 YEARS OLD. 33 INCHES HIGH.

GLADIATOR.

SAMSON.

Compliments of Charles S. Stratton

152 NASSAU ST NEW YORK.

Above: *This pipe (about the size of a matchbook) and many other personal belongings of Tom Thumb (Charles Stratton) are on display at the P.T. Barnum Museum. Photo by Neil Swanson. Courtesy, P.T. Barnum Museum*

Facing page: *This poster of "The General" was likely used as a promotional piece following his appearances before Queen Victoria. Courtesy, Historical Collections, Bridgeport Public Library*

Top: *Paper doll figures of Tom Thumb and his wife were available from Barnum's circus. Several sets of clothes were included with each doll, and it was possible to dress Thumb in many of the costumes he wore when he performed for Queen Victoria. Photo by Neil Swanson. Courtesy, P.T. Barnum Museum*

Above: *These are some of the clothes and costumes belonging to Charles and Lavinia Stratton. The six-inch ruler indicates the small scale of the clothing. Photo by Neil Swanson. Courtesy, P.T. Barnum Museum*

Charles S. Stratton,

KNOWN AS

PHOTOGRAPHED BY E. T. WHITNEY & CO., NORWALK, CT.

GENERAL TOM THUMB.

The smallest man alive. Born in Bridgeport, Conn., January 4th, 1838. He has appeared three times before Her Majesty Queen Victoria, and also before most of the crowned heads of Europe. His performances have been witnessed by upwards of Twenty Millions of Persons.

WHITNEY & Co., have the General's assurance that this is the last picture he will have taken in character. They will furnish copies by mail, in each or all his characters, for 25 cents each. Direct, E. T. WHITNEY & Co., Photograph and Fine Art Gallery, Norwalk, Conn.

The "smallest man alive" poses for the last time in character, circa 1860. Since he was four years old, Charles Stratton traveled the world with P.T. Barnum, entertaining millions. Copies of this photo were available for twenty-five cents. Courtesy, Historical Collections, Bridgeport Public Library

back his purchase of the American Museum. He filled his newest prize with numerous odd attractions, including the Fejee Mermaid (a combination monkey and fish), the Wild Men of Borneo, the bearded lady Josephine Clofullia, and Chang and Eng, the original Siamese Twins. Barnum became a national favorite.

But the attraction that catapulted the big man to international fame was Bridgeport's own twenty-five-inch boy, Charles S. Stratton, better known as Tom Thumb.

Barnum met Stratton in November 1842 while visiting his brother, who operated the Franklin Hotel in Bridgeport. Barnum had

heard of a remarkably small child, and at my request, my brother Philo F. Barnum, brought him to the hotel. He was not two feet high; he weighed less than 16 pounds, and was the smallest child I ever saw that could walk alone; he was a perfectly formed, bright-eyed little fellow, with light hair and ruddy cheeks, and enjoyed the best of health. He was exceedingly bashful, but after some coaxing, he was induced to talk with me and he told me that he was the son of Sherwood E. Stratton of Bridgeport, and that his own name was Charles S. Stratton. After seeing him and talking with him, I at once determined to secure his services from his parents and to exhibit him in public.

Barnum hired Stratton, who was just four years old, for three dollars a week plus traveling and board expenses for his mother. (Stratton's parents were normal sized.) In December 1842 Barnum "announced the dwarf on my museum bills as 'General Tom Thumb.'" (Though

Barnum often referred to Stratton as his dwarf, he was actually a midget. Midgets are proportioned normally, but on a smaller scale.) Barnum devoted numerous hours educating and training his tiny prodigy for singing and dancing. Tom Thumb had a "great deal of native talent" and Barnum hired him and his parents for a year at seven dollars per week, plus fifty dollars at the end of the engagement to exhibit him anywhere in the country. As Tom Thumb became a public favorite, it wasn't long before Barnum upped his weekly salary to twenty-five dollars. Barnum for a time was reluctant to contract Tom Thumb for any great length of time for fear he would grow and force him to abort his smallest-man-on-earth campaign.

It turned out that Barnum's biggest problem with the midget was counting the money he made from him. (Tom Thumb reached a height of only forty inches.) The pair spent three years in Europe, including London and Paris, where Thumb played and danced before the "crowned heads of Europe." He even performed for Queen Victoria at Buckingham Palace.

In 1862 Barnum hired another midget, Lavinia Warren of Middleboro, Massachusetts. Stratton and Warren were married February 10, 1863, in New York and resided in a mansion at Bridgeport's Main Street and North Avenue. The Tom Thumb Conservatory, as it was known, was demolished in 1952 to make room for a parking lot for City National Bank. Tom Thumb established Barnum as the most celebrated showman of the times, and in turn Barnum became Bridgeport's greatest public relations man.

While Barnum delighted in all the attention, he urgently wanted to be recognized as an impresario of "legitimate" performers. The "Swedish Nightingale" Jenny Lind, the most celebrated European soprano, represented a much different kind of Barnum showcase. In 1848, Barnum completed his innovative oriental-style home Iranistan, and featured it on his letterhead in a pitch to bring Lind to the United

82

Facing page: *On September 1, 1850, Barnum introduced to America the "Swedish Nightingale," Jenny Lind, the celebrated European soprano. In less than a year, Lind concert receipts totaled more than $700,000. Courtesy, Historical Collections, Bridgeport Public Library*

Right: *Charles Stratton catapulted P.T. Barnum to international fame after Barnum met Stratton in November 1842 while visiting his brother, Philo, who operated the Franklin Hotel in Bridgeport. Courtesy, Historical Collections, Bridgeport Public Library*

Below: *Barnum and Tom Thumb spend three years in Europe, including London and Paris, where Thumb entertained royalty. Courtesy, Historical Collections, Bridgeport Public Library*

States. Lind surmised that she wanted to visit a place that had such a beautiful house. Before she had even set foot in America, Barnum started an avalanche of publicity and thousands covered the wharves in New York to watch her arrival on September 1, 1850. Lind gave ninety-five concerts for Barnum in nineteen cities in less than a year. The receipts totalled more than $700,000.

*　　　*　　　*

By 1850, Barnum's home life centered on Bridgeport; its transportation and nearness to New York was just what he wanted.

"Its situation as the terminus of the Naugatuck and the Housatonic railways, its accessibility to New York, with its two daily steamboats to and from the metropolis, and its dozen daily trains of the New York and Boston and Shore Line railways are all elements of prosperity which are rapidly telling in favor of this busy, beautiful, and charming city."

It was in the last thirty years of his life that Barnum's architectural work infused the city with beauty. He teamed up with two English brothers, George and Charles Palliser, to design and build inexpensive single-family "Model Gothic Cottages" in the area of Main, Broad, Whiting, and Atlantic streets. The brothers' first project was laid out over what had been the municipal cemetery on Cottage Street. Barnum advocated the establishment of a rural park-like burial ground, got state approval, and raised the funds to transfer the 4,000 interments to the new Mountain Grove Cemetery. Many people complained about the transfer of their relatives and friends, as truckloads of bodies were hauled over to Mountain Grove by George W. Pool, a retired butcher hired by Barnum. Pool apparently had little regard for matching the deceased with the correct headstone, and it seems he didn't empty the old municipal cemetery when he made the transfers; even in recent years from time to time

skeletons and headstones have been dug up among the houses at the old Cottage Street location.

"The cottages they designed here between 1874 and 1878, of the most fashionable architectural lines and unbelievably modest price tags, were a smashing success with homebuyers," said Charles Brilvitch, a Bridgeport architectural historian, of the Pallisers' and P.T.'s project. "They began replicating this success all over town, and soon all of Connecticut was clamoring for Palliser houses."

Brilvitch, for one, is quite familiar with the Barnum myth. He resides in one of Bridgeport's architectural beauties, the Octagon House, built in 1856 by clothier Nathan Gould at Barnum Avenue and Harriet Street. Numerous newspaper accounts credit Barnum with building the house and charging the curious twenty-five cents to see "a round house on a square lot."

The Pallisers wrote design books with basic patterns, signaling the emergence of mail-order architecture in America. In 1880, Barnum and the Pallisers started a new South End development, building mansion-scaled Victorian duplexes. They saved money on foundation costs and the houses remained affordable for the working class. In 1982 the block bound by Austin, Gregory, and Atlantic streets and Myrtle Avenue was officially listed as a Historic District in the National Register of Historic Places.

Barnum constantly looked for ways to beautify Bridgeport. In 1863, he proposed that Bridgeport's shore on Long Island Sound, at that time strewn with rocks and boulders, should be cleared out, opened along the entire waterfront, and transformed into a park. He predicted that such an improvement would increase the taxable value of the property in the area, enrich the city treasury, be an attraction to visitors, and increase development.

Barnum felt that "it dwelt upon the absurdity, almost criminality, that a beautiful city

Barnum's third Bridgeport home, Waldemere, completed in 1869, remains today as separate residences at Atlantic and Rennell streets in Bridgeport and One Pauline Street in Stratford. Courtesy, Historical Collections, Bridgeport Public Library

Phineas Taylor Barnum and Charles Stratton (shown here circa 1844) enjoyed enormous, worldwide success. Stratton began working for Barnum at age four, appearing first at Barnum's American Museum in 1842. Courtesy, P.T. Barnum Museum

like Bridgeport, lying on the shore of a broad expanse of salt water, should so cage itself in that not an inhabitant could approach the beach."

Barnum faced stiff opposition from many "old foggies," who complained that people anxious to see salt water and inhale the breeze from the sound could take boats at the wharves. Barnum convinced several landowners to donate land and he purchased and donated about $20,000 worth of land himself. Hundreds of workmen graded inaccessible approaches to the beach and laid out walks and drives. The rocks and boulders over which Barnum had attempted to cross by foot and horseback were used to build a seawall. Paths were opened, trees planted, and a bandstand and Civil War Soldiers' and Sailors' Monument were erected. Barnum presented this new improvement to the city and called it Seaside Park. "I do not believe that a million dollars, today, would compensate the city of Bridgeport for the loss of what is confessed to be the most delightful public pleasureground between New York and Boston," Barnum wrote.

In the summer of 1866, with Barnum's wife's health declining, a physician recommended that the family move nearer to the seashore. Barnum's first house, Iranistan, had burned to the ground in 1857. A few years later he built his dream house, the elegant Lindencroft, which was adorned with statuary and fountains, trees and shrubbery and beautiful flowers. Lindencroft was sold July 1, 1867. He moved into his completed house Waldemere (Woods by the Sea) in June 1869, another house built with the highest in comfort,

keeping in mind always that houses are made

to live in as well as to look at, and to be homes rather than mere residences. So the house was made to include abundant room for guests, with dressing rooms and baths to every chamber; water from the city throughout the premises; gas, manufactured on my own ground; and that greatest of all comforts, a semi-detached kitchen, so that the smell as well as the secrets of the cuisine might be confined to its own locality.

Two sections of Waldemere remain today as separate residences, one at Atlantic and Rennell streets, and the other at One Pauline Street in Lordship, across Bridgeport's harbor, the residence owned by actress Nancy Marchand. Barnum's last Bridgeport mansion, Marina, was built in 1889 for his second wife, Nancy Fish, after the death of Charity. The University of Bridgeport eventually acquired Marina and demolished it in 1961 to build the Marina Dining Hall.

*   *   *

It wasn't until the last twenty years of his life that Barnum's circus won international fame, nevertheless the tireless worker served one term as mayor in 1875, winning by 200 votes over Democrat Frederick Hurd. Barnum, a staunch Democrat until his friendship with Republican Abraham Lincoln, won the election as a Republican despite the Democrats' 500-voter majority. Democratic chants branded him a flimflam showman who cared nothing for public service.

Barnum was truly one of Bridgeport's first progressive mayors, fighting for numerous public improvements (including an abundant, citywide water supply), called on the police department to crack down on vice, and successfully warred against Sunday liquor sales. Barnum vehemently spoke out against the drinking of alcohol and often spoke of reform. "Caring for all, partial to none," was one of his mayoral slogans.

A vintage Barnum publicity stunt: in 1888 the Stratford Avenue Bridge was replaced by a new iron structure. To assure everyone of its safety, Barnum paraded a dozen elephants weighing some thirty-six tons onto the bridge. Barnum, hatless and white haired, is standing in the middle of the group. The hatless man standing next to Barnum is Patrick Coughlin, Bridgeport's first Irish mayor. Photo by Corbit's Studio. Courtesy, P.T. Barnum Museum

"Before there can be any reform in Bridgeport," he told an alderman, "there will have to be a few first-class funerals."

Barnum possessed good humor and had a razor-sharp wit. At one of his temperance lectures, a heckler asked whether alcohol hurt a man internally or externally. Barnum shot back, "Eternally."

"Spiritous liquors of the present day are so much adulterated and doubly poisoned that their use fires the brain and drives their victims to madness, violence and murder," he told the Common Council.

The money annually expended for intoxicating liquors, and the cost of their evil results in Bridgeport, or any other American city where liquor selling is licensed, would pay the entire expenses of the city (if liquors were not drank) including the public schools, give a good suit of clothes to every poor person of both sexes, a barrel of flour to every poor family living within its municipal boundaries, and leave a handsome surplus on hand. Our enormous expenses for the trial and punishment of criminals, as well as the support of the poor are mainly caused by this traffic. Surely then it is our duty to do all we can, legally, to limit and mitigate its evil.

Barnum sapped every ounce of mayoral power and the magic of his words to lead Bridgeport. He fought persistently with the Common Council in defending the Board of Police Commissioners' right to maintain the ultimate authority in the police department. During his

farewell speech to the council, he urged all to hold no grudges.

Occasional thunder and lightning are needful to the preservation of a pure atmosphere. If those who invoke the hurricane are prompted by pure and disinterested motives, their action will be approved. I am glad to believe that you have endeavored to study and promote the best interests of the city. In my efforts to be faithful to duty, I have never felt the slightest personal animosity, and I entertain for each and every member of this Council sincere wishes for their happiness and all the public approval which their actions merit.

And now, gentlemen, as we are about to close our labors in a harmonious spirit, and bid each other a friendly farewell, we have like the Arabs, only to 'fold our tents and silently steal away,' congratulating ourselves that this is the only 'stealing' which has been performed by this Honorable Body.

*   *   *

Barnum's circus career took off in 1870 with the formation of his immense circus. "The Greatest Show On Earth" consisted of a museum, menagerie, and eventually a grand three-ring circus that required 500 men, numerous horses, and a seventy-car freight train to transport it through the country. Bridgeport became the circus capital of the world when Barnum selected it as the winter headquarters—the site was a ten-acre lot in the West End along Wordin Avenue, Norman Street, and Railroad Avenue. Daily, downtown Bridgeport was treated to visits from the most famous circus characters, including William F. "Buffalo Bill" Cody.

On November 20, 1887, an evening fire destroyed the winter headquarters, killing nearly all the animals except for several elephants and a lion which escaped into the streets and nearby barns. Barnum's "sacred" white elephant was killed in the blaze. Barnum, the eternal optimist, immediately began erecting another winter headquarters.

"I am not in show business alone to make money. I feel it my mission, as long as I live, to provide clean, moral, and healthful recreation for the public to which I have so long catered," Barnum explained.

Throughout his life, Barnum was cursed by fires; his Iranistan home, New York museum (twice burned), and winter headquarters all were hit by fire. In 1880 Barnum formed a partnership with circus associate James A. Bailey, who carried on the circus after Barnum's death. The Barnum and Bailey Circus was sold to the Ringling Brothers in 1907, and the new owners moved the headquarters to Sarasota, Florida, in 1927.

Even in the last years of his life Barnum never lost his enthusiasm for a masterful publicity stunt. One of his last Bridgeport gimmicks took place in 1888. The Stratford Avenue Bridge was replaced by a new iron structure and Barnum assured everyone of its safety by parading twelve elephants weighing thirty-six tons onto the bridge.

In the fall of 1890, a stroke confined Barnum to his home. In his final letter to his partner James Bailey, the Greatest Showman on Earth reflected on his career:

Never cater to the baser instincts of humanity, strive as I have always done to elevate the moral tone of amusements, and always remember that the children have ever been our best patrons. I would rather hear the pleased laugh of a child over some feature of my exhibition than receive as I did the flattering compliments of the Prince of Wales. I am prouder of my title 'The Children's Friend' than if I were to be called 'The King of the World.'

I regret exceedingly that my bodily weakness prevents my being present at the exhibition in New York, for I veritably believe that if I

Just as in the first Barnum Festival Parade in 1949, there is always a best float among floats. The Lycoming Girls Club won best float award in the Barnum parade in 1962. Their float featured a Gemini capsule orbiting the earth. The girls' costumes were truly space-age for 1962. Bridgeport Brass president Herman W. Steinkraus conceived of the festival as a way to reunite the city, then suffering a postwar slump. Courtesy, Historical Collections, Bridgeport Public Library

In 1949 Bridgeport saluted the greatest showman on earth with the Barnum Festival. The King and Queen event, Tom Thumb competition, Jenny Lind Concert, grand parade, and the midway, shown here at Seaside Park, represent some of the special features associated with the Barnum tribute. Courtesy, Historical Collections, Bridgeport Public Library

could again see the rows of bright-faced children at our matinees and observe their eyes grow round with wonder or hear their hearty laughter, it would do me more good than all the medicine in the world.

I am too weak to write more now, but let me entreat you to never allow the honorable and honestly acquired title of 'The Greatest Show on Earth' to be in any way disgraced or lessened in fame. Go on as you have begun and I know you will continue to prosper.

Barnum died five days later on April 7, 1891. The public and press reacted with intense sorrow. "The death of Barnum ends a unique career, and no singular combination of traits and talents survives to compete with his memory," wrote the *New York Tribune*. "It is probably safe to say that not more than half a dozen persons now living, including reigning sovereigns, are known by name to so many millions of their fellow beings as was Barnum."

"The death of P.T. Barnum may not 'eclipse the gaiety of nations,' but it takes out of the world one who has added more to this gaiety than perhaps any other man who has ever lived," noted the *New York World*.

"Bridgeport has long since outgrown the influence of any one man, but still so far as civilization has penetrated, Bridgeport has been associated with his name and is known as the city in which he made his home," wrote the *Bridgeport Standard*.

Bridgeport has indeed outgrown the influence of any one man, but no man has had more influence on Bridgeport than P.T. Barnum, a man who cherished friendships with Abraham Lincoln and Mark Twain, a man so famous that he wrote of receiving letters from foreign countries addressed simply "P.T. Barnum, America" and a man who made Bridgeport a better place to live.

Barnum lives on in Bridgeport; no less than forty businesses, streets, and enterprises are named for him or his family, including Barnum Avenue, Barnum School, and of course, the Barnum Museum and the Barnum Festival. Playwright Mark Bramble even captured Barnum in a Broadway show of the same name in 1980.

In life and in death, Barnum has benefited Bridgeport. He willed the money for the museum that recalls the step-right-up spieling of his circus life. It is there that hundreds of thousands have rediscovered Tom Thumb, Jenny Lind, and P.T. himself. "Barnum's the most important 19th Century figure in the development of Bridgeport," said museum curator Robert Pelton.

In 1949, so that Barnum's "kind acts may live forever," Bridgeport saluted the showman with the Barnum Festival, an idea generated by Bridgeport Brass executive Herman W. Steinkraus. It includes the King and Queen event, the Jenny Lind Concert, the Tom Thumb competition, and numerous other special features, capped by the grand parade, all saying thanks to the Greatest Showman on Earth and Bridgeport's first citizen.

Barnum's impact was worldwide. During one of his visits to England, Barnum listened to the Bishop of London making a farewell speech. The Bishop closed by saying, "I hope I shall see you in heaven." Barnum smiled and answered, "You will if you are there." So will all of Bridgeport.

With Pleasure Beach Amusement Park on the horizon, the Lake Torpedo Boat Company yard, at the foot of Seaview Avenue, is seen here in 1922. Owner Simon Lake submitted a submarine design to the U.S. War Department in 1893, but the government decided against construction at that time. Courtesy, Historical Collections, Bridgeport Public Library

CHAPTER V

All That

Brass

"Industria Crescimus— By Industry We Thrive"

—*city motto, adopted 1875*

When Bridgeport's city fathers introduced this city motto saluting the development of Barnum's East Bridgeport, few could have realized that some forty years later their city would have clearly earned its reputation as the industrial center of the country. If the true worth of a city is measured by how much it has contributed to progress, then the contribution of Bridgeport's labor force, inventiveness, and industrial prominence have left its mark nationwide. Bridgeport has boasted of being the sewing machine and corset capital of the world, and it was the armament center of the nation during the two world wars. Its manufacturing produced an assortment of offbeat and progressive firsts, including model trains, luxury cars, aerosol sprays, and undergarments. Its Yankee ingenuity invented the pull-chain light socket, and the micrometer, which is used in various industries to measure small distances and diameters. Add to that the aviation genius of Igor Sikorsky and the enterprising Dymaxion automobile design of R. Buckminster Fuller.

*   *   *

Barnum's East Bridgeport set the tone for citywide manufacturing, and the race was led by the sewing machine industry. After Barnum's Jerome Clock Factory failed, sewing machine partners Nathaniel Wheeler and Allen

Wilson left Middletown, Connecticut, to occupy the clock factory's East Washington Avenue building in 1856. Ten years later Elias Howe, Jr., of Spencer, Massachusetts, who had successfully defended his 1845 sewing machine design against patent infringers, manufactured machines from a large building at Howe and Kossuth streets which had a dock for shipping machines to New York buyers. Wheeler, Wilson, and Howe revolutionized the clothing industry, and sewing machine manufacturing remained Bridgeport's major industry through the end of the nineteenth century.

The city of Bridgeport was just thirty years old at this time and was making its first giant step in rapid growth, advancing from its earlier comb and hatmaking and patent leather industries, and the anchoring carriage and saddlery industries.

Of the early sewing machine entrepreneurs,

Sewing machine manufacturing in Bridgeport was the city's major industry through the end of the nineteenth century. This drawing of the machine made by partners Allen B. Wilson and Nathaniel Wheeler in 1852 was the beginning of the industrial revolution that put Bridgeport on the map. Courtesy, Historical Collections, Bridgeport Public Library

The Singer Sewing Machine Company absorbed the Wheeler and Wilson Company in 1905. Singer was the first to offer installment plan purchasing, which put the sewing machine within the reach of nearly everyone. Courtesy, Historical Collections, Bridgeport Public Library

Wheeler won the credit for making the machine a commercial success through simplified machine operation and improvements that reduced the costs of manufacture. Singer, which absorbed the company in 1905, introduced an installment-buying sales system which further supported the industry. By train and commercial freighter, thousands of sewing machines left Bridgeport as the nation's population and demand for clothing burgeoned during the Civil War. Another Bridgeport company of national importance was the Union Metallic Cartridge Company, founded in 1867. The New York dealer of munitions located its plant on Pauline Street in East Bridgeport and manufactured arms during the Civil War.

The mid-nineteenth century also was a growth period for banking. Between 1850 and 1860 three banking institutions were chartered that became the forerunners of today's Citytrust. People's Bank was chartered in 1842, and Mechanics and Farmers Bank was chartered in 1871. The Connecticut National Bank had its

This twenty-six-piece marching band from the Wheeler and Wilson Factory posed for this postcard photo in the late 1800s. Parades were popular and all the major industries had a band. Before becoming a heavily industrial city, Bridgeport factories produced hats, patent leather, and was the home of a number of saddlery and carriage shops. Courtesy, Robert Clifford Collection

People's Bank, on the corner of Main and Bank streets, was chartered in 1842. The First National Bank occupied the second floor of this building, seen here circa 1870. Courtesy, Historical Collections, Bridgeport Public Library

attracting capital and promoting business interests in the city.

The Bridgeport Brass Company, incorporated in 1865, operated from a sprawling plant on Housatonic Avenue. It got its start from the brass-framed hoop skirts which became popular in the 1860s. When styles changed in 1870, the company concentrated on making kerosene lamps and parts, and later it made the first flat copper sheets for photoengraving purposes and a variety of brass parts for plumbing equipment, automobile tire valves, shell casings, and parts for flashlights. America's first micrometer originated in the brass shop. During World War II, Bridgeport Brass invented the DDT aerosol bomb, used in tropical jungles to destroy disease-carrying insects. After the war, the product was marketed for commercial use

Originally built in 1806 (shown being remodeled in 1856), the Bridgeport Bank was the first organized bank in Bridgeport. Courtesy, Historical Collections, Bridgeport Public Library

beginning as the first banking institution in Bridgeport, organized as the Bridgeport Bank in 1806.

In 1860, Bridgeport's ninety-six manufacturing establishments employed 2,196 males and 1,131 females. The sewing machine and carriage making companies together employed 1,000 people.

The men who ran these companies were the most go-getting of an extremely dynamic breed of early entrepreneurs who, during the emergence of steam power, advanced Bridgeport toward its most spectacular growth period. Brass, machine tool, and corset companies would make Bridgeport a world leader in those fields and, years later, the electrical equipment industry would join their ranks. The expanding industrial climate was aided in 1875 by the founding of the Board of Trade, which was active in

Right: *Workers here trim edges in the final process of manu-facturing sheet brass in 1909. Beginning with brass hoops for skirts in the 1860s, Bridgeport Brass later produced parts for brass lamps, shell casings, and tire valves. Courtesy, Historical Collections, Bridgeport Public Library*

Below: *Bridgeport Brass invented the DDT aerosol bomb dur-ing World War II. DDT was used to kill disease-carrying in-sects, and after the war the product took off with dozens of commercial applications. Courtesy, Historical Collections, Bridgeport Public Library*

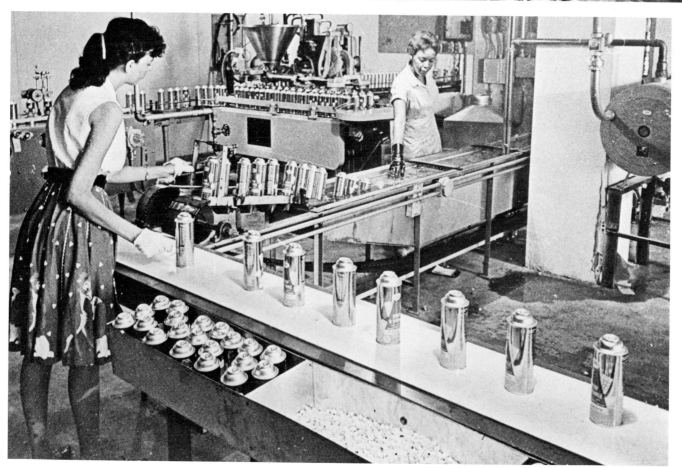

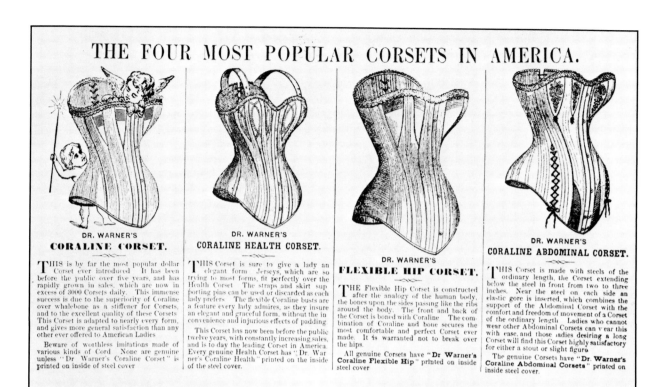

Above: *Dr. I. DeVer Warner and his brother, Dr. Lucien C. Warner, developed the first fitted undergarments and the first A-B-C-D bra sizes. In 1912 the Warners opened the largest corset manufacturing plant in the world, occupying two city blocks in Bridgeport's South End. Authentic Warner corsets had "Dr. Warner's Coraline" printed inside the steel cover. This advertisement ran in 1883. Courtesy, Historical Collections, Bridgeport Public Library*

Facing page: *Founded in 1888, Harvey Hubbell's machine tool company at State and Bostwick Avenue developed many electrical conveniences still in use today. The building is still occupied today by Hubbell's company. Courtesy, Historical Collections, Bridgeport Public Library*

under the Bridgeport Brass Aer-A-Sol trademark.

Bridgeport's manufacturing prominence paved the way for another industry—machine tools. Edward P. Bullard, following a wave of industrial pioneers who left their home states for Bridgeport, realized that with all this growth, companies would need machines to make machines. He established the Bullard Company at Broad Street and Railroad Avenue in 1880 and produced tools for the manufacture of sewing machines, bicycles, textile machinery, and machines used in railroad repair shops and shipbuilding plants.

Harvey Hubbell founded a machine tool company at State Street and Bostwick Avenue in 1888 that became prominent for manufacturing wiring devices. Hubbell developed the rolled-thread screw, the electric pull-chain light fixture (which complemented Thomas Edison's light bulb), and the duplex interchangeable receptacle plug. Before Hubbell's creation, electrical wires were soldered into the wall outlet.

While Bridgeport served as the sewing machine capital of the world, it also became the world leader in corset manufacturing. Dr. I. DeVer Warner and his brother, Dr. Lucien C. Warner, based their Warner Brothers Company at 325 Lafayette Street in 1874, developing a long line of women's undergarments, including the two-way stretch girdle and the first line of bras utilizing the A-B-C-D sizing system. Warner's fitted corsets made the old tie-in style obsolete. As a result of the influx of out-of-state female workers, the Warners opened the Seaside Institute, an educational housing facility for women. First Lady Frances Folsom Cleveland attended the Seaside Institute dedication ceremonies on November 5, 1887. The facility later became the headquarters for the *Bridgeport Herald*. In 1912, Warners' became

"Unhampered by the Interstate Commerce Commission, immune from freight rate regulation, and undetected as yet by the Government." This was from an advertisement for the popular mechanical trains introduced by the Ives Manufacturing Company in 1901, which are still praised by collectors today. Ives employees posed for this portrait around 1910. Courtesy, Historical Collections, Bridgeport Public Library the largest corset manufacturer in the world, expanding its plant to fill two city blocks in the South End, and employing 3,300 workers.

Companies such as the Warners' mirrored a period of ingenuity that included diverse inventors and risk takers. In 1871, William R. Frisbie baked five-cent pies from a house on Kossuth Street and delivered them by horse and wagon. In 1915 his son built a three-story bakery which produced more than 50,000 pies per day twenty years later. This bit of news might have been lost in city history had it not been for company employees flinging the heavy metal pie tins during lunch break (thousands found the bottom of the Pequonnock River) and Yale students skimming them on the New Haven Green. The Wham-0 Manufacturing Company spotted Yalies tossing the pie tins in the 1940s and developed their own plastic model (Frisbees), which have since soared through every yard, beach, and park in America.

Bridgeporter Charles F. Ritchel also soared— 200 feet over the Connecticut River in the world's first propeller-powered balloon flight on July 13, 1878. Ritchel controlled his hydrogen balloon through the action of foot pedals. He is also credited with inventing roller skates. His *Bridgeport Post* obituary reports he had 150 inventions, "all of them moneymakers," but his marketing inability failed to turn a profit. He died broke at age sixty in 1911.

The Ives Manufacturing Company, founded in 1868 on Water Street, instigated the wind-up toy craze, and steered the nation's railroad network into the home in 1901 by producing the first mechanical trains to run on tracks. "Unhampered by the Interstate Commerce Commission, immune from freight rate regulation, and undetected as yet by the Government," whistled the Ives advertisement for the miniature clockwork railroad system. The Ives Company closed in 1932, but its trains remain precious collector's items.

While the Ives Company invention relied on rails in 1901, that same year Gustave White-

head relied on his propeller-driven aircraft in what was arguably the first airplane flight in history—two years before the first flight of Wilbur and Orville Wright at Kitty Hawk, North Carolina. Whitehead was a German immigrant who experimented with aircraft as early as 1897 in several East Coast cities before making his home on Pine Street in the West End where he built his aircraft. On August 14, 1901, as witnessed by a *Bridgeport Herald* reporter, Whitehead made four flights, ascending 200 feet and traveling about one mile. Six months later, Whitehead flew for about seven miles over Long Island Sound. Whitehead was apparently much too occupied with flying than promoting his accomplishment and when he really needed it had little documentation to support his air flights. Author Stella Randolph, who wrote two books on Whitehead, uncovered his feats in the 1930s. William O'Dwyer of Fairfield, whose more recent book, *History By Contract*, continues Randolph's research, and reports the Smithsonian Institution acknowledges the Wright brothers because their airplane could be obtained for display. Smithsonian officials and the Wright family signed a contract in 1948 agreeing that the plane must be returned should someone else be given credit for being the first to fly. As for Whitehead, he failed to market his aircraft and died penniless in 1927.

By air or land, Bridgeport labor produced many innovations. The Locomobile Company of America, which developed luxury cars that sold for more than $11,000 in 1922, proclaimed it produced the best-built car in America. The company policy emphasized comfort above all, and its objective was to build a limited number of exceedingly lavish Locomobile cars to perfection. Not more than four cars per day were assembled by hand to extend intimate attention to each car and owner. The company's limousine model had cut-glass side lamps, a tiffany shade covering the dome light, trim of sterling silver, an electric telephone allowing passengers

On the steps of Holy Rosary Church at East Washington and Harriet Street, the Frisbie Pie Company baseball team poses for this picture about 1935. In 1871 William R. Frisbie baked pies that sold for five cents and were delivered by horse and wagon. In 1915 his son built a three-story bakery on Kossuth Street and by 1924 nine tons of pies left Bridgeport every day. Before power became available on the East Side in 1905, Frisbie built his own powerplant in his basement. Photo by B. Brignolo, Brignolo Studios. Courtesy, Historical Collections, Bridgeport Public Library

Right: *On August 14, 1901, Gustave Whitehead took his #21 aircraft for four flights, witnessed by a Bridgeport Herald reporter. Whitehead experimented with aircraft in several East Coast cities as early as 1897, but, unable to market his aircraft, he died penniless in 1927. Courtesy, Gustave Weisskoph Museum*

Below: *This January 1986 photo shows a modern reconstruction of Gustave Whitehead's 1901 plane, undertaken by engineers from Pratt and Whitney, Pitney Bowes, and workers from the SST project. Andy Kosch is the director of construction. Photo by Neil Swanson*

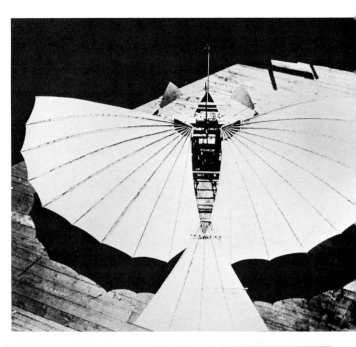

Left: *Whitehead posed in 1901 with his daughter, Rose, in the shade of his aircraft just months before his first flight. The craft's two propellers were carved from wood and were powered by an engine of Whitehead's own design. Courtesy, Gustave Weisskoph Museum*

Below: *Shown here without the propellers and with weighted wings to prevent an unplanned lift-off, the similarity of this 1986 reconstruction to Whitehead's original aircraft is striking. When completed, the craft will fly with wooden props and a steam engine, just as Whitehead's did eighty-five years ago. Photo by Neil Swanson*

Facing page: This car, seen here in a 1948 photo, was the first American-built car to win the prestigious Vanderbilt Cup. The 1906 Locomobile set a speed record during the October 24, 1908, race, reaching a top speed of 64.38 MPH. At the time this photo was taken, the car belonged to Peter Helck. Courtesy, Historical Collections, Bridgeport Public Library

Above: In the late 1800s and early 1900s, the city expanded its water distribution system, especially for fighting fires. When P.T. Barnum became president of the Bridgeport Hydraulic Company some twenty years after its 1857 creation, the expansion of the water supply and the replacement of worn-out pipes began. Workers here are unloading the huge pipes to connect the city to the supply. Courtesy, Robert Clifford Collection

Facing page: *This special 1917 Type Désobligéant Town Model was designed for Elsie Vanderbilt. In 1922, a Locomobile cost more than $11,000, a price only the rich could afford. Each car was hand-built with such conveniences as sterling silver trim, cut-glass side lamps, and even a telephone to speak to the driver. Courtesy, Historical Collections, Bridgeport Public Library*

Right: *The Carlson Brothers opened a carriage shop in 1909 and with the introduction of the automobile they began to produce metal truck bodies as early as 1912. Truck bodies like the Couplex Cab shown here circa 1920 were built to fit the chassis of many different manufacturers, such the White Model 60 shown. By 1936 the brothers had developed the Metro Truck, a cab that was ideal for many types of delivery purposes. Courtesy, Robert Clifford Collection*

to speak to the driver, and a concealed toilet case with a mirror. The company, which set up shop in Bridgeport in 1900, pioneered the development of steam, gasoline, and electric automobiles, but fell victim to the post-World War I depression. In 1922 it was taken over by General Motors founder William C. Durant, whose middle-priced models could not save the company from closing several years later.

R. Buckminster Fuller rented space in the old Locomobile plant and wasn't so successful with his Dymaxion invention, a three wheeled, cucumber-shaped vehicle that streaked 120 miles per hour. His urge for mass production received little interest from auto makers. Fuller went on to invent aluminum houses and the geodesic dome.

Two other Bridgeporters, William and Philip Carlson, took advantage of the growing automobile market. The Carlson brothers were Russian Jews who opened a carriage repair shop in 1909, produced metal cab bodies for trucks in 1912, and by 1936 developed the Metro Truck, a spacious cab used by dairies, bakeries, and the U.S. Postal Service.

The advancement of Bridgeport inventors and business leaders coincided with the progress of public utilities. Gas light came to Bridgeport in May 1849 when the state legislature chartered the Bridgeport Gas Light Company. Two years later the company, located on Housatonic Avenue, had seventy-six private customers and twenty-six public street lamps.

Bridgeporters greeted the coming of gas with opposition, insisting the night should be left alone because illumination would increase the most frequent crime—drunkenness. Electric power emerged in the early 1880s. In 1885 the city's two electric light companies—Thompson-Houston and Brush Electric Company—merged into the Bridgeport Electric Light Company on John Street. Bridgeport had more than 100 streetlights by 1890, and the fee was based on lamp size and number of hours in service before the installation of meters in 1894. On January 30, 1900, the Bridgeport Electric Light Company and New Haven Electric Light consolidated under the name United Illuminating. In 1908, the company operated twenty-four hours a day, marking around-the-clock electricity availability and significantly changing residents' habits of working until dark and going to bed shortly after.

Bridgeport had a limited public water supply during its first fifty years as a city. The city was dependent on several springs until 1853 when the need for an extensive supply, particularly to fight fires, was addressed. The Common Council named Nathaniel Greene to lay water pipes under principal streets so a full supply for the city could be furnished. Greene and others organized the Bridgeport Water Company which formed Bunnell's Pond in northern Bridgeport, filled by the water of the Pequonnock River.

In 1857, the Bridgeport Hydraulic Company was founded, but the city's wait for an adequate supply source, the replacment of worn-out pipes, and quality water main locations didn't end for twenty years, when P.T. Barnum became president of the company. Bunnell's Pond served as the city reservoir until Bridgeport Hydraulic expanded reservoirs in Easton, Fairfield, and Shelton.

Bridgeport's first telephone company—the Telephone Dispatch Company—opened on Main and Fairfield in July 1878, six months after New Haven became the first city in the world to have a commercial switchboard. Thomas B. Doolittle, who first suggested the use of hard

Above: *The Hincks and Johnson Carriage Company was one of at least nine carriage shops in Bridgeport during the late 1800s. Courtesy, Historical Collections, Bridgeport Public Library*

Facing page: *The Southern New England Telephone Company grew out of the original Telephone Dispatch Company, formed in Bridgeport in 1878. Operators are at work here circa 1930, the year that SNET converted to rotary-dial operation. Courtesy, Historical Collections, Bridgeport Public Library*

drawn copper for telephone lines, headed the Bridgeport phone company which numbered 100 subscribers, including Barnum. *The Story of Bridgeport,* written by Elsie Danenberg in 1936, credits Mrs. Augustine Gray as being the first woman exchange operator in the world. Southern New England Telephone Company was formed October 2, 1882, and moved about the city until settling into its present site at John and Courtland in 1930—the year Bridgeport service converted to dial operation.

*   *   *

Buoyed by the muscle of the immigrant groups, Bridgeport was building a solid industrial base while heading for its strongest period of growth in history during World War I. In the years just prior to the war, Connecticut was in the throes of an industrial slump with many factories working only three or four days per week. Bridgeport had become one of the most progressive cities in New England and although it suffered pains to employ and house the newcomers of the immigrant surge, it was prepared to meet the challenge.

In 1915, the English, French, and Russian armies placed heavy munitions orders with Remington Arms and the Union Metallic Company, the largest manufacturers of firearms and ammunitions in the allied countries. The Boston Avenue building was the marvel of its time—thirteen buildings a half-mile long covering eighty acres of floor space. The plant manufactured bayonets, guns of small and large caliber, and the Browning machine gun which fired a belt of 250 rounds of ammunition in about twenty seconds. At one point the company hired a new employee every twenty minutes and by 1916 it employed over 22,000 persons. The national troop-guarded zone known as "Remington City" became recognized as one of the most important and protected spots in the world.

Above: *The explosion of sixteen tons of gunpowder on May 14, 1906, virtually leveled "Success Hill." Not long after the accident, the area became known as the Remington Nature Preserve and many paintings of hunters with Remington arms were made for advertisements. Courtesy, Robert Clifford Collections*

Below: *Founded in 1867, the Union Metallic Cartridge Company became the Remington Arms Company in 1915. By the time the United States entered World War I, it was the nation's single largest factory, employing more than 22,000 workers. The plant produced seven million rounds of ammunition a week—two-thirds of American ammunition production. Courtesy, Historical Collections, Bridgeport Public Library*

The Bridgeport Chamber of Commerce, founded in 1915, organized the Bridgeport Housing Company which constructed war workers housing projects, including Seaside and Lakeview Villages and Black Rock Gardens.

Remington wasn't the only Bridgeport company that contributed greatly to the defense of the nation. The Locomobile Company manufactured Riker army trucks and Bridgeport Brass produced shell casings. The Lake Torpedo Boat Company, led by submarine designer Simon Lake, produced R-21 submarines that were launched at the foot of Seaview Avenue.

War contracts totaling in the millions catapulted Bridgeport as the leader in statewide prosperity. Bridgeport was called the Arsenal of Democracy and Mayor Clifford B. Wilson's progressive leadership spawned the "Essen of America." The *New York Times* maintained that "regardless of how the war is affecting others, it is demonstrating itself good business for Bridgeport and Bridgeport people."

But pains of growth accompanied Bridgeport's economic prosperity. Roughly 100 strikes marred the open-shop city in the summer of 1915 as Bridgeport became a main target of labor's drive for an eight-hour day. Bridgeport received international attention as national

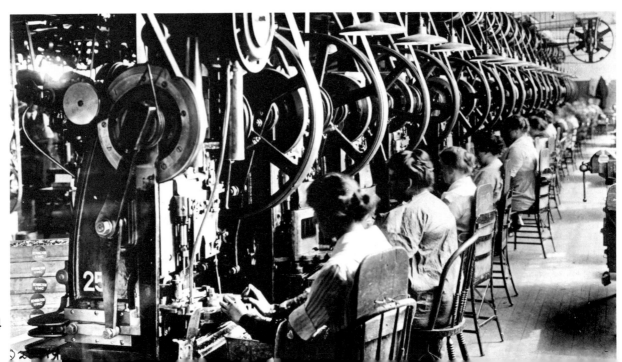

union leaders targeted Remington as the cornerstone of their labor fight. Strikes by building trades, iron workers, machinists, and others lit up the front pages. The walkouts generally included only small numbers of workers at any one time, and factories carried on without major interruption, but the persistent union agitation and the threat of Bridgeport factories being held up during the production of war munitions forced employers to grant concessions.

One of the standoff Remington strikes settled on July 23 left officials of the International Association of Machinists and the National Bridge and Structural Iron Workers claiming victory in securing an eight-hour workday. Company officials, however, maintained that strikes collapsed because they had planned for eight-hour workdays prior to the job action to prevent the city from being plunged into an industrial war. Either way, workers made strides for their eight-hour days and Bridgeport companies continued in their prosperity.

While more than 8,000 served in "the war to end war," thousands of skilled and unskilled workers flooded the city. As a result, rents rose by 50 percent, and Remington Arms and the federal government constructed hundreds of homes to fill the housing gap. The expanding trolley, police, fire, school, and street lighting services were financed by increased taxes and bond issues.

The national fear of radicalism generated during this period threatened order and stability in the state and spread into Bridgeport as well. In March 1919, Bridgeport Police raided the Industrial Workers of the World city headquarters and confiscated a truckload of Communist literature.

Nevertheless, by 1920 the city was the state's leader in industrial employment, and it emerged from World War I as the industrial center of the nation. But the end of the war caused the demand for products to fall, and Bridgeport faced some serious troubles within the emerging peacetime economic picture.

Simon Lake's Lake Torpedo Boat Company produced submarines as early as 1897, the year he submitted plans to the U.S. War Department. In 1918, he began building R-21 submarines for the government, along with O-series, N-series, and S-series submarines. Courtesy, Historical Collections, Bridgeport Public Library

Remington abandoned its huge Boston Avenue munitions plant for a Barnum Avenue location and the plant was occupied by General Electric, which commenced the manufacture of wiring devices. But the impact of the Depression forced a period of crisis for Bridgeport. Acute unemployment led Mayor Edward Buckingham to hire the jobless to perform municipal custodial chores for fifty cents an hour. In 1930 roughly 1,000 men each month repaired streets, painted buildings, and cleaned sidewalks; these tasks added some much-needed relief to the ranks of the unemployed that had swollen to more than twice the number from the previous year. But the worst was yet to come.

The city borrowed $500,000 in 1931, and in order to stretch the work relief funds, it slashed work hours and cut the hourly wage to thirty-five cents an hour, prompting Public Welfare Director Angus Thorne to lament "we can't give them much less." The city also gave to the needy direct payments called scrip—certificates given to merchants in exchange for food and clothing; the merchants were reimbursed by the city in cash.

But 1932 was the year of crisis. Mayor Buckingham desperately pulled out every trick possible to feed and cloth thousands of jobless, down-and-out citizens. The city turned vacant lots into gardens, and hundreds of aliens were dropped from the relief rolls so the city could care for its own destitute citizens. City employees contributed as much as 10 percent of their wages to help the needy, and thousands of dollars were cut from city departments, including $150,000 from the Board of Education.

Above: *With the lower peacetime demand for arms after WWI, Remington Arms no longer needed eighty acres of factory and moved to Barnum Avenue. General Electric has moved into Remington's huge Boston Avenue buildings and is the largest manufacturer in Bridgeport today. Photo by Neil Swanson*

Facing page: *Mayor Edward T. Buckingham's second term, during the Depression, led him to hire the jobless to perform municipal chores for just fifty cents an hour. As the economic crisis worsened, wages fell to thirty-five cents an hour, and in 1932 Buckingham asked city employees to accept a 20 percent cut in salary for two years. Courtesy, City of Bridgeport*

The work program was even eliminated in favor of food and clothing handouts, although thirty-two businesses jointly spent $750,000 on factory refurbishing to create jobs.

Conceding that Bridgeport was one million dollars in debt and could not meet its payroll, Buckingham made his most drastic—and politically dangerous—decision in asking all city employees to accept a 20 percent salary cut for the next two years. A group of prominent businessmen also urged a reduction of municipal expenses to the 1917 level, which launched angry protests from city employees who argued they shouldn't shoulder the burden of the Depression. To top that off, Buckingham's administration was criticized for overspending on repairs to the Stratford Avenue Bridge.

Waiting in the wings during the crisis was Socialist Jasper McLevy, who proclaimed that the answer to economic relief started with governmental reform and proper spending. The next year, 1933, McLevy captured city hall for the first of his twenty-four years in the mayor's office. It also marked the year Franklin Delano Roosevelt and the federal government took an active role in bailing out cities, as cash relief flowed from Washington. In 1934 the state Emergency Relief Commission, which supervised the spending of millions of federal dollars, launched numerous statewide building programs constructing hospitals, airports, roads, and town halls. All parts of the state benefited from the program, including Bridgeport, where Park Avenue was widened and extended to meet the Merritt Parkway.

Although a few labor unions had been formed sixty years earlier and had strengthened with the city's industrial growth, the labor movement enjoyed great progress and gathered clout as workers throughout the state joined the Connecticut Federation of Labor. Many union locals were formed in Bridgeport plants. Bridgeport was now working its way out of the Depression and had once again found economic prosperity as World War II approached. Led

Above: *With Igor Sikorsky at the controls, his VS-300 helicopter lifts inches off the ground in September 1939 during its first flight test. Courtesy, Sikorsky Aircraft*

Facing page: *Russian-born Igor Sikorsky is credited with being the father of the modern helicopter. Backed by United Aircraft in 1938, he was able to continue experiments begun in Russia around 1910. With the outbreak of World War II, Sikorsky Aircraft on South Avenue developed the world's first helicopter assembly line. Courtesy, United Technologies Corporation*

by skilled toolmakers, workers in this period established the era of the machine tool industry which made products for nations all over the world. This period also established the genius of Igor I. Sikorsky.

Worried by the German seizure of Czechoslovakia in 1939, France placed huge contract orders with the United Aircraft Corporation which then expanded the Chance-Vought Division, maker of Corsair fighter planes. A new plant was built by the Sikorsky Division in Stratford where half of the 11,000 Corsairs produced during World War II were manufactured. The gull-winged Corsair, first flown at the Bridgeport Municipal Airport in 1940, was the fastest shipboard fighter in the world, reaching speeds of more than 400 m.p.h.

Meanwhile, the Sikorsky Division in January 1941 had won a government contract for the R-4 model helicopter, which was used extensively in the war by American and British troops for rescue work. Russian immigrant Igor I. Sikorsky, the father of the modern helicopter, had won the backing of United Aircraft in 1938 for the development of the first practical helicopter. The war spawned the world's first helicopter assembly line at the Sikorsky Aircraft Bridgeport plant on South Avenue.

Bridgeport was once again a beehive of activity, a workingman's paradise where people could count on work when all else failed, where visitors and observers on passing trains could see the perpetual illumination of factories at work.

But Bridgeport once again learned that its dependence on war would come back to haunt it during the peacetime transition. Bridgeport's Chamber of Commerce Post-War Planning Council offered, through industrial site improvements, a solution for the false security offered by the demands of the war. The Connecticut Turnpike, which stormed through the edge of the downtown district, was touted as an urban renewal plan to eliminate dilapidated housing. And as unemployment slapped 15,000 residents, Bridgeport Brass Executive Herman Steinkraus' launching of the Barnum Festival in 1949 was perceived as more than a means to salute Barnum. It also served to take residents' minds off the post-war troubles by infusing civic pride. Chance-Vought departed for Dallas the same year, but its plant was occupied two years later by Avco, a builder of military turbine engines.

This model VS-300 helicopter was flown in a test flight over Stratford meadows in the early 1940s. Sikorsky's VS-300 was the first successful helicopter in the Western Hemisphere. Courtesy, Historical Collections, Bridgeport Public Library

Organized labor's reaction to mass layoffs forged strikes, including a 1946 work stoppage by the United Electrical Workers which briefly shut down General Electric. "Unions were recognizing that they were a potent force collectively," according to Michael J. Sorrentino, one of the emerging labor leaders of the period, and president of the Greater Bridgeport Labor Council since 1971. Sorrentino recalls this as a vibrant period for labor, when at UEW local 203 meetings, fights often broke out involving card-carrying Communists who wanted a larger say in union decisions. "I had to be a rough tough guy those days. I dished out my share of bloody noses." It got so tough that a Bridgeport Police Department car was stationed at Harding High School outside every local 203 meeting.

Bridgeport city employees, who had borne the burden of the Depression, demanded better conditions, and in one precedent-setting case the first municipal union was formed. The Fire Department-Bridgeport International Union of Firefighters slashed the firefighters' eighty-four-hour work week to seventy-seven in 1946 and down to forty-two hours by 1957. The fire union leaders also were successful in having an ordinance rescinded which forbade the formation of unions by city employees.

But like many industrial cities, something else was happening to the city. Bridgeport was getting old. Its rundown factories needed repair, its shabby downtown a facelift. More than that, the heyday of the machine tool industry in the 1950s was slowly losing its grip. Japan, which had been bombed into the ground, was forced into building modern facilities, and produced casting and aluminum which cut through the heart of Bridgeport's machine tool industry. The Japanese and its cheaper work force grabbed the basic market in cars and machine tools and eventually in the electronics industry. In order to cut shipping costs, Bridgeport companies moved closer to the Midwest where the car makers were located, others

A nationwide strike against General Electric in 1946 by the members of United Electrical Workers briefly shut down the company's Bridgeport factory. A police car was often parked outside local 203 meetings held at Harding High School to head off anticipated violence. Courtesy, Historical Collections, Bridgeport Public Library

Few things are still handmade these days, but until recently, Topstone Cigars were being rolled and packed by hand in Bridgeport, as this man did in 1950. The factory, located at 256 Middle Street, was the last cigar factory in the state. Photo by Fred Schulze. Courtesy, Historical Collections, Bridgeport Public Library

moved south for the luxury of cheaper labor, and parent companies closed antiquated Bridgeport plants. The post-World War II years saw Underwood, Singer, Columbia Records, Bridgeport Brass, Dictaphone, and others either relocate or shut down. The once powerful Remington, which was purchased by the Du Pont Company in 1933, slowly moved departments to other plants in other cities. The industry void chipped away at the city's tax base.

The 1950s also saw many middle-class Bridgeporters, made prosperous by the war, leave the city for the status of the suburbs, in search of better homes, more property, and better schools. But census figures show that rushing to the suburbs wasn't as fashionable in Bridgeport as in Connecticut's two other major cities, Hartford and New Haven, which showed far greater population decreases. While the influx of blacks and Hispanics in the 1950s and 1960s filled housing units in the East Side, South End, and West Side, Bridgeport pulled north with a housing boom, and the North End provided a suburban atmosphere within the city limits.

People's Bank became the powerhouse financial institution in the city during this period, its growth spurting when bank president Samuel Hawley mass marketed mortgages. The bank offered cheaper VA mortgages, and found ways for people to buy their own homes.

In recent years, Bridgeport has remained dependent on the military contracts secured by Sikorsky which employs thousands and subcontracts to the remaining skilled, but smaller machine trades.

The city has developed a growing professional status as accountants, physicians, and particularly lawyers (who have located law firms near the city's two state courthouses and the Federal District Court), have been attracted by Bridgeport's cheaper rental space. Bridgeport business and industry faces a period of transition from a military and machine tool industrial base to a professional, retail, and sports entertainment

Fred Roberto (right), once the secretary treasurer of Local 191 United Brotherhood of Teamsters, was a very powerful union force. He was succeeded by Anthony Rossetti in 1985. Photo by Frank Decerbo. Courtesy, Post Publishing Company

center. Led by Fairfield-based commercial real estate developer United Properties, the city is experiencing its greatest commercial development in recent history. United Properties is responsible for the 12-screen movie theater complex in Black Rock, a Home Depot and Super Stop & Shop stores in the North End and a Downtown retail complex that is home to Bob's Discount Furniture.

The city is also in the early stages of amassing a major sports entertainment complex in the South End, featuring Harbor Yard, home of the popular Bridgeport Bluefish baseball team and an adjacent 10,000-seat indoor sports arena that will host professional hockey, big-time college basketball and concert attractions.

Sylvia Gomes, the daughter of Portuguese commercial fishermen, shows off a lobster along her parents dock in the East End. The talented Sylvia made her parents and city proud in 1999 by winning the Miss Connecticut title and finishing in the top 10 of the Miss America 2000 pageant where she performed the song "The Promise" on the piano in the preliminary talent competition. Sylvia has made a promise to youth groups as an influential peer mentoring advocate. Photo by Ron Blanchard

CHAPTER VI
The
Park City

"When you're not on Broadway, everything is Bridgeport."
—Arthur "Bugs" Baer,
syndicated columnist

Every run-of-the-mill vaudeville comic harbors a debt of gratitude to Bridgeport. When all else failed, Arthur Baer's crack evoked enough laughter to keep loads of vaudevillians off the unemployment lines. Baer's 1915 remark was adapted by numerous show people, who added a twist of their own. George M. Cohan used to go around saying, "After New York, everything is Bridgeport." In fact, he used to say it so often that everyone gave him credit for coining the phrase. For many years Daddy Warbucks lectured Little Orphan Annie about Bridgeport in the musical *Annie,* and it provided the biggest laugh in the first act. Bridgeporters generally have considered the expression a rotten put-down, despite the vaudevillians' claim that the punch line would mean the same if connected to another city.

Entertainer quotes about Bridgeport were common over the years. From the 1920s through the war years, Bridgeport became known as a magnet for New York's theater and pageantry, a decent stop off between New York and Boston. It also garnered a reputation as something of a decent tryout town. If those fussy, working-class ethnics from Bridgeport liked it, so would just about anybody. Bridgeport's savage critics could flatten any turned-up actor's nose into mashed modesty. As a result, John Barrymore reportedly said, "If you think you're great . . . play Bridgeport."

Decades after Barrymore's barb, Paul Newman blurted out something else about the city. In 1973, after making a movie in Bridgeport, he called the city a "depressing little town." A resident of genteel Westport, Newman hasn't filmed a movie in Bridgeport since, and Bridgeporters aren't exactly getting down and beating the rug over it.

*   *   *

Bridgeport had little in the way of entertainment in the early days. Its introduction to show business was a few dramatic lectures. The first theatrical house was organized in the Gay Nineties by Lewis Christian Segee, who presented shows on the second floor of his Steamboat Hotel on State Street.

The emergence of Italian immigrant Sylvester Z. Poli, who established himself as a renowned sculptor in New York and then founded numerous theaters throughout the country, launched Bridgeport as a respectable theatrical community and beautified the downtown. Poli started a string of theaters that took his name with his purchase in 1902 of the Hawes' Opera House on Fairfield Avenue. He built his first show house in Bridgeport during the Christmas week of 1912, that would become known as the Globe Theater, on Main Street. Poli lured many of the bigger vaudeville headliners of the time, including Eddie Cantor and Al Jolson. In 1922 Poli opened Bridgeport's twin architectural beauties—the Palace and Majestic theaters. Roughly fifty Broadway stars, including Mae Murray and Johnny "Torchy" Hines, attended the theaters' openings on September 4. Previous to Poli's arrival, the city's theaters had benches or wooden chairs. Poli gave them comfort and beauty. The theatrical structures featured 6,000 seats, mirror and gold leaf decorations, plasterwork, marble and crystal chandeliers,

curved balconies, and stained-glass screens.

In the next ten years, several theaters, ballrooms, and eateries would fill Bridgeport's downtown. The city seemed to have something to meet every need: hotels, entertainment, dining, shopping. Bridgeporters would take in a show at the Palace, walk next door for a one-dollar pasta dinner at the Spaghetti Place, walk a block for a sundae at the Goodie Shop (which called itself "the best place in the city to get your candies and ice cream"), and then shop at Howlands or D.M. Read's.

By 1936, Bridgeport had more than twenty theaters, enough for every neighborhood. They were more than just places to watch a movie for ten cents. The Strand handed out dinner sets to families during the Depression, and its outside concession stand was popular with children—so popular in fact that inventory literally disappeared. The girls' bathroom window was located just in back of the concession stand, and children would make frequent trips to the bathroom, jump on each other's shoulders, reach out the window and quickly fill their pockets with candy behind the cashier's back. This practice, say those who remember filling their pockets, went on for years.

As the swing tunes and the jitterbugs jumped in Bridgeport dance halls such as the Ritz Ballroom during World War II, Columbia Records was the cornerstone of the city's entertainment industry. The forerunner of Columbia was the American Graphophone Company, the world's first manufacturer of talking machines. The company, founded in 1888 by Thomas H. MacDonald in a plant on Barnum Avenue, leased to the public the machines that were developed by Thomas Edison and refined by Alexander Graham Bell.

While many other factories made munitions and arms during the war, Columbia Records made music. In 1941, its 825 workers manufactured roughly 100 million records for such Columbia stars as Benny Goodman, Kay Kayser, Count Basie, Gene Autry, and Gene Krupa.

Sylvester Z. Poli, an Italian immigrant, received early recognition for his wax sculptures in New York. He went on to establish theaters throughout the U.S., and he opened Poli's Palace Theatre in Bridgeport seen here in the mid-1930s. Courtesy, Theatre Historical Society

Right: *In 1922 Poli's Majestic Theatre, and its twin, the Palace, opened on Main Street. Poli's first showhouse, the Globe, opened Christmas week in 1912 and attracted entertainers like Eddie Cantor and Al Jolson. Courtesy, Theatre Historical Society*

Below: *The chandeliers and fine metalwork of Poli's theater lobbies distinguished them from those built today. Note the posters advertising double features, something rare in modern theatres. Model airplanes hanging from the ceiling were also an interesting touch. Courtesy, Theatre Historical Society*

*If you were lucky enough to attend the opening of Poli's
Palace theatre on September 4, 1922, you and 3,600 other people would have seen what a "Palace" really was. Poli's Palace
was truly beautiful, with gold leaf and mirror decorations, elegant plasterwork, and stained glass. Courtesy, Theatre Historical Society*

Bridgeporter Edward Krolokowski, who gained stardom with his Polish polkas, made all his recordings with Columbia. Columbia assumed the leadership in the record-making industry and modernized factory equipment, presses, and machinery. It switched from cylinders to lateral-cut flat discs of hard rubber, introduced the double-faced disc, produced the first recorded complete symphony (Beethoven's Seventh), and introduced the 33-1/3 r.p.m. LP. Columbia designer Frank C. Kinley won the patent for the automatic stop, his invention for making phonographs stop when they played to the end of the record.

In February 1941, Columbia scurried to recall copies of an explanatory leaflet printed to accompany albums of Richard Strauss' *A Hero's Life* symphony. The leaflet explained that Strauss' work was among Adolf Hitler's favorites and offered a musical picture of Hitler's Nazi propaganda.

In 1964, despite pleadings from Mayor Samuel Tedesco and Connecticut Governor John Dempsey to stay, Columbia ended record production here, citing the high cost of operation and a large, outdated facility. The Columbia complex today is a professional office building known as Columbia Towers.

Numerous Columbia artists appeared at Bridgeport's favorite nighttime spots—the Lyric, the Pleasure Beach Ballroom, and in particular, the Ritz Ballroom. The Ritz came to Bridgeport through the efforts of two Bridgeport dancers, George S. McCormack and Joseph R. Barry, who moved their Brooklawn Dancing Pavillion, at Brooklawn and Capitol, to a larger,

Facing page: *Columbia took the lead in record-making technology with developments such as the flat disc, double-sided disc, and long-playing "microgroove" record. The "Magic Notes" seen on these U.S. and English pressings from the 1940s was a company trademark. Photo by Neil Swanson. Courtesy, Ruth Swanson*

Below: *As the forerunner of Columbia Records, the American Graphophone Company made music in more ways than one. Like most large industries at that time, the company fielded a marching band for local parades. Courtesy, Robert Clifford Collection*

trolley-accessible area on Fairfield Avenue in 1923. The Ritz was the most elegant dance palace in the city, with mural decorations, crystal chandeliers, a dance hall the size of an airport runway, and the biggest of the big bands—Louis Armstrong, Tommy and Jimmy Dorsey, Artie Shaw, Rudy Vallee, and Guy Lombardo (who set the all-time fan attendance mark, attracting 4,400 "Ritzites").

Just like every other theater in the city, the Ritz fell victim to the rage of post-World War II television. As the 1950s, 60s, and 70s passed, the Lyric, Strand, Globe, Ritz, Palace, and Majestic all closed. The day the music died in Bridgeport was New Year's Eve 1961, when couples danced at the Ritz for the last time.

Ritz owner Joseph Barry leased the old dance hall to a furniture company that year. A fire in June 1970 destroyed the old dance palace.

The Park City has been home to its share of famous entertainers. Robert Mitchum was born on Logan Street in the city's East End and as a child he was noted for his poetry while at McKinley School. Mitchum has had little or no contact with the city since his parents moved to Delaware during his youth. (But he did recently write a letter to the family now occupying his old house.)

Chuck Mitchell, who grew up on Pequonnock Street in the Hollow, has won fame late in his career as the red-neck saloon owner Porky Wallace in the 1982 box office smash *Porky's*. Mitchell returns frequently to Bridgeport to visit relatives on the Upper East Side.

Both Mitchum, who had the lead role, and Mitchell, a bit part, appeared in the television mini-series *Winds of War*, which was produced and directed in 1983 by Bridgeport native Dan Curtis.

Albert "Johnny" Altieri, the long-time page boy who was discovered by Philip Morris executives at the Stratfield Hotel, won fame as the "call for Philip Morris" voice in the tobacco firm's radio and television commercials. The seventy-one-year-old Altieri worked as the Philip Morris page boy from 1935 to 1960 and retired as a company sales representative in 1982. He remains today a Bridgeport resident.

Alfred Patricelli, a forty-year city resident, has promoted beauty pageants in Bridgeport and throughout the country for more than fifty years. From 1959 to 1977 Patricelli was the executive director of the Miss World-USA pageant, a stepping-stone for the careers of Lynda Carter, Marjorie Wallace, and Donna Dixon. Patricelli lost the prestige of the Miss World-USA directorship when a U.S. District Court judge stripped him of the title in a dispute with the pageant owners. The persistent Patricelli has struggled the last eight years in promoting his new pageant, Miss Venus USA,

which he annually stages at the Klein Memorial.

Novelist Maureen Howard, who was born in Bridgeport in 1930 and graduated from Central High School, has blended many of her Park City experiences into her award-winning books, including *The Facts of Life* and *Bridgeport Bus.* Howard has not lived in Bridgeport for about thirty years, but returns to the area to visit friends and relatives.

In 1969, Bridgeport-born songwriter Paul Leka was so uninspired by the opening words to a song scheduled to be the B-side on a 45 record that he tossed in the chant "Na, na, na, na, hey, hey, goodbye." Pretty soon, everybody around the world was singing it and it made Leka a lot of money and an established songwriter. *Na, Na, Hey (Kiss Him Goodbye)*, sung by a trio of Bridgeport boys called Steam, has since sold roughly three million records.

Leka has come a long way since his Tin Pan Alley song-peddling days in New York City. At twenty-four years old in 1964, he wrote songs for a publishing company owned by Bobby Darin before he discovered REO Speedwagon as a staff producer at CBS records. For the last fourteen years the Bassick High School graduate, who also wrote the hit songs *Green Tambourine* and *Rice is Nice,* has been a producer and arranger for many pop artists at his Connecticut Recording Studio on Main Street. Musicians such as Stevie Wonder, Rita Coolidge, Kris Kristofferson, and the late Harry Chapin have recorded music at Connecticut Recording.

But Bridgeport has had relatively little in the way of entertainment these recent years. The Greater Bridgeport Symphony attracts the largest crowds to the city's only full-fledged theatrical auditorium—the Klein Memorial Auditorium, opened in 1940 through money bequeathed from the estate of prominent city lawyer Jacob Klein. The Cabaret Theater, launched in 1977, has suffered several financial setbacks but continues to provide nostalgic shows and original revues by local talent, as does the Polka Dot Playhouse at Pleasure

Whether on the screen or at the wheel of Bob Sharp's Datsun 280ZX race car, Paul Newman is a force to be reckoned with. While filming in Bridgeport in the early 1970s, Newman made the comment that the city was "a depressing little town." Newman claimed that then-Mayor Nicholas Panuzio had called the city "the armpit of New England." Photo by Neil Swanson

Beach. And, through the promotion of Klein Memorial Director Dennis Dean, Kennedy Stadium has been the scene of popular concerts in recent years, including performances by the Beach Boys and Kenny Rogers.

Over the past fifteen years several movies have been shot in Bridgeport that have become storm signals for the city's image. When directors needed the presence of run-down housing or a smokestack, Bridgeport has fit the bill. O.J. Simpson and James Coburn filmed a bank robbery scene for the 1978 movie called *Firepower* in Bridgeport. The climactic scene for the 1983 film *Without A Trace*, starring Judd Hirsch, was filmed in the South End. In the film, Hirsch plays a cop who locates a missing New York City child among Bridgeport's decrepit housing. But the 1972 film that Paul Newman directed, *The Affect of Gamma Rays on Man-in-the-Moon Marigolds,* is the one for which every Bridgeporter has forever blamed Newman, for allegedly branding their city the "armpit of New England."

Newman didn't actually coin the phrase. He gave the credit to Mayor Nicholas Panuzio. In the November 1973 issue of *Cosmopolitan* magazine, Newman said, "I shot (the movie) in Bridgeport, you know, and I filmed what was there. It's a terribly depressing little town—the mayor calls it the armpit of New England."

Mayor Panuzio upheld his reputation as a polished orator with this response in the *Bridgeport Sunday Post:* "It's asinine to even have to deny that I would say such a thing about my hometown. And, as I said, I haven't been to the movies too much in the past few years so I don't have Mr. Newman's intricate knowledge of that part of the human body."

* * *

Bridgeport has been called the Park City for roughly a century. Ever since the mid-1880s, when the Park City Dye Works appeared in the city directory, dozens of businesses have incorporated the moniker into their names. Just where the name originated from may never have been officially recorded. No available mayoral addresses, Park Commission, Common Council, or Board of Trade (established before the Chamber of Commerce) minutes officially declare Bridgeport the Park City. It apparently established itself through word of mouth.

One account of how Bridgeport earned its pet name comes from a column written by James H. Sterling of the *Evening Times* in September 1922. Around 1880, as other Connecticut cities enjoyed nicknames, inquiries were sent throughout Bridgeport for a fitting name. Nothing clicked until *Morning News* reporter Arthur French proclaimed: "What's the matter with calling Bridgeport the 'Park City?' " So French seems as worthy as anyone to receive the credit.

Mayor Philo C. Calhoun was the first to actively lobby for the establishment of public parks in the Park City. In his mayoral message in 1857 he said, "It is to be regretted that provisions have not long since been made for the selection and purchase of ground for a public park. The want for such a place in our crowded limits for the free circulation of air and healthful exercise is seriously felt by our citizens, and universally remarked by visitors."

While William Noble and P.T. Barnum set aside Washington Park for public use in 1851 during the initial development stages of East Bridgeport, the five-acre tract was not officially transferred to the city until 1865. That year, Barnum, Captain John Brooks, Captain Burr Knapp, and George Bailey donated the initial thirty-five acres toward Seaside Park. Architects Frederick Olmsted (who designed Central Park in New York City) and Calvert Vaux designed the park site, and city land purchases and gifts from more than seventy donors added about 200 more acres by 1915—a breakthrough year for the beautification of Seaside.

Led by Mayor Clifford B. Wilson and city planner John Nolen, Bridgeport became one of the first cities in the nation to sponsor a Board of Recreation. The city built a bath house, developed sports facilities, and purchased swing sets and seesaws for Seaside Park, and built the Perry Memorial Arch (named for William Perry, who willed money for city improvements), which serves as the formal entrance to the park at the foot of Park Avenue. The arch was designed by Henry Bacon, who numbers among his works the Lincoln Memorial in Washington. The now 340-acre Seaside Park covers two and a half miles of waterfront.

Frederick Olmsted also designed Beardsley Park, whose initial forty-three acres was donated in 1878 by James Beardsley, a farmer who insisted that the land be used for no other purpose than as a public park. The city dedicated Beardsley's statue at the Noble Avenue entrance to the park in 1909.

Connecticut's only zoo has progressed rapidly from the two-bear exhibit that was first displayed in Beardsley Park in 1922. The 33-acre zoo now features hundreds of animals, from Siberian tigers to monkeys, and attracts roughly 100,000 visitors annually.

Pleasure Beach is perhaps the one park left that is a sad reminder of the demise of the premier summer resorts of New England dating from the Gay Nineties. Tourists from throughout the northeast traveled by trolley and ferry-

The Perry Memorial Arch is a familiar site to Bridgeport parkgoers. The arch stands at the entrance to the 340-acre Seaside Park, and was designed by Henry Bacon, the designer of the Lincoln Memorial in Washington. Photo by Neil Swanson

boat to visit the original thirty-seven-acre area also known as the "Million Dollar Playground." J.H. McMahon and P.W Wren, two wholesale liquor dealers and land developers, turned the barren, sandy island into an amusement park in 1892. Three years later, a brochure of Pleasure Beach advertised a roller coaster, boardwalk, miniature railroad, skating rink, arcade, merry-go-round, a 5,000-seat colosseum, wooden horse rides on a rail (for which the park later took the name Steeple Chase Island before returning to its original name), and a track which was one of the prestigious stops on the bicycle racing circuit. It also boasted of the Pleasure Beach legend which alleges that the island was chosen by Captain Kidd for burying vast treasures.

"No exorbitant prices, an honest dollar's worth for all," was the motto. The Pleasure Beach Cafe served broiled lobster and soft shell crab for fifty cents, broiled blue fish for forty cents, and clams on the half shell (when local oyster beds were abundant) for twenty-five cents a dozen.

McMahon and Wren, as well as other private operators, ran into some financial troubles with the help of the fires that have cursed the island through the years; the first came on August 18, 1907, and destroyed the grandstand and weaving horse-rail ride. The Bridgeport Board of Park Commissioners bought the park

for $220,000 in 1919 and took over full operation in 1938, running the park during its most glorious days. Through the Depression it was a place to relax—on the glittery carousel, roller coaster, or in the big band ballroom. In its heyday, Pleasure Beach attracted hundreds of thousands each year. In the 1950s the amusement center began to falter through the city's willingness to allow it to deteriorate, and due to declining tourist revenues.

The park became a campaign issue in Samuel Tedesco's victory over Jasper McLevy in 1957. The Tedesco administration tried reviving the park through a massive public relations campaign, but the amusement center closed in 1960 and steadily sank into disrepair. The left-over buildings, ballroom, and rides fell victim to fires, vandals, and wrecker balls. Just about every year since, Pleasure Beach has been promoted as the ideal location for a jai alai fronton, dog racing track, gambling casino, college campus, jail, or resort center. Lots of talk and ideas, but little else. The fifty-three-acre peninsula (the U.S. Army Corps of Engineers used landfill dredge from Bridgeport Harbor to increase its size by sixteen acres and connect the island to Stratford in 1947) has resembled a ghost town except for the 600-foot T-shaped pier, the last relic of the former amusement center, which survives as a local fishing haven for snapper blue anglers. The pier sustained heavy damage when Hurricane Gloria swept the area in late 1985. However, the city is receiving federal assistance to restore the structure.

For the past twenty years, the seventy-six-year-old Pleasure Beach carousel, complete with organ and hand-carved chariots and galloping horses, has been the topic of numerous restoration proposals ranging in value up to $160,000.

Bridgeport has more than forty other parks, from the 320-acre Fairchild Wheeler Golf Course developed in 1930, to the .13-acre Wood Park acquired in 1880. Much of the

Left: *The "Million Dollar Playground," Steeple Chase Island, or Pleasure Beach, circa 1895. It had many names but they all described the thirty-seven-acre amusement park known to many as the place to be in the Gay-Nineties. The Dodge'em was among the many attractions offered by the park. Courtesy, Robert Clifford Collection*

Below: *Compare this 1985 photo to the earlier one and you see just how much things have changed at Pleasure Beach since its closure in the 1960s. Nearly every year, ideas for the land's usage surface, ranging from a dog-racing track to a casino to a jail. Today, police dogs are trained at the former amusement park. Photo by Neil Swanson*

This elite group of sixteen men served as lifeguards for the Pleasure Beach Park in 1927. Being young, tan, and blond wasn't considered a requirement to protect the hundreds of thousands of beachgoers that visited the park. Courtesy, Corbit's Studio

Facing page: *In 1907 a fire at Pleasure Beach destroyed the grandstands and consumed the large building at right. The Pleasure Beach Ballroom was again destroyed by fire in 1973. Today few of the original buildings remain. Courtesy, Robert Clifford Collection*

These before and after photos show the effect of the 1907 fire on the Steeple Chase horse ride. The ride was not rebuilt after the fire. Courtesy, Robert Clifford Collection

Above: The great Pleasure Beach carousel horses are now housed in a new building at the Beardsley Zoo. Photo by Kathy A. Weydig

Facing page, top: September 27, 1985, meant "Gloria" to the State of Connecticut and much of the Northeast. Seaside Park was struck by 130 MPH winds and tides twelve feet above normal. An estimated 185,000 United Illuminating customers were left without power. Photo by Neil Swanson

Below: Hurricane Gloria also damaged the pier at Pleasure Beach. Once 1,500 feet long, the pier is now about half that length. Photo by Neil Swanson

The World Tropics building at the Beardsley Zoo features exhibits from a South American rain forest. Connecticut's only zoo has emerged as one of the state's top tourist attractions under the leadership of Zoo Director Gregg Dancho. Photo by Kathy Weydig

parkland was either bought or donated after 1915 when city planner John Nolen proposed land acquisitions to beautify Bridgeport. Today Bridgeport boasts 1,374 park acres, one for about every 104 people - which is just about the figure the federal government has determined cities need to accommodate residents.

*   *   *

Bridgeport parks have extended the perfect showcase for many of its sports stars, whether they be on a local or professional level. Louis Brock, a champion rope climber, was one of the first. Brock pulled his weight to the eastern rope climbing championship in 1881, with the hand-over-hand method. Bridgeporters (and Brock) crowed regularly about the 138-pound Brock's 16.5 inch biceps which measured larger than those of ex-bare knuckles champion John L. Sullivan, who made the downtown Tremont Hotel his home for awhile.

In the Gay Nineties, Bridgeport boasted a champion roller team which won the Southern New England league title for three straight years. Led by center George "Dumpy" Williams, the team was a scrappy quintet on roller skates that played in a rink on Lumber Street.

Legendary golfer Gene Sarazen learned how to play golf in his teen years, circa 1915, at Beardsley Park which featured a golf course before construction of the Beardsley Zoo.

Bridgeport also had a rather bizarre sense of sportsmanship as well, particularly at the turn of the century. Around 1905, Bridgeport could safely broadcast that it had the only true rattlesnake club in the country. One spring, a bunch of newspaper editors, including The Herald's Richard Howell, organized and manned a rattlesnake club. Armed with forked sticks, the scribes sojourned to the nearest place they could find rattlers—Kent Mountain in Kent, Connecticut—where an Indian named Big Chief Pan, head of the Schaghticoke Indians, helped them to find the timber rattlers. He also provided his sure-cure whiskey snakebite remedy which promised to save even the weakest man from the most poisonous snake attack. The trick was to scout out the snake, thrust the forked stick behind its head, and lean down and grab the snake and stuff it into a burlap bag. The unpardonable crime was to injure a snake in the catching; points were scored based on the handling of the timbers.

The popularity of these annual expeditions spread so rapidly that the head curator of reptiles at the American Museum of Natural History in New York joined the snake seekers, who generally exhibited their catch at Bridgeport gun and tobacco shops. The only accident involving both man and snake came when a rattler lodged its fangs into the hand of charter member Charles E. Wheeler, who was cured by a venom-sucking teammate and several instant gulps of Chief Pan's Sagwa remedy. The club died of natural causes with the commencement of Prohibition when the main ingredient of Pan's remedy—whiskey—became unavailable. It was probably the first sporting event in Bridgeport history that gave a bunch of newspaper people a good excuse to get out and drink.

But the rattlesnake club didn't have nearly as much fan support as the city's jam-packed wrestling matches at Eagle's Hall. Wrestling was probably Bridgeport's favorite early day spectator event; sports page play by local papers regularly drop-kicked the New York Yankees for wrestling and would banner screaming headlines as early as World War I. Such greats as "the huge" Polish grappler Larry Zybyszko and the "South African Boer" Peter Nogert would square off in Bridgeport arenas.

Bridgeport hasn't restricted itself to the offbeat sporting life. It has produced many local players who have performed in the professional ranks of the mass media-supported sporting events. James. H. O'Rourke, son of one of the first Irish families to settle in the city, played outfielder and catcher in major league baseball for twenty-one years in the late 1800s and was inducted into the Hall of Fame in 1945. At the

turn of the century O'Rourke developed Newfield Park in the East End, which gave life to many baseball organizations including the Bridgeport Bears, an Eastern League professional franchise that folded in 1932. Newfield Park played host to many great baseball players. Lou Gehrig, who led Hartford's entry in the Eastern League before starring with the Yankees, played many games in Bridgeport, as did Babe Ruth, who made exhibition appearances while with the Bronx Bombers.

The first unassisted triple play in major league baseball was turned by a Bridgeporter. On July 19, 1909, while playing shortstop for Cleveland in the American League, Neal Ball snared a line drive, touched the runner off second base, and tagged the runner coming from first.

Bridgeport native George "Kiddo" Davis starred at Bridgeport High School before playing on the New York Giants World Series championship team in 1933. Davis, who compiled a lifetime average of .282, batted .368 in that World Series. Bridgeport's most recent entry into the majors is Kurt Kepshire, a star pitcher with Central High School, who chucked for the National League champion St. Louis Cardinals in 1985. Many of Bridgeport's baseball prospects have toiled in the Senior City League, a showcase of area talent for more than 100 years.

After returning home from World War II in 1947, Bob Sherwood's urge to play baseball was so great that he poured his last cent into building a sports stadium, founded the Bridgeport Bees minor league baseball team, and played centerfield for it. Sherwood and Carl Brunetto bought 6.5 acres in the North End and built Candlelite Stadium which included fields for baseball, football, and a one-fifth-of-a-mile track for stock car and midget auto racing. With the resurgence of minor league ball after the war, Sherwood entered the Bridgeport Bees, a farm team of the Washington Senators, into the Colonial League and later hired Hall

of Fame slugger Jimmy Foxx as manager. The team was noted for developing black and Cuban players just after Jackie Robinson broke baseball's color barrier. One of the star players, José Blanco, even had his wedding ceremony at home plate. Sherwood's team folded in 1953 as attendance declined with the emergence of television.

Certainly one of the greatest team dynasties in the history of organized sports was forged by the Brakettes, who in the last quarter century have won eighteen national softball titles, two world championships, and more than 1,500 games. Since Raybestos Division General Manager William S. Simpson organized and sponsored the team in 1947, the names of Bertha Tickey, Joan Joyce, Barbara Reinalda, and Kathy Arendsen have helped to make the Brakettes America's best women's softball squad. Bridgeport developer F. Francis "Hi-Ho" D'Addario, who died in a plane crash March 5, 1986, took over sponsorship of the team in 1985 after Raybestos, the long-time sponsor, ran into financial difficulties.

D'Addario also owned Bridgeport's Hi-Ho Jets professional football team from 1968 to 1973 which featured players such as John Dockery and Earl Christy, both of whom played on the New York Jets' 1969 championship team. The Bridgeport Jets, playing in the Atlantic Coast football league, initially drew large and enthusiastic crowds into Kennedy Stadium. Though the Jets never won a league title, their game in Orlando, Florida, probably did more to impact the women's movement than any other team or game anywhere. The Jets featured a 235-pound linebacker named Wally Florence, who hit anything in sight, and Orlando fielded a 5'2", 110-pound female extra-point kicker, who some thought brought to the team little more than a lot of attention. On one extra-point try, Florence lined up, barreled through the Orlando offensive line, and crunched the female kicker into the turf. Network television picked up footage of the locally filmed game, and the Jets were captured throughout the country. All the attention couldn't save the Jets from folding in 1973.

The biggest turf and court wars in Bridgeport high school sports have been waged between Harding and Central High, as each has recorded its dominant years in both football and basketball. Their Thanksgiving Day football clashes have often turned out more than 10,000 spectators. Central has graduated standout athletes such as Frank "Porky" Vieira and George "Kiddo" Davis while Harding boasts Charles Tisdale, one of the city's top high school quarterbacks, and Wes Mathews and John Bagley, both of whom currently play in the National Basketball Association. The two arch-rival coaches who have touched the lives

of many of the city athletes were Harding's Steve Miska and Central's Eddie Reilly, the first honored sportsman of the Greater Bridgeport Old Timers Association in 1958. Other influential coaches still active include Emmett Spillane, veteran sports editor of the *Bridgeport Post-Telegram* and Perry Pilotti, the founder of the Arctic Sports Shop, who has coached on a local level for four decades. In his position as the American representative of the Italian Baseball and Softball Federation, Pilotti has arranged for many Americans to play baseball in Italy, and he is liaison for Italian baseball in the Commissioner's Office of Major League Baseball, developing exchange programs and tours, and coaching Italians on baseball. He is also an advisor to the Italian Olympic Baseball Committee.

The man who has triggered the most attention on the Bridgeport sports scene recently is the 7'6" Sudanese, Manute Bol. University of Bridgeport (UB) hoop fans appropriately coined him "Basket Bol." For one year, Bol was a giant exclamation point for the UB program, scoring twenty points per game, rebounding, and swatting shots. Practically every major newspaper and sports magazine has profiled UB coach Bruce Webster's discovery. Citing financial problems, Bol left Bridgeport after one season in 1984-85 to play in a newly founded professional basketball league, and then jumped to the NBA's Washington Bullets who drafted him the league's second round in 1985.

Facing page: *Bridgeport has always had a great number of clubs, both ethnic and political. Here the 7th District Democratic Club poses for its team picture in front of the FDR club. Photo by B. Brignolo, Brignolo Studios. Courtesy, Historical Collections, Bridgeport Public Library*

Top left: *A popular Park City sporting event during the early 1900s was the one-mile hill climb sponsored by the Automobile Club of Bridgeport. On May 30, 1907, Harry D. Gates of the Fairfield Automobile Company drove a 16 HP Reo to the finish line in two minutes and sixteen seconds. Photo by Neil Swanson. Courtesy, Robert Clifford Collection*

Above: *You might say that the 1984-85 basketball season was the year of "Basket Bol." Seven-foot-six-inch Manute Bol towers over the other players considered tall in their own right. One newspaper story claimed Bol had chipped his teeth on the rim while still learning the game. Photo by Barry Tenin. Courtesy,* People Magazine

A Jasper McLevy tradition: an evening victory motorcade on Main Street following the former roofer's 1941 mayoral election. A tireless soapbox campaigner, McLevy was respected as the workingman's friend who took patronage out of politics and cut Bridgeport's $16-million municipal debt in half during his twenty-four years in office. Courtesy, Historical Collections, Bridgeport Public Library

CHAPTER VII

Jasper McLevy

"God put the snow there . . . let Him take it away."

—attributed to Jasper McLevy

It's the spring of 1939 and Bridgeport's Public Works Director Pete Brewster is taking another needling about his tardy snow removal operations from reporters. The scene is Billy Prince's bar on State Street, where the truth or the near truth about city operations flowed freely for a good many years. "Napoleon," as Brewster's scribe friends called him, grew angrier with each sip of his beer and each jab from the probing reporters.

How, they repeatedly insisted, could Brewster allow so much time to elapse before firing up city snowplows to clear the streets? Brewster, of course, had been smarting since the previous November when *The Herald* had plowed him for "waiting 'till the sun shines" to clear the streets of snow. "Napoleon fails to fight storm, thousands suffer," the scandal sheet's headline declared. "Sole responsibility for the terrible condition of Bridgeport streets following last weekend's double snowstorm rests with Director of Public Works Peter P. 'Napoleon' Brewster," crowed the story's opening paragraph. And, for practically every week that winter, *The Herald* poked fun at Brewster's snow-plowing direction. After all, the city had initially appropriated only $300 in the budget to cover the cost of snow and ice clear-

This 1938 Bridgeport Herald *cartoon criticizes Peter P. "Napoleon" Brewster, director of public works, for his lack of speed in snow removal, but Socialist Mayor Jasper McLevy's penny-pinching city budget was the real culprit. Cartoon by Jess Benton. Courtesy, Historical Collections, Bridgeport Public Library*

ance that year.

So, with several months of persistent nagging catching up to him, Brewster picked this moment in Billy Prince's to break his long-standing silence. "Let the Guy who put the snow there take it away," he cut loose. Bridgeporters were never satisfied by the excuses given for the lack of snow removal, but this was the Depression, and although many vociferous complaints about mushing through the snow had piled up, residents had by then grown accustomed to their penny-pinching Socialist Mayor Jasper McLevy.

With each passing winter and with more taxpayers' complaints about the snow-covered streets, the story of how Jasper McLevy said "God put the snow there, let Him take it away," has been told countless times in front of fireplaces, in snow-stranded vehicles and, yes, in bars. Jasper McLevy, down through the

years, involuntarily received the credit for a line coined by his long-time and trusted employee. But for Bridgeport, it represented a sign of the times and the tight-spending of a reform mayor who helped lift Bridgeport out of bankruptcy and out of the dog days of the Depression.

Jasper McLevy was Bridgeport's mayor from 1933 to 1957, one of the longest tenures for a chief executive officer of a city of any size. That feat alone would be worth admiring, but for twelve straight municipal elections, Democrats, Republicans, and independent voters marched into voting booths to elect a Socialist as their mayor. Yet the Socialist affiliation was generally meaningless to those who supported him. They were loyal to a man who showed there could be honesty in government; someone who lived up to practically every campaign promise and kept taxes and spending to a minimum . . . a man who would be known to them as just Jasper.

A few days after McLevy died in November 1962, William J. Walsh, the *Bridgeport Post* political reporter who covered McLevy for many of his twenty-four mayoral years, wrote: "To say that his death marks an end of an era is too trite, for this puts the emphasis on time rather than personality. Jasper McLevy was an era all by himself. His imprint on the city was the greatest since a distant predecessor in the mayor's chair—P.T. Barnum."

McLevy introduced the civil service system into Bridgeport to cut off the patronage that dominated political power in the past; convinced the state to maintain key city bridges and highways; made garbage collection a city function; revamped the sewage system with trunk sewers leading to disposal plants; supported slum clearance to pave the way for low-to-moderate-income housing units; and slashed in half the $16-million bonded indebtedness that he had inherited. Voter confidence in McLevy grew so strong that some even suggested that he could grow grass in the streets.

Right: *November 9, 1955: McLevy's last victory tour motorcade down Main Street. He had always been a far more visible candidate and mayor than his predecessors. Courtesy, Historical Collections, Bridgeport Public Library*

Below: *Twenty four years after McLevy was first elected, The Champ left City Hall for the last time on November 9, 1957. His successor was Samuel Tedesco, a man he had defeated in the 1955 race by 5,300 votes. Courtesy, Historical Collections, Bridgeport Public Library*

And in a way, he did that too—he built esplanades.

*   *   *

McLevy was born in Bridgeport on March 27, 1878, to two Scottish immigrants. The oldest of nine children, he left school in the eighth grade and went to work in local factories before joining his father's roofing trade, which he eventually took over years later when his father died from a fall off a roof. His inspiration to join the Socialist cause came from reading Edward Bellamy's *Looking Backward.*

McLevy was the last—and perhaps best—of the soapbox campaigners. Thirty years before he became mayor, he tirelessly campaigned on street corners and in front of factory gates for various elective city positions, with practically no success. A Scot with a weather-beaten face from his days as a roofer, he took to the streets with cracked hands and a battered felt hat. In those early days, McLevy didn't command much of an audience, so he'd plant a heckler in the crowd to trigger some give-and-take on the issues at hand. Often the heckler would shout,

153

"If you don't like it here why don't you get out." McLevy would reply, "I not only like it here, but I like it more than you because I want to improve it."

McLevy's first political success came in 1903. Although he lost his bid for the city clerk's position, voters soundly accepted his petition drive for a referendum to ask for the appropriation of free textbooks for elementary school children. McLevy modeled himself after the man re-elected as mayor that year, Denis Mulvihill, the Irish stoker. McLevy admired Mulvihill for becoming the city's first workingman's mayor—shattering the white-collar tradition of installing Yankee chief executive officers. In the following years, McLevy ran for a variety of municipal and state offices, including alderman, state representative, and state senator, receiving in some cases a few dozen votes in local races. Nevertheless, he continued to build his name recognition and attended nearly every Common Council meeting after 1900, building his knowledge of city affairs and parlaying his union activities into boosting a small electoral base. He had helped organize the Central Labor Union and was a leader in the Slate and Tile Roofer's Union, rising to become international president of the organization three times. And through his gritty union activities he learned to out-talk and out-pound the opposition with brilliant political rhetoric.

In 1911 McLevy took to his mayoral soapbox for the first time, maintaining that the only cure to the evils of patronage was civil service, an eight-hour work day, municipal ownership of utilities, and tighter spending— the Socialist platform he would continually espouse as he began building credibility with national Socialist Party leaders such as Norman Thomas, the long-time presidential nominee of the party. In McLevy's first mayoral race, the Socialist drew votes from elements disgusted with the political machine of Republican Town Chairman John T. King (perhaps the greatest

McLevy came right from the rooftop to become Bridgeport's mayor. The day after his 1933 victory, he first finished a roofing job before assuming office. Courtesy, Historical Collections, Bridgeport Public Library

political boss in city history), who nevertheless led Clifford B. Wilson to the first of five consecutive mayoral victories. McLevy, riding the fervor of the early labor movement, finished a respectable third, drawing 3,625 votes, 2,000 votes behind Wilson.

McLevy was up against the most charismatic politician of the times. King, a charming, calculating, brilliant strategist, had formed political clubs throughout the city for the sole function of doling out jobs in his patronage system. King had reversed the Democratic trend of Irish political leaders, building his power base in the Republican Party and becoming a national committeeman. He formed a political friendship with Allan F. Paige, a Yankee Republican in the shadow of the Mulvihill and Edward T. Buckingham mayoral years, and built a powerful patronage machine, a double machine. While King realized McLevy drew some anti-establishment votes from him, he also knew that the McLevy factor would siphon off more votes from the Democrats. All the things King stood for—power, patronage, political clubs—McLevy furiously fought against, but King wanted McLevy to run. And McLevy helped King's candidate become mayor.

McLevy often said that the Democrats were "spare tires" to the King machine and someday "when people get sick enough of this municipal circus we are liable to have a blowout that will affect all their tires." Still King became quite fond of McLevy as a politician and insisted he would make him mayor someday if only he turned Republican. Speculation centered on whether King financed McLevy's campaigns, since King spoke so highly of McLevy.

McLevy ran for mayor (and a variety of other offices) almost every election year after 1911, his vote generally unimpressive, but still a factor in the King-Wilson victories. McLevy, who married his childhood sweetheart Mary Flynn in 1911, preached the labor movement, and his voice was heard regularly in legislative halls in the battles to establish the Workman's Compensation Law and the Public Utilities Commission in 1913.

During the King-Wilson era, Bridgeport emerged as a major industrial city and as the country's arms and munitions center. Parks were beautified, dental programs instituted in schools, and dirt roads given a coating of expensive pavement. But much of the money spent on the city came from King's bonding policies. King strayed from the commonly known pay-as-you-go system to build up the city. It worked for quite some time, but King's machine became vulnerable as the city's bonded debt grew.

In 1921, Democratic Town Chairman John Cornell and his mayoral candidate Fred Atwater convinced voters the city needed spending re-

form, and King was dethroned, if only for one term. The two became embroiled in a fight for party control which King quickly exploited, and his precision figuring surfaced once again in the 1923 election. Realizing several hundred Germans were active in the Socialist Party and regularly supported McLevy, he nominated F. William Behrens, a German and local butcher, for mayor. King's strategy was to borrow just enough votes from McLevy for a victory over the Democrats. That election McLevy received 330 less votes than the previous one, precisely just enough votes for King's candidate to sneak past the Democrat.

During the 1920s, try as he might, McLevy could not convince the voters that both parties were no-good scoundrels and that the Socialist Party presented the only honest choice. McLevy's tireless love for the soapbox continued on street corners for biennial runs for mayor and governor. Although McLevy would not be elected mayor for another seven years, 1926 became a breakthrough year and resulted in the most radical change in Bridgeport's government. An investigation by State Tax Commissioner William H. Blodgett found that Bridgeport had not collected more than three million dollars in back taxes covering several years and three administrations. Blodgett said $38,000 in abatements had been granted on the night before the 1923 election, in what he described as "clean up night," and over the ensuing two-year period his investigation revealed abatements amounting to $400,000 for King's political friends. On top of that, the 1922 city tax book had suddenly disappeared. Blodgett cited sixty-seven cases of illegal abatements and charged the city with flagrant financial mismanagement.

"Bridgeport," said Blodgett, "is one of those towns that doesn't collect their taxes very well. That way of doing things came into vogue in Bridgeport years ago; it is ingrained there and people have become tempered to it."

As a result, the state legislature enacted the

Above: *Mayor McLevy and his second wife, Vida Stearns, celebrating their last mayoral victory on November 9, 1955. McLevy had married Stearns, an artist, in 1929, but kept the marriage a secret for five years until* The Herald *discovered the marriage certificate in the Office of Vital Statistics. His first wife, Mary Flynn, had died many years earlier. Courtesy, Historical Collections, Bridgeport Public Library*

Facing page: *Bridgeport Mayor Hugh Curran greets Vida McLevy Parsons at dedication ceremonies renaming the old City Hall as McLevy Hall on November 1, 1967. McLevy had suffered a stroke in 1960, forcing him into political retirement. He died on November 19, 1962. Courtesy, Historical Collections, Bridgeport Public Library*

"Ripper Bill," which ripped financial home rule away from Bridgeport. Under the bill, the governor appointed the tax collector, tax attorney, and the Board of Apportionment and Taxation, which set the city's millage rate. The Ripper Bill also cut into the political spoils of John T. King, who died in 1926, leaving no one to rally the Republican Party. McLevy actually denounced the Ripper Bill as "destroying the principle of home rule in Bridgeport," and he later used it as ammunition to forever blame the Republicans and Democrats.

Behrens managed to win the last of his three terms in 1927, which would be the last Republican victory in Bridgeport until 1971. Behrens' administration collapsed with the news of a bridge scandal involving the newly constructed Yellow Mill Bridge on the East Side. Charges of graft concerning the construction of the bridge surfaced and flushed out greater revelations. Members of the bridge commission which approved the construction contract had become secret members of a dummy corporation organized by the construction company. Essential bridge materials passed through the dummy corporation, some supplied by a contractor who was actually a bridge commission member. An investigating committee estimated the city made an overpayment of $183,000.

The Democrats seized the opportunity and brought back Edward T. Buckingham, a Yale graduate, who was beaten by the King machine in 1911. Buckingham promised voters no more "cost plus" contracts and won the scandal vote for a victory. While Buckingham banged away at the Republicans' bridge scandal, McLevy's chief charge against Behrens was that he increased the city bonded debt up to $14,828,000. In 1929, the 50-year-old McLevy polled only 1,968 votes, yet it was his highest mayoral vote since 1911, and he carried on, running for governor in 1930, gradually earning respect from the electorate through his effective workingman's political rhetoric. During his 1930 race for governor, he authored the following campaign letter to the live letter column of the *Bridgeport Post*:

I note by the evening papers that Dean Wilbur Cross declines to discuss with me the issues of the campaign and through his State Chairman P.B. Sullivan says 'It's bears, not chipmunks, we want' and further says that he hopes that I will not take any offense at the suggestion that during this campaign we are gunning for bear and can't waste any time or ammunition on chipmunks.

But really, are not my Democratic opponents starting out on a very ambitious hunting expedition, for hunters who haven't even shot a chipmunk for many years? Either the hunters have been poor or the ammunition faulty—or both! Many a good hunting trip has been ruined, however, by the squirrels nibbling holes in the bottom of the powder pouch.

There are more squirrels in Connecticut than bears, my kindly opponents, so why should I take offense at being labeled a little chipmunk? You will need a lot of little chipmunks, P.B., in this campaign to put your Dean across—so don't ride too high in your gilded chariot.

Great oaks from little acorns grow and great political parties from little chipmunks grow. A thought that is well to keep in mind, my worthy opponent.

Wilbur Cross was elected Govenor of Connecticut, but the patient McLevy would get more than even some eight years later.

*   *   *

Six months after Buckingham came into power on the crest of the Yellow Mill Bridge scandal, his administration allowed a contract for the repair of the Stratford Avenue Bridge at a cost of $33,000. After months of work, however, the repair costs had run beyond $150,000. Buckingham explained than an engineering contract mistake low-balled the repair figure at $33,000, and that bridge conditions were actually worse. But the public wasn't buying Buckingham's excuse. As it turned out, bridge repairs totaled roughly $280,000. Whether Buckingham was telling the truth or not, Bridgeporters had experienced their fill of bridge scams. It appeared that the question wasn't whether there would be a bridge scam this year, but which bridge would be involved.

Buckingham, meanwhile, had other problems—Bridgeport started feeling the stock market crash of 1929. The slowdown came harder and heavier with each passing month, and the worst was yet to come. Unemployment rose at record rates; the city borrowed millions to meet the welfare crisis. Charges of municipal corruption or the exposure of a political pork barrel may not have overjoyed voters in the past, but they could more easily swallow

the scams and forgive the elected officials during times of prosperity. In the eyes of the voters bearing the worst of times during the Depression, this practice grew too costly. With people out of work, they had time to listen to McLevy, who was now emerging as the 'I told you so' front-runner. He had warned before the disclosure of the bridge scandal that the city would overspend on the repairs, just as the Republicans had done years before. McLevy earned respect as the champion of the taxpayer. With his battered campaign hat and frayed shirt, his street corner crowds grew and intensified.

"They used to talk about the Socialists dividing up the wealth," McLevy told the crowds. "That makes the two old parties like the thief yelling 'Stop, thief' to detract attention from themselves."

McLevy also hammered Buckingham's exlusive use of a black limousine and two chauffeuring police officers during the economic crisis. Buckingham played into McLevy's hands by sneering at his shabby shirt, questioning this man who would be mayor. McLevy countered, "There are a lot of workmen's shirts in Bridgeport."

Still, McLevy was up against Democratic Town Chairman Cornell's powerful political machine, which had a campaign fund of roughly $60,000. Street money was everywhere for the Democrats, but McLevy had no campaign fund, no organization. He had but the nickels, dimes, and quarters of factory workers.

The 1931 poll results garnered Buckingham 17,889 votes, McLevy 15,084, and the Republicans showed a poor third. But McLevy had elected a slate of Socialists: an alderman, three sheriffs, and two selectmen. For McLevy, twenty years after he first trumpeted his cause on street corners, it was just a matter of time. People didn't care anymore that he was a Socialist. McLevy could now build a political organization based on his latest showing. He stepped up his push for civil service to eliminate the political spoils the two parties had ex-

On his sixtieth birthday, McLevy, his wife Vida, and their dog Lassie spend a quiet weekend at their country retreat in Washington, Connecticut. Courtesy, Historical Collections, Bridgeport Public Library

Mayor McLevy seemingly spent as much time discussing city issues at Van Dykes, his favorite spot for morning tea, as he did at City Hall. Here he is chatting with his longtime City Treasurer John Shenton. Photo by Fred Schulze. Courtesy, Historical Collections, Bridgeport Public Library

ploited, directing his calls to the blocs of ethnic voters.

The city's financial crisis deepened, albeit with some flashes of humor such as public debate over whether the monkeys at the zoo should continue to receive their bananas. But McLevy didn't find anything funny about the city's financial situation. Workdays were cut and scrip was handed out. The tax board discovered that $1,500 had been used to pay for the private phones of various city officials, including the mayor. On New Year's Eve 1932 it was announced that the city's cash had been exhausted and the payroll could not be met. City employees were paid two weeks late when Bridgeport Hydraulic, Bridgeport Gas Light Company, and Southern New England Telephone Company made advance payments of $340,000 on their tax bills. The Chamber of Commerce reached into the business community to form the committee of 100 to determine ways to soften the burden of the Depression.

In the spring of 1933, only months from election time, Buckingham announced he would accept a state job and not seek reelection, leaving James L. Dunn, president of the Common Council as the Democratic candidate for mayor. Voters were now clearly ready for a radical change and they registered their restlessness in the voting booth. McLevy received 22,445 votes, more than 6,000 votes ahead of Dunn. It was now official. Jasper McLevy had come into power on the sins of the Democrats and Republicans and he would attack the two parties unmercifully for the next twenty-four years.The morning after McLevy celebrated his victory with friends and relatives, he stripped the political signs off his battered green truck, loaded his roofing materials into it, and drove off to finish a roofing job in Southport. Bridgeport citizens blacked in beards on McLevy photographs, comparing "Honest Jasper" with "Honest Abe" Lincoln, but McLevy told everyone he just wanted to be known as "the same old Jasper;" he held his inaugural luncheon in a diner a few blocks away from City Hall. The first action he took as mayor was to discard the black limousine the Democratic mayors had used.

McLevy was not only a patient politician, he was a lucky one too. Eight days after his election, the federal government announced it would assume Bridgeport's largest Depression expense - 1,000 persons on city relief rolls. In the years ahead, McLevy became the most visible and predictable Bridgeport mayor ever. Never a desk mayor, he would stop in to his third floor office in the red brick City Hall on State Street for about an hour in the morning, then make on-the-job inspections at the Public Works garage or sanitation department, and lunch on corned beef and tea at Van Dykes on Main Street. McLevy

would often saucer his tea - transferring the hot liquid to his saucer, he'd then lean forward to sip. Some Bridgeporters would be absolutely horrified at the sight of their mayor saucering his tea, but they grew accustomed to it. After lunch Jasper would go back into the field until 4 p.m., return to City Hall for an hour or two, return home for dinner cooked by his sister Mabel, then go out to city meetings. Jasper had few friends outside of politics and inside he never groomed an heir. Three of his most trusted employees were City Attorney Harry Schwartz, Comptroller Perry Rodman, and City Clerk and Campaign Manager Fred Schwartzkopf.

McLevy clearly lived up to his workingman's promise. The five-foot-nine-inch mayor wore a wrinkled blue or grey suit, a shirt with frayed collars, sometimes a sweater over his vest, a battered hat, and a funny-looking tie. He never owned or rented a tuxedo and always preferred the corner setting of a diner to the banquets he loathed. McLevy rarely went to church except for funerals and retained the rigid marks of a strict Presbyterian upbringing; he never smoked or took a drink. His informal conversation was loaded with pungent curse words rivaling the speech of any blue-collar worker. He was a patriotic mayor, appearing at every parade waving an American flag. Indeed, he was a people's mayor.

He was also a strictly private man. His 1929 marriage to Vida Stearns remained a secret for five years, until the Herald dug up a copy of their marriage certificate from the Office of Vital Statistics. (McLevy's first wife had died many years before.) They maintained that they kept their marriage a mystery and lived in separate houses so Vida Stearns could care for her ailing father, Edmund Stearns. Some said that Edmund Stearns had a secret distaste of McLevy's desertion of Socialist principles, which also created dissension between McLevy and national Socialist leaders. But McLevy clearly was elected as a reform

Above: *Whether it was at home in Bridgeport or at his weekend cottage in Washington, Connecticut, McLevy showed an unending affection for his dog, Lassie, a constant companion. Courtesy, Historical Collections, Bridgeport Public Library*

Facing page: *Jasper McLevy, Bridgeport's Socialist mayor, served the city for twelve terms, from 1933 to 1957. Local officeholders and city employees, as well as the Singer Sewing Machine Company Band, posed for this 1936 photo with the "Official Family." Courtesy, Historical Collections, Bridgeport Public Library* mayor and not a Socialist. He repeatedly lectured people on honesty and morality, but did not often dip into Socialist principles such as the abolition of private wealth.

McLevy and his wife often took weekend holidays to their farm in the hills of Washington, Connecticut, with his collie "Lassie," who was the only living thing (including his wife) who ever received a public demonstration of affection from him.

Locally, McLevy built up layers and layers of trust and honesty, but he also became one of the giants on the state political scene. He continued running for governor many times after being elected mayor, and in 1934 he carried Bridgeport in the gubernatorial race, outpolling his old foe Governor Cross by 4,000 votes. He was largely responsible for the election of three Socialist state senators and two representatives, who comprised the city's entire legislative delegation at Hartford. With seventeen Democrats and fifteen Republicans in the Senate, McLevy skillfully secured the balance of power to win his legislative proposals by dealing with the Republicans, who in turn enacted McLevy's programs for the return of "home rule," state maintenance of key bridges and highways, a centralized purchasing department, and civil service (the system that would hire prospective city workers based on tests results, eliminating much of the spoils that McLevy denounced so regularly).

The civil service regulations were compiled by City Attorney Harry Schwartz, one of McLevy's most trusted advisors. By living up to his word that politics would not control the city, McLevy became the guardian angel of civil service and actually created his own political machine by solidifying the devotion of all city employees whose positions were protected by the strong civil service system. In years past, City Hall would be just about cleaned out after an administration's defeat. But under civil service, city workers enjoyed the greatest job security, drawing the fire of post-McLevy era mayors and department heads, whose authority to transfer and terminate was limited by the regulations.

McLevy had now become a legitimate state power, but his greatest political triumph was ironically an election he didn't win. Continuing his biennial pursuance of the governor's seat, McLevy's ability to earn credibility through the scent of scandal peaked in 1938. The corner-

stone of his gubernatorial campaign stemmed from the revolt against graft scandals involving the city of Waterbury and the Merritt Parkway. McLevy received an astonishing 166,000 votes on the Socialist ticket, roughly 64,000 votes behind the new governor, Raymond E. Baldwin, who would later serve as Chief Justice of the State Supreme Court. While the Waterbury and Merritt Parkway scandals tainted both of the major parties, McLevy's image of honesty siphoned enough votes from Governor Cross to swing the election to Baldwin with a 2,688 vote plurality. Politically, McLevy had gotten even with Cross who eight years earlier had labeled him a chipmunk.

*   *   *

In McLevy's first six years, federal relief spending in Bridgeport reached ten million dollars, yet McLevy seemed to grow more and more frugal on how it, and particularly city money, would be spent. For instance, in 1940 McLevy spent only $10 all year on office supplies and $89.44 on postage, telephone, and telegraph service. McLevy retained only one

secretary and his initial $7,500 mayoral salary was increased quite infrequently, reaching only $10,500 during his twenty-four years in office. His salary was far below the incomes of mayors running cities of comparable size. Often McLevy never spent unless it was absolutely necessary. For instance, the original snow and ice removal appropriation of 1939, the year complaints bombarded Public Work's Director Pete Brewster, was only $300. But the city ended up dipping into the general fund to spend $13,000 to plow the streets.

In 1939, McLevy shot down a proposal to pay $4,500 a year toward retaining a full-time school physician, even though federal money would have fully funded the first two years, paid for the physician's car, and would even have added assistance for many more years.

City health officials scoffed at McLevy's argument, insisting an additional $4,500 wouldn't affect the city budget and amounted to a mere seventeen cents per student.

When it came to federal money, McLevy said he couldn't be sure how long it would last. One of the expenditures he did allow was the installation of many miles of esplanades to enhance the city's beauty. They became known as "Jasplanades." He also spent money on the expansion of residential sewers that had initially emptied into Long Island Sound. Maintaining that the city needed a clean shorefront, he initiated the unglamorous sewage disposal project, laying trunk sewers that flowed uniformly to two disposal plants.

During his twenty-four years, four federal low-cost public housing projects creating 2,539 units were constructed, along with two state developments that added 1,280 moderately priced rental apartments. McLevy spoke often of slum clearance, but initial credit for constructing housing projects belongs to Father Stephen J. Panik. As many of the East Side's framed houses aged and fell victim to numerous fires, Father Panik proposed a predominantly federally funded housing project that would be affordable to the Depression-era citizens. McLevy initially opposed the project because the city's contribution would amount to 10 percent or roughly $650,000.

Father Panik took his proposal to the people with a public hearing. McLevy threatened to veto the proposal if the council approved it, and there he heard his first chorus of boos as mayor. The battle lines were drawn—Father Panik, a Czechoslovakian immigrant, had the city's liberal elements, McLevy had the Chamber of Commerce representing the interests of builders and landlords, who viewed public housing as a threat to their businesses. But most of the support grasped the hand of Father Panik. McLevy did an about-face on the issue and successfully appealed to the state to ease the city's financial contribution to the project.

Above: *In a rare photo, McLevy poses with Father Stephen J. Panik, who battled McLevy and subsequently won the mayor's support for slum clearance that led to the establishment of the Father Panik Village Housing Project. Courtesy, Historical Collections, Bridgeport Public Library*

Facing page: *The rains came in November 1949, but it didn't stop McLevy from his ninth victory motorcade. Courtesy, Historical Collections, Bridgeport Public Library*

By 1940, ground was broken on what McLevy called "the biggest event in the history of Bridgeport." McLevy often boasted that his socialist administration launched Bridgeport as a pioneer in the field of slum clearance when actually Father Panik was the force behind it.

McLevy also had some of his toughest battles with city employees, who agitated for better working conditions and more pay—the very things McLevy had fought for during his days as a union organizer. In 1945, the city's fire department was the first to break the ice with McLevy on the formation of a municipal union and it subsequently became the most active department in the city. In those days, firefighters earned about forty-three dollars for eighty-four hours of work per week. With the grueling hours taking their toll on department members, firefighters Joseph Shanahan, a lieutenant, and

Facing page: *The last of the soapbox campaigners stumps in front of a factory gate during his unsuccessful 1954 run for the governorship. McLevy's last term as mayor would begin the following year, as the Socialist began to outlive his support base. Courtesy, Historical Collections, Bridgeport Public Library*

Above: *McLevy cuts the cake on his seventy-first birthday, with his wife, Vida, and Lassie. McLevy gradually lost popularity among voters from 1949 until his defeat in 1957. In the 1951 election his 53 percent plurality was his lowest since his first victory in 1933. Photo by Fred Schulze. Courtesy, Historical Collections, Bridgeport Public Library*

Pat M. Sherwin, a private, enlisted the help of Joseph Cleary, a Teamster official with the American Federation of Labor. Reasoning that much of the city's private sector had been organized, and with the full backing of the *Bridgeport Herald*'s labor editor Jack Butler, they convinced McLevy to rescind a 1920 ordinance that forbade the formation of any municipal unions. But, a clause in their first union contract forbade the right to strike.

In 1946, firefighters' weekly hours were reduced to 77.5 hours and in 1948 fell to seventy-two. In 1949 the fire officials received overwhelming support on a referendum calling for a fifty-six hour work week, and firefighters' hours were reduced to forty-two in 1957, McLevy's last year in office. It wasn't until 1955 that a statewide act was passed requiring all municipalities to recognize unions as a bargaining unit.

In the years McLevy sought re-election, he received little competition from the other parties. In fact, Cornelius Mulvihill and Edward Sandula, the leaders of the Democratic and Republican parties, often threw in political unknowns as the biennial sacrificial lambs. Nevertheless, to save face, they had to run somebody, so they would generally pick out a local businessman, buy him a pair of new shoes and a suit and send him out for a licking. Any erosion in McLevy's popularity came painfully slow for the two parties. But some signs of hope came after World War II when several factors began to build up against McLevy.

In 1949, McLevy turned seventy-one years old and more than ever retained a frugal spending posture. During this period, Bridgeport experienced a housing boom as the city pushed northward. Along with their new homes, residents insisted on the same city services—police, fire, paved streets, sewers—as the rest of the city received. McLevy was criticized for not providing those services. Still others criticized him for not planning for redevelopment, for putting patches on top of patches as facto-

ries became antiquated and the city's downtown aged. McLevy's supporters maintained that no man could overcome the city's dependence on the war.

In 1951, McLevy's once-staggering vote percentages started to weaken. His 53 percent of the vote, although comfortably ahead of the other two parties, represented the lowest total since his 1933 victory. But more than anything else, the one factor catching up to McLevy was time. In his first mayoral victory, McLevy received support from various middle- and lower-income ethnic groups who remained faithful as long as they were able to vote. McLevy had outlived his vote base, and the newer, younger electorate didn't have the same allegiance to him. The Democrats meanwhile drew added strength from blacks and Puerto Ricans who moved into the low-income housing projects McLevy had helped to bring into the city.

In 1955, the Democrats nominated Samuel Tedesco, a forty-year-old lawyer who had not even been born when McLevy first ran for mayor. Democrats targeted as supporters Tedesco's numerous fellow Italian Americans and mainstream Democrats and the influx of minorities. Tedesco finished 5,300 votes behind McLevy. After that showing, Democratic leaders said it was just a matter of time, and in 1957, with enough voters believing the time was right for a younger man to lead the city, Tedesco defeated the seventy-nine-year-old McLevy by 161 votes. In a near-record city election turnout of 53,779 voters, the Democrats smashed the twenty-three-year-old Socialist control of the Common Council. In defeat, McLevy wryly cracked: "I suppose I could go back to the roofing business"—twenty-five years after he last did work on a roof. Promising that he would run for mayor as long as his health permitted, he lost to Tedesco by 15,000 votes in 1959, his last campaign for city office.

A stroke in 1960 forced McLevy into political retirement. One of his last public appearances came during the 1962 Barnum Festival,

Late in his career, McLevy was denounced for his penny-pinching tendencies. Photo by John Hayduk. Courtesy, Historical Collections, Bridgeport Public Library

which had always been one of his favorites. Jasper McLevy died November 19, 1962. More than 500 people attended the funeral of the man they called "Champ."

They paid tribute to the man's honesty when the city so desperately needed it, to his devotion to his city, to his frugal spending, low taxes, one cent parking meters. They hailed his open-door policy to the local grocer, political and labor leaders, a carpenter looking for a job, and even to a voter with a leaky roof.

A quarter of a century later McLevy is either denounced for being too cheap to redevelop the city and plow the streets, or he is revered as Bridgeport's greatest mayor.

As reported by the Bridgeport Post *on April 7, 1913, the mysterious explosion in the doorway of Kleinberg's Pawn Shop may have been the work of the "underworld," and the Secret Service investigated the blast. The damage, estimated at $18,000, blew out windows and destroyed much property for one whole block on both sides of the street. Three men were injured. Courtesy, Robert Clifford Collection*

CHAPTER VIII

Politics, Police, and Perpetrators

"Some towns play political softball, other towns play hardball . . . in Bridgeport they play hand grenades."

—Philip L. Smith, 1984

If Phil Smith had accomplished nothing more as chairman of Bridgeport's Charter Revision Commission, his assessment of Park City politics captured what most have tried to express but didn't quite know how. No truer words were ever spoken.

In his address to the commission, Smith had solid reason for delivering this flavor of real-world politics. In the previous decade alone Bridgeport's political pot of blood has featured car firebombings in front of Republican campaign headquarters and the home of one of its mayors, accusations of mayoral candidates accepting campaign donations from the mob, a conviction for taking illegal campaign donations, a mayor wearing a bullet proof vest, charges of mayoral corruption, double-dealing and racism, allegations of vote buying, stealing, and cheating, and absentee ballot scandals.

Say hello to Bridgeport politics—the favorite game in town.

*   *   *

John T. King emerged as Bridgeport's first political giant. The Yankees' control of the city remained powerful when he initiated his power base in the Republican Party through citywide political clubs which had one purpose: controlling votes through patronage. Splitting up the spoils was clearly a function of the Yankee politician, but King refined it, generating an earlier-day yuppie fraternity in these clubs. The number of jobs persons could hand out depended on the number of votes they could deliver. Patronage flourished in every city department, and from about 1911 to 1926 it was all handed out under the direction of one man—King. But it wasn't just the Republicans who wound up with the jobs, Democrats could win their fair share of positions. In the pre-King era, when a new administration was voted into office everybody got thrown out of work no matter what position they held. But the control of political clubs resulted in some longevity, stability, and King's double machine—when one leader controlled both political parties. In this way the Republicans found work, the Democrats found work, King remained king, and everybody was happy. It took a special politician to pull it off, and King electrified it.

King earned a high national recognition factor in Bridgeport as a Republican national committeeman whose high-roll dealings outside of Bridgeport caught up to him. He got linked to the Teapot Dome scandal in which some members of President Warren G. Harding's administration were tied to wrongdoing regarding the nation's oil reserves. King, who never faced criminal charges, died in 1926.

King set the standard for the city's greatest political bosses, but several years after his death, a man who had no money, no jobs to hand out, and few workers, stepped forward to rival and perhaps surpass King's political genius. While King built his strength and prestige with patronage, Jasper McLevy solidified his power through legislation that did away with the political spoils—he introduced the civil service system. In 1935, McLevy's shield of civil service cut through the heart of the patronage system, but, whether planned or coincidental, it actually built McLevy a triple machine, supplying job protection to a grateful voting bloc of city employees regardless of party affiliation. For years McLevy had shouted that the patronage system would be the ruination of

Riding the strength of Republican John T. King's machine, Clifford B. Wilson spent ten years in office and began Bridgeport's surge as the dominant industrial center in the nation. Courtesy, Historical Collections, Bridgeport Public Library

the city. Yet when McLevy dealt with state Republicans for the passage of civil service, he insured security for thousands of workers, and as a result, insured their indelible loyalty to him. They no longer had to worry about losing their jobs when a new administration came in.

McLevy's ultimate test of strength was challenged when the Republicans resurrected Clifford B. Wilson, the anchor of the old King-machine golden era, to face McLevy in 1935. It was a matchup of two of the greatest Bridgeport mayors, but Wilson represented the old-time politics and a threat to civil service while McLevy evoked job security.

Although McLevy dominated Bridgeport politics for twenty-four years, the Democrats and Republicans had strong party leadership during and after McLevy's era through several men, including Democrat Cornelius Mulvihill and Republican A. Edward Sandula. They were pragmatic politicians who could deal with

McLevy when they knew they couldn't beat him, grabbing any leftover spoils to feed their parties. Mulvihill engineered Samuel Tedesco's defeat of McLevy in 1957 and launched what would become fourteen consecutive years of Democratic mayoral control in Bridgeport. Shenanigans (or, it's not how you play the game, but winning that counts) have played a big factor in past Bridgeport elections, and one story has it that prior to the 6 a.m. poll-opening for the 1957 mayoral election, a leading Democratic figure slipped into a voting booth at Barnum School and rattled off a number of votes for Tedesco. Two hundred votes seems to be the figure old time politicians recall.

Right: Many veteran political observers agree with McLevy's declaration that the 1957 election was stolen from him when a leading Democratic figure padded opponent Samuel Tedesco's tally by 200 votes. McLevy lost by 161 votes. Courtesy, Historical Collections, Bridgeport Public Library

Below: Democratic Town Chairman Cornelius "Connie" Mulvihill, here greeting John F. Kennedy in Bridgeport just days before Kennedy won the 1960 presidential election, dominated Democratic politics from the close of World War II until his death in 1963. Courtesy, Elizabeth Walsh

Above: *On October 16, 1959, Republican mayoral candidate Edward Sandula (left) shared a torchlight rally with running mates Doris Mitchell and the fledgling James Stapleton. In 1969 the "happy family" broke up when Stapleton overthrew Sandula's grip on the party, to become a dominant city Republican force. Photo by Ed Brinsko. Courtesy, Post Publishing Company*

Facing page: *In 1978 Marie Scinto (left), a charter member of James Stapleton's upstart Republican Action League, became the first woman to serve as head of a Bridgeport political party. Courtesy, Post Publishing Company*

Tedesco defeated McLevy that year by 161 votes. While Mulvihill assumed a double machine, his friendly rival, Sandula, was more than willing to work with him to keep a firm grip on his Republican Party. Sandula tried to cultivate young, inexperienced people in the Republican Party who would look up to him and join his so-called strategy to build for the future, when actually the last thing he wanted was to have a Republican become mayor who could immediately undermine his stature in the party by challenging his leadership position. Sandula's downfall started when he lured a young attorney named James Stapleton to run on his mayoral ticket for city clerk in 1959.

The Republicans took another of their predictable biennial beatings that year, but Stapleton, writing his own political literature for campaign mailings, secured enough support to win a Board of Education seat in the next city election and build himself a small yet loyal following within the party. In 1968, Stapleton brought the house of cards tumbling down. Bridgeport's Charter Revision Commission placed several questions on the ballot, including a call for a four-year mayoral term and pay for aldermen. Stapleton was the only one who spoke out against the proposals during a Republican Town Committee meeting. Stapleton's boldness drew Sandula's wrath, who blasted his protege for deviating from the party's wishes. But Stapleton charged that the only thing Sandula cared for was sticking to a patronage deal cut with Democratic Mayor Hugh Curran, who supported the four-year term.

Stapleton had hit a nerve. Pressing his anti-charter revision issue, he won the editorial support of the *Bridgeport Post*. Stapleton and an insurgent following even placed ads in the paper denouncing the charter revision. Their efforts resulted in the proposed measures being shot down at the polls three to one. Incensed, Sandula vowed to finish Stapleton in the Re-

publican Party. But Stapleton, with the anti-charter group as a nucleus, formed a group to take over Bridgeport's Republican Party.

Stapleton could never beat the entrenched Sandula forces in a primary with the existing Republican voter registration list, so he decided to form a new party. Calling themselves the Republican Action League (RAL), Stapleton cultivated talented people who had not been given the opportunity to flourish under Sandula's regime. They included long-time Board of Education member Anita Vogel, Nicholas Panuzio, who headed the Student Center at the University of Bridgeport, and Marie Scinto, a homemaker who came from a political family and would later become the first woman in city history to serve as a town chairman. Using the battle cry "let's get rid of Sandula the boss dictator," and calling on voters to smash the double machine by restoring the two-party system, the RAL organized an army of notaries and marched door to door throughout the city; from the beginning of 1969 to the spring of 1970 roughly 5,000 Democrat and independent voters switched to the Republican Party, nearly doubling the total GOP voter registration. Stapleton then had a voter list that Sandula didn't control.

The RAL had its registration list, but when it needed a mayoral candidate, none of the Republican leaders stepped forward. Stapleton didn't want to be mayor. Neither did Anita Vogel. For that matter, neither did just about anyone else who was offered the opportunity. The eventual candidate was an unlikely one: Nicholas Panuzio, an affable, rotund administrator at the University of Bridgeport. But he was willing, and turned out to be a sleeper, pleasantly surprising his associates with enthusiastic oration and a nice feel for the blue-collar person of Bridgeport.

The RAL and Panuzio beat Sandula's endorsed candidate for mayor in the 1969 primary. The fact that Panuzio was beaten handily by Hugh Curran in the general election did

Above: *Some refer to State Comptroller J. Edward Caldwell as the "Chairman of the Board" of Bridgeport's Democratic Party. Caldwell served eight consecutive terms as a Bridgeport senator. Courtesy, Caldwell Family Library*

nothing to dampen spirits. Stapleton's next step was to challenge the Sandula-controlled town chairman George Ganim. No problem this time with fielding a candidate: Stapleton stepped forward. Before the actual town chairmanship election, Stapleton and Sandula calculated that they each had twenty-five of the fifty town committee votes. Strangely enough, on the night of the 1970 election, a committee member and Sandula supporter disappeared giving Stapleton a one-vote victory—and the town chairmanship.

For the first time in twenty-five years, the Republican Party had a new leader. In 1971 the party, invigorated by fresh leadership, again sent Panuzio to face Curran, who had adopted a surprise mini-tax to offset a city deficit. The Republicans seized the badly-timed mini-tax as the cornerstone of their campaign. In the closest mayoral election in Bridgeport history, Panuzio defeated Curran by nine votes, returning the Republicans to City Hall and the two-party system to Bridgeport for the first

Below: *No post-McLevy politician has sparked journalists' interest more than John Mandanici, Bridgeport mayor from 1975 to 1981. Whether it was defying corruption-seeking FBI agents or brashly pushing through a 50-percent pay increase for himself, "Mandy" always made a great story. Photo by Neil Swanson. Courtesy, Fairfield County Advocate*

time in more than forty years. And in a vintage display of Bridgeport political sportsmanship, on the night of Panuzio's victory a couple of Democrats dropped through the ceiling of the Town Clerk's office in City Hall to try and cast a few more absentee ballots to secure a victory for Curran. They were thwarted though, so the story goes, when they found the ballots were stored in a closet sealed with masking tape.

This was the beginning of two prosperous Republican years. In 1970 and 1971, the RAL helped to elect Sidney Dworkin as judge of probate, Stewart McKinney as 4th District congressman, Lowell Weicker as United States senator, Thomas Meskill as governor, and it assisted a state senator and five state representatives into office. Panuzio, who was reelected in 1973, abandoned his mayoral seat late in his second term for a presidential appointment in Washington, leaving President of the Common Council William Seres to finish out the last fifty-five days. The Democrats regained City Hall in 1975, behind the brash and colorful A&P store manager John Mandanici, who quickly built one of the most powerful political organizations in the state. Mandanici likened himself to the "Archie Bunker" voter. He kept taxes down while evoking a no-nonsense attitude that endeared him to many voters, but also made him enemies.

Mandanici's political fortune began to break apart in 1978, when he demanded a city pay raise package that provided him a 50 percent increase, raising his salary from $28,000 to $42,000. "Mandy," as he was called, maintained the move was necessary to attract a higher grade of candidate for the mayor's office. While few questioned the need to modernize the mayor's salary, Mandanici's insistence that the hike be made in one step started a wave of public criticism. Eventually, the Common Council approved his proposal, but the mayor was denounced by several aldermen, the Civil Service Commission, and the *Bridgeport*

Post's editoral chief Joseph Owens.

Mandanici was to face many more problems. A turning point in Bridgeport political history, and a contributing factor to Mandanici's defeat in 1981, came one year earlier with the election of Margaret Morton as state senator. Morton, a black funeral home director who had served eight years in the state house, defeated incumbent Salvatore DePiano by eight votes in a bitter, racially divided primary. Morton said Mandanici had consented to her succeeding DePiano upon his appointment as city tax attorney. When Mandanici and DePiano "double-dipped" (DePiano held both jobs at once), Morton went ahead with her primary challenge, noting that every city housing project was in her district.

"I felt I was a loyal Democrat," said Morton. "They had reneged on their promise that there would be no double-dipping. I wanted to make peace but they wanted to make war." Morton's victory infused hope into a black community which had experienced little involvement in

Margaret Morton's 1980 state senate election was a major victory for blacks in city politics. Photo by John Hayduk. Courtesy, Post Publishing Company

Left: *In 1983 Charles B. Tisdale, the former director of Action for Bridgeport Community Development and a member of President Jimmy Carter's administration, became the first black to win the mayoral nomination of a major political party in Bridgeport. Photo by Neil Swanson. Courtesy,* Fairfield County Advocate

Right: *When it comes to mayoral debates, few put on a better show than John Mandanici and Leonard Paoletta. The bitter rivals, seen here debating in the Bridgeport Common Council chambers in 1983, faced each other in three general elections. Photo by Dennis Bradbury. Courtesy* Fairfield County Advocate

city politics. She had opened the door for other blacks such as Charles Tisdale, who served as an aide to President Jimmy Carter and earlier had served as director of the city's Action for Bridgeport Community Development program. In 1983, in fact, Tisdale parlayed his record and the increasing black political involvement to win the Democratic mayoral nomination, the first time in history either major party had endorsed a black candidate for mayor.

In 1981, Bridgeport endured its most vicious mayoral campaign ever, pitting Mandanici against Republican Leonard Paoletta, a former city tax attorney who capitalized on a series of federal indictments and party infighting that had splintered Mandanici's administration. Mandanici himself was told by federal authorities that he was a potential target of a federal grand jury investigation into the city's Comprehensive Employment Training Act operations, an investigation that spread into other aspects of his adminstration. The intensity of the campaign was heightened in August when the FBI employed a local car thief, Thomas E. Marra, Jr., to lure Bridgeport Police Superintendent Joseph Walsh, a target of a federal grand jury investigation, into a bribe. Walsh turned the

tables on Marra and arrested him for attempted bribery. The botched sting attempt catapulted Bridgeport onto the front pages of national and international newspapers.

Mandanici made political hay of Paoletta's attorney relationship with Marra, claiming Paoletta helped to instigate the federal mission, and he also accused Paoletta of accepting campaign donations from two of Marra's associates linked to organized crime. Paoletta in turn hammered Mandanici for his indictment-filled administration and for further smearing an already seamy city image.

Two months after the sting attempt, Marra's car was firebombed outside of Paoletta's campaign headquarters, and a few weeks later, two cars parked in Mandanici's driveway were firebombed in the middle of the night. If that wasn't enough, Paoletta's house was burglarized. When the sparks settled, voters handed Paoletta a sixty-four-vote victory. The scars that were inflicted by the political hand grenades of the 1981 campaign were still raw more than two years later when Paoletta tried to fire Walsh from his civil service position on a number of allegations, which Walsh successfully defended in court.

Police Superintendent Joseph A. Walsh, hands raised, casts away two FBI agents trying to rescue informant Thomas E. Marra, Jr., following a federal bribery sting attempt against Walsh. Photo by Frank W. Decerbo. Courtesy, Post Publishing Company

Fights between politicians and police officers really aren't an unusual thing in Bridgeport. The position of superintendent of police was created in 1895 out of a political conflict between John Rylands, the police chief, and city leaders led by W.E. Grant, a police commissioner who wanted to get rid of Rylands. The Board of Police Commissioners (unlike during the Walsh affair more than eighty years later) were evenly split on Rylands' future. But city leaders opposing Rylands convinced the state legislature to abolish the office of chief of police. With Rylands out of a job, Eugene Birmingham, on April 23, 1895, was installed as Bridgeport's first superintendent of police.

The seed for Bridgeport's early day police force was planted with the founding of the borough of Bridgeport in 1800. As shops sprouted around the city and the potential for fire increased, a "public watch," comprised of volunteers who patrolled city streets, was formed. Roughly one year after Bridgeport's 1836 incorporation, twenty-five special constables were appointed to preserve the peace, and were granted the power to make arrests. Drunks caused most of the problems in Bridgeport's early days, and until a legislative act created a

Facing page, top: *Bridgeport police were mounted on bicycles in 1900, but by 1914 the mounted force had graduated to Indian motorcycles. Photo by Seeley. Courtesy, Historical Collections, Bridgeport Public Library*

Left: *The first chief of police in Bridgeport (front row, center) was Chief W.W. Wells, whose 1869 salary amounted to $100 per month. Standing next to Wells is Mayor J. Morford. Courtesy, Superintendent of Police Joseph Walsh*

In the early 1800s volunteers formed a public watch to patrol Bridgeport streets, looking out for criminal activity and protecting against fires. Soon after the borough's incorporation as a city, twenty-five constables were appointed, eventually forming independent police and fire departments. The horse-drawn steam pumper above was photographed circa 1912. Courtesy, Historical Collections, Bridgeport Public Library city court in 1868, the mayor was also the local judge, a source of power many later mayors probably wish they could have utilized. A reorganization of the police department in 1869 created a chief of police (who earned $100 per month), a captain, two sergeants, and not more than twenty patrolmen. Bridgeport's mounted police force was created in the year 1900, although the city's finest rode bicycles instead of horses.

Through the years city police and firefighters have battled numerous elements of disaster and corruption, although most of the early disasters came from ferocious downtown fires or careless pedestrians and stray animals hit while crossing the nearby Water Street train tracks. The tracks were elevated in 1902 to everyone's relief. Mother Nature has thrown her share of curve balls at Bridgeport. The blizzard of March 1888 buried Bridgeport in drifts of snow as high as fourteen feet and some up to one mile long. The storm paralyzed the city for three days, ripped chimneys off roofs and roofs off shops; streets lamps and electric lights all went black and railroad trains stuck in the drifts were socked with more drifts no sooner had shovel brigades cleared the tracks. The Blizzard of 1888 was replayed in February 1934 when roughly twenty-eight inches of snow fell on the city, and again in February 1978 when Governor Ella T. Grasso closed down the state and ordered a ban on all non-essential traffic until work crews could clear away snow on the streets.

Perhaps the worst hurricane to hit Bridgeport arrived on September 21, 1938. The storm pounded Bridgeport's shoreline with menacing winds and violent waves, uprooted city trees, and heavily damaged the Black Rock Yacht Club and a major portion of the Pleasure Beach pier.

Several violent rainstorms created havoc in Bridgeport during the 1950s, including raging waves and jet winds on November 7, 1953, which destroyed nine cottages on Pleasure

Beach and flooded Seaside Park. Parking meters and cars were nearly submerged in the rain-swollen municipal parking lot at the rear of the Bridgeport Railroad Station.

Murders in the Park City's early days were infrequent, but on June 18, 1891, Jacob Scheele, a German national, was the last man to be publicly hanged in the city. Scheele shot to death a New Canaan, Connecticut, constable who was preparing to arrest Scheele, a saloon-keeper, at his home for violation of the town's dry laws. Just seconds before his execution at the Fairfield County Jail on North Avenue (which had been constructed twenty years earlier), the sixty-three-year-old Scheele announced to a crowd of police and selected city leaders: "Gentlemen, I am willing to die. I have changed my mind and now do not want to stay here. I wish you all goodbye and I hope the Lord Father in Heaven will pardon me." Hangings were transferred to the Wethersfield State Prison four years later.

On July 11, 1911, the wreck of the Federal Express in the West End killed fourteen people and injured forty-seven others when the train ran across a switch point at the Fairfield Avenue overpass at sixty miles per hour. The train jumped the tracks and plunged twenty feet into a roadway, destroying the locomotive and five cars. The impact turned the iron cars to scrap, rails were twisted and torn, and several headless bodies were found among the wreckage. The train was one hour late and was apparently speeding to make up time. Among the passengers were members of the St. Louis Cardinals baseball team, including manager Roger Bresnahan, a future hall-of-famer, who rescued many people injured in the wreck. The crash was the second most disastrous in the history of the New York, New Haven & Hartford Railroad Company, topped only by the loss of forty-four lives in 1853 when a train plunged from an open drawbridge in Norwalk, Connecticut.

One of the most intriguing hoaxes in Bridge-

On March 12 and 13, 1888, a blizzard blanketed Bridgeport with twenty-two inches of snow. Looking north from Gilbert Street toward the First Congregational Church, residents are seen digging out on Broad Street. Photo by Bronson's Photograph and Gallery. Courtesy, Historical Collections, Bridgeport Public Library

port history occurred in 1938, and as one *Bridgeport Post* account suggested on December 16, "nothing in local criminal history quite compares" to the McKesson and Robbins case. On December 16, Frank Donald Coster, the rich and respected president of the Fairfield-based McKesson and Robbins pharmaceutical company, shot himself in the head in his palatial Fairfield home. This would be front page news in any event, but just one day earlier Coster had been unmasked as the notorious New York swindler Philip Musica, whose lengthy bank-swindling activities earned him more than one million dollars a quarter of a century earlier. Musica had remarkably managed to put that behind him with a new name, new parents, and an impressive educational background that tranformed him into the financial-genius head of a major drug company and earned him a listing in "Who's Who in America." An investigation into the disappearance of some eighteen million dollars in company assets revealed that Coster had diverted cash to pay blackmail money to New Yorkers who knew him as Musica, the Italian immigrant swindler. All these revelations, however, didn't prevent McKesson and Robbins from prospering after Musica's death.

Bridgeport's Romanesque-style railroad station, vacant after the 1975 construction of a new railroad terminal, was destroyed by a fire on March 20, 1979, while the city's elite gathered at a St. Patrick's Day dinner in the Algonquin Club. The 203-foot long, 75-year-old building, of terrazzo and marble floors and red slate roof set with copper gargoyles on the tower, grew from the city's need for an elevated train system. The supervising architect was Bridgeporter Warren R. Briggs, who planned a station "pleasing to the eye and suitable to the surroundings." Police blamed the cause of the blaze on arsonists.

"The House of Happenings," a little, four-room house at 966 Lindley Street, produced one of the Park City's most bizarre stories. The

On July 11, 1911, the Federal Express train jumped the Fairfield Avenue overpass at sixty miles per hour, destroying the locomotive and five train cars. Among the passengers were members of the St. Louis baseball team, who survived the rail-twisting crash and posed for this photo (top of page) taken on top of an overturned Pullman. Both photos courtesy, Historical Collections, Bridgeport Public Library

house gained national attention in November 1974 when the owners claimed to have heard strange noises, curtains being ripped down, a television set being crashed to the floor, a refrigerator being lifted off the ground—a regular haunted house. Police, firefighters, and noted demonologists Ed and Lorraine Warren said they witnessed the strange occurrences. Thousands of curious onlookers lined Lindley Street, causing massive traffic tie-ups and forcing the police department to close the street to traffic. But Police Superintendent Joseph Walsh would have none of it. He maintained that the 10-year-old foster daughter of the family that owned the house admitted to staging the series of incidents. "There are no ghosts in Bridgeport," Walsh reassured.

*   *   *

Not all the city's perpetrators were ghostly or nameless; most that the city has known were those that could be seen, people more regularly identified as Dutch, Cigars, Tommy the Blond, or Fat Franny. In the last ten years, federal authorities have launched a massive crackdown on organized crime, gradually weeding out an element that had thrived when Bridgeport was thought of as one of the most wide-open mob cities in the country. Just how and why these men known as capos and soldiers operated so freely in the city has been open to speculation. The lack of manpower and resources has been the standard answer of the city police; federal authorities have claimed the only thing lacking was enthusiasm for the task. A clearer picture of the present-day Mafia element emerges by looking back to the Prohibition era.

Connecticut was one of two states that did not ratify the Eighteenth Amendment, which prohibited the manufacture, sale, or transportation of intoxicating liquors. State lawmakers cried that such a law was an infringement on the rights of citizens. Although the state was technically forced to abide by the federal law, Bridgeport law enforcement did little to enforce it. As a result, Bridgeport blossomed as a place where bootleggers could operate with little trouble. When Prohibition became law in 1919, the city had already earned its reputation as a hard-drinking, hard-fisted town. The patrons of the downtown speakeasies, many of them Irish, German, and Italian laborers, were not going to be deterred from their evening cocktail by lawmakers in Washington.

And for those who preferred privacy, there was always the option of making your own at home. It could be a messy chore, though, and ceilings splattered with home brew were not uncommon. The more fastidious moved their stills to outdoor locations. A wooded area in the North End developed into a noted haven and to this day retains the name "Whiskey Hill." Its remote stills were renowned for their quality, volume, and egalitarian sales practices. All customers, cops included, were welcome. But while the cops were customers, there were appearances to maintain. There were occasional raids.

It took the efforts of United States Treasury Department to put any noticeable dent in the local traffic. As a rule they did not inform local authorities of impending raids for fear a connected cop would alert a friendly still operator.

What wasn't being brewed locally was being smuggled. Whether by harbor or hearse, liquor flowed through the city. Close to New York,

but far enough away to provide some sanctuary, Bridgeport became attractive to men whose business practices occasionally drew the attention of law enforcement agencies. There were scores, but perhaps the most flamboyant and famous of them all was a man named Arthur Flegenheimer, better known as Dutch Schultz, the man U.S. District Attorney Thomas E. Dewey called the "biggest gangster" in New York City. Bridgeport's reputation as a wide-open town was an invitation for guys like Schultz, even after the repeal of Prohibition in 1933. Schultz spent substantial time in 1935 living at the Stratfield Hotel where he'd play cards with cops, lawyers, and heavyweight businessmen who thought of him as something of a celebrity. For Schultz, Bridgeport was a pleasant place to visit while avoiding the persistent inquiries of federal authorities. But if Bridgeport had a reputation, it was nothing compared to Schultz's.

"Dutch Schultz has given the Bridgeport Police Department 24 hours to get out of town," was the way *Bridgeport Herald* columnist Harry Neigher described the gangster's arrival here. But the last thing Schultz wanted in Bridgeport was trouble. He had plenty of that

An undertaker's wagon arrives to begin the removal of the fourteen people killed in the Federal Express wreck. Forty-seven others were injured. Courtesy, Robert Clifford Collection

In the only known posed photo granted to a photojournalist, Gus Curcio in March 1984 denied involvement in the 1981 mob-style execution of Frank Piccolo. Though acquitted of the Piccolo-related charges, Curcio was jailed on several other federal charges. Photo by Neil Swanson. Courtesy, Fairfield County Advocate

elsewhere. As it turned out, two days after Schultz got out of Bridgeport to watch the Max Baer-Joe Louis title fight in Yankee Stadium in September, federal authorites arrested him in New Jersey on tax evasion. About one month later Schultz was blasted to death in a Newark, New Jersey, restaurant.

Schultz was never a player in Bridgeport's underworld, just a visitor. The two men who ran the rackets with little trouble in the city during the 1930s and 1940s were Ernie and Frank Cozza, who built up quite a lucrative bootlegging, gambling, and prostitution operation. Later it would be men such as Thomas "Tommy the Blond" Vastano, Frank "Cigars" Piccolo, and Francis "Fat Franny" Curcio and his brother Gus, who would take over the action.

But it was only until the late 1970s that the wise guys had free rein in Bridgeport. Led by federal prosecutors Richard Gregorie and William Keefer, the U.S. Justice Department's Organized Crime and Racketeering Strike Force and the Federal Bureau of Investigation decided to move in earnest. Armed with court-authorized wiretaps, they started closing in on the local operations of the Vito Genovese and Carlo Gambino organized crime families. In some cases, they apparently didn't move fast enough. For example, someone eliminated the need to continue a federal grand jury investigation of Vastano, a Genovese soldier, by shooting him to death in his Stratford backyard.

Two shotgun blasts disconnected Piccolo in September of 1981 while he stood at a public phone booth on a Saturday afternoon on Main Street. Just months before, Piccolo had been indicted for allegedly extorting money from the king of the Las Vegas strip, entertainer Wayne Newton. Gus Curcio, who had operated in Piccolo's shadows in the rival Genovese operation, was arrested in connection with Piccolo's murder, but was eventually cleared. The Strike Force investigations culminated when the Curcio brothers and numerous other underworld figures were sentenced to double-figure jail terms.

Whether it was federal authorities or inter-mob rivals concerned with preventing leaks by colleagues in the secrecy of the grand jury room, the combined zeal of these two organizations put a serious crimp in organized crime activity in the early 1980s.

But while the feds had success in one area, they played Keystone Kops in another—the infamous sting attempt against Bridgeport's feared and revered lawman, Police Superintendent Joseph A. Walsh, on August 18, 1981. Two months earlier, federal authorities disclosed that both Walsh and his long-time associate, Inspector Anthony Fabrizi, were targets of a grand jury exploring possible violations of the Racketeer Influenced Corrupt Organization Act. In Walsh's forty years as a cop, he had earned praise as one of the department's finest officers, a detective who could figure out what phone number a person was dialing just by listening to the dial turn. His reputation was enhanced during the hot summers of the 1960s when Bridgeport avoided the kind of racial violence that plagued other cities during the civil rights movement. But where there is power like his, there is envy, and Walsh was rumored to have had a dark side, too.

"The Boss," as almost everyone who knew Walsh called him, fought with mayors and police boards for control of the department and with minority members of the force who claimed Walsh's department discriminated aginst minorities. Numerous charges of police brutality alleged that Walsh's management style encouraged the beatings. Whatever allegations surfaced, Walsh rose from the clouds of dust as the shrewdest, most powerful and charming politician in Bridgeport.

Federal authorities, however, had concluded that Walsh not only condoned corruption, but was corrupt himself. They employed a 28-year-old convicted car thief, Thomas E. Marra, Jr., whose family had known Walsh for decades, to bribe the superintendent to gain back the city's lucrative towing contract (which Walsh had revoked in May) for his uncle's garage. The federal investigation brought together the most powerful law enforcement officials in the country, including David Margolis, the chief of the national Strike Force operations, who ultimately authorized the mission.

As Marra, following lengthy discussions with Justice Department officials, headed to the downtown meeting spot with Walsh and wearing a concealed recorder, so too did the superintendent conceal a recorder, and he crooned the tune "Little Things Mean a Lot" on his way to the meeting. Federal officials hadn't counted on the fact that Walsh was prepared for a set up. While Walsh maintained "it didn't take a genius to figure out what was happening," Marra confessed later that the idea of stooging against a man he'd known all his life was too much for him, and he had gotten word to him.

Whatever the stories, it was clear the federal informant did everything strike force prosecutor Gregorie and FBI agents told him not to do: he brought up the subject of money, got

out of his car to talk to Walsh, and then made the bribe offer.

Walsh waited until Marra had handed him the envelope of cash, then arrested him for attempted bribery and called his men who were staked out in the old firehouse on Middle Street, for backup. Mass confusion and a tense stand off between two law enforcement agencies followed as FBI agents rushed to Marra's assistance and demanded that he be released. Walsh refused the agents' claims while his men dropped Marra's trousers to his ankles and removed the recording device and then took Marra into custody. (U.S. District Court Judge T.F. Gilroy Daly later dismissed the bribery charge against Marra, ruling that he was acting under the direction of the federal government and lacked criminal intent.) Photographs taken by *Bridgeport Post* photographer Frank Decerbo, who Walsh tipped off to be on the scene, appeared in international newspapers as the botched federal sting led newspaper, television, and radio reports. Walsh, for that episode, emerged as the righteous hero, and local government officials squeezed every drop of political opportunity out of the affair. An embarrassed U.S. Justice Department shuffled home. Marra, reverting to his old car thief habits, returned to jail on state and federal charges.

The "Bridgescam" affair proved at least one thing: in Bridgeport it's often difficult to separate the politics, the police, and the perpetrators.

Bridgeport police arrest Thomas E. Marra, Jr., after Marra offered Police Superintendent Joseph Walsh a bribe. Marra was acting for the FBI in that agency's attempt to uncover corruption. The bribery charges against Marra were dropped. Photo by Frank Decerbo. Courtesy, Post Publishing Company

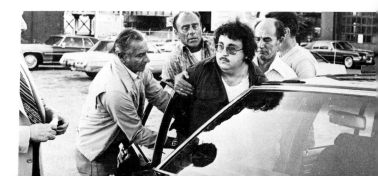

Francis "Hi-Ho" D'Addario was possibly the most important and influential businessman in Bridgeport. He controlled a construction company, an oil company, and a radio station in Bridgeport, and the Jai Alai Fronton in Milford. He is seen here at the site of the old Bridgeport Brass Company building, which he purchased in 1983. Photo by Wayne Ratzenberger. Courtesy, Post Publishing Company

CHAPTER IX

Fighting the Image...Bankruptcy

"Bridgeport...where the circus never left town."
—James G. Clark, writer

Strange as it may seem, the ghost of Jasper McLevy still surrounds Bridgeport nearly thirty years after he left office. From 1933 to 1957 Bridgeport had only one mayor—McLevy. Since then the city has had nine and it is no less a tribute to McLevy's influence that the old-time Bridgeporter and the new have waged many a heated debate over his impact on the city.

The patience of the older voter who remembers and cherishes McLevy's reform and honesty expired relatively quickly against those men and woman who succeeded the Socialist mayor. Yet the attitude of the newer, younger voter suggests that McLevy's failure to infuse the city with urban renewal forged the deterioration of neighborhoods, the loss of industry, a vacant downtown, and ultimately an ugly image.

For bad or good, Bridgeporters now live in the post-McLevy era—an era that has in some ways brought out the best and the worst in the city. The city has experienced a decrease in the white population as it joins the rush to the suburbs, a North End housing boom, redevelopment, new highways, sweeping social changes involving the minority community, the fall of the machine tool industry, the exodus of several major businesses, the collapse and rebirth

In 1957 Bridgeport elected Samuel Tedesco as its new mayor. Downtown redevelopment highlighted his eight years in City Hall and Tedesco said, "McLevy was a nice man, but he let the city crumble just so he could keep the taxes down." Photo by Ed Brinsko. Courtesy, Post Publishing Company

of neighborhoods, the transition from manufacturing to the service industry, and the hopeful vision of downtown revitalization.

Some of the post-McLevy mayors have universally agreed on approaches to these changes, while strongly disagreeing on other concepts and implementations for a progressive city. But clearly one standout and common issue each mayor has forcibly confronted is an albatross that has choked Bridgeport progress for more than a quarter century: the problem of a monotonous image.

And in some cases these mayors have been

commonly accused of being a major contributor to the city's image problem.

*　　*　　*

Bridgeport is actually no different than any other northeast city victimized by a dependence on the temporary demands of wars. Antiquated business equipment and the urgent need for modern facilities has taken its toll. People have lost jobs because of corporate strategies to cut shipping and repair costs by moving closer to car makers; firms have headed south for cheaper labor costs or they have taken advantage of the cheaper Japanese work force, who have grabbed the basic market in the car, machine tool, and electronics industries—all of which Bridgeport has thrived on for years.

McLevy may have been frugal to a fault with city money by his refusal to raise taxes to support education and mend city streets and provide other services, but it wasn't his fault that the Singer Company left Bridgeport, that Columbia Records found it cheaper to move departments to New Jersey and New York, or that the technological advances of Japan left Bridgeport factory equipment antiquated.

Samuel Tedesco was the first mayor who inherited this fallout and a city desperately in need of a facelift. "When we took office the city was in bad shape," Tedesco recalled. "The roads were in bad shape, the schools were in terrible shape. McLevy was a nice man, but he let the city crumble just so he could keep the taxes down."

Less than two months after Tedesco took office in November 1957, the $464-million Connecticut Turnpike opened to traffic from Greenwich to New Haven. The planning and construction of this first major highway to race through Bridgeport had been many years in the works, and during the planning stages the route the interstate would take touched off much debate and discussion. McLevy persistently argued for State Highway Commissioner Albert Hill's southerly route, and disagreed with the Chicago engineering firm, H.W. Lochner Company, that suggested a north-central route through the newer section of the city. McLevy argued that such a northerly route would displace too many citizens. The southerly span, however, would overlook the West End, South End, and East End, as McLevy wanted, covering the deteriorating and gloomier sections of the city sprouting depressed housing and billowing industrial smokestacks; the most prominent of these was the United Illuminating Company's Harbor Station, finished in 1957 to complement the old Steel Point Plant across the harbor. This view of the old city, following a drive through an increasingly corporate Fairfield County, has done little to soften an outsider's view of Bridgeport. Tedesco embraced the turnpike route as maximizing accessibility to Bridgeport without massive displacement of city residents.

The cornerstone of Tedesco's eight years was urban renewal, and the lawyer fostered the biggest facelift in the city in forty years. He admittedly was willing politically to live and die by it. In his initial days as mayor in March 1958, he came under fire from picketing preservationists when he announced the upcoming demolition of the city's Gothic jewel, the Harral-Wheeler House, built in 1848 for Bridgeport mayor and saddlery entrepreneur Henry Harral and later purchased by sewing machine leader Nathaniel Wheeler. Candidate Tedesco had campaigned to save the building for a possible museum, but stated as mayor that money could not be raised to restore the home. Nathaniel Wheeler's son, Archer, left the house to the city for educational or park purposes, but nearly thirty years later Tedesco revealed "the Wheeler family was on my back to demolish the place because they felt it wasn't worth keeping up." The only artifacts left from the home are preserved at the Smithsonian Institution and in a first floor room of City Hall.

Demolition of almost any kind was frequent during the Tedesco years. In 1962, Tedesco launched the city's first urban renewal program—the fifty-two-acre State Street redevelopment project. While fifty-two acres may have seemed petty compared to Mayor Richard Lee's extensive renewal accomplishments in New Haven, for Bridgeport this project was indeed massive. Backed by federal money from the Kennedy administration, the project began in September 1962, with Tedesco sledge-hammering the first blow. The Chamber of Commerce's "Brand New Bridgeport" battle cry was raised by Redevelopment Chairman Arthur Clifford, and practically anything old in the State Street area—residential structures, churches, service stations—were bulldozed in favor of the Lafayette Plaza shopping mall, the new Route 25-8 connector (which rushed through the North End of the city), and the twelve-story People's Savings Bank, the first high-rise building construction in the city in nearly forty years.

Bridgeport's new commercial district was bounded by two highways and the Pequonnock River. All residences were removed from the redevelopment area, which contained no housing developments. Years later the lack of downtown housing became a major criticism of the State Street redevelopment project because no citizens were left in the immediate area to support the downtown businesses.

Other Tedesco projects included the construction of eight schools (including the new Central High School) and Kennedy Stadium, and the transfer of City Hall from State Street into the old Central High School facility on Lyon Terrace, which placed nearly all city departments under one roof for the first time.

While development progressed under Tedesco, the rigors of the mayor's office handed him a severe case of burnout. In addition, financial concerns led Tedesco not to seek a fifth term in 1965 and instead to accept a state judgeship.

Tedesco's city attorney Hugh Curran, a reserved, silver-haired Irish-American, followed Tedesco as a mayor who attempted to promote Bridgeport's resurgence through renovations of the Barnum Museum, the Bridgeport Public Library, and city parks. Curran also addressed the concerns of the black community by developing Model Cities, and the Action for Bridgeport Community Development program.

While Bridgeport had its share of isolated store firebombings, window smashings, and militant gangs due to the social turbulence of the late 1960s and early 1970s, the city did not suffer the racial hostilities that other cities did during that era. Curran credited a "rapport and dialogue with the black community," and praised Police Superintendent Joseph Walsh as a "fearless leader" whose meetings with minority groups defused tensions. Perhaps a more telling reason, however, is the location of the city housing projects, which are not concen-

trated into a single area and are removed from white neighborhoods. Most members of the predominantly low-income black community reside in separated city housing projects such as Father Panik Village, P.T. Barnum Apartments, and Beardsley Terrace Apartments, which are all something of communities unto themselves.

Although Bridgeport did not suffer the pains of violent racial tensions, racial discrimination lawsuits sought action against racial imbalances within the police and fire departments, and during the late 1970s and early 1980s these actions prevented hirings of any sort until the federal courts ordered sweeping changes. Before 1972 Bridgeport's Police Department had no black supervisors and only a handful of black officers, who were usually detailed to the least desirable sections of the city. Blaming the low numbers and poor job assignments on a steady flow of racial discrimination from Joseph

Walsh, the Civil Service Commission, and the mayor's office, Police Officer Ted Meekins formed a chapter of the Guardians, a national organization that specializes in protecting the civil rights of minority police officers.

Demanding that more minority police officers be hired and given equal job assignments as white police officers, the Guardians spent a hectic decade involved in court suits, investigations by federal agencies, and agreements worked out by federal judges. The first major victory for the Guardians came in 1972 when U.S. District Court Judge Jon Newman issued a ruling that the police department had discriminated against minorities and ordered the immediate hiring of minority officers.

Facing page and below: *The Route 25-8 connector (seen here under construction), which offered greater accessibility to and from the suburbs, was evidence of downtown development during the 1960s. Photo Frank W. Decerbo. Courtesy, Post Publishing Company*

Six years later U.S. District Court Judge T.F. Gilroy Daly determined that examinations for positions in the fire department discriminated against minorities. The court then ordered the city to pay millions of dollars to hundreds of minority applicants who had suffered from the discriminatory practices of the two departments. Judge Daly in 1982 found continued widespread discrimination and issued a remedy order that produced numerous police department changes, including the appointment of black and Hispanic officers to specialized divisions. A few months after Daly's ruling came an agreement worked out by lawyers for the Guardians and the city requiring that four Hispanics or blacks be hired for every five white police officers. This came after the Guardians' suit claimed that questions on the entry level test were discriminatory. Throughout the litigation, Superintendent Walsh argued that the Guardians' court action only served to tie up hirings and stall minority involvement. Yet in ten years, Meekins and the Guardians succeed-

ed in adding more than 100 minority police officers to the force.

* * *

As Bridgeport approached the mid-1970s, city officials hoped to land that one major development project that would infuse some life into the downtown. Pleasure Beach seemingly every year was mentioned as a site for a gambling casino or a race track. Mayor John Mandanici often spoke of constructing a downtown civic center, but the funding and interest from the state never materialized as arguments poured in from opponents who questioned whether people would support a civic center.

Bridgeport's Jai Alai Fronton was one of those development projects touted as the savior of the city. Sports entrepreneur David Friend, of Hollywood, Florida, and president of the Connecticut Sports Enterprises which promoted the facility, was awarded a state license to open the facility in 1974. Numerous civic groups opposed the construction, arguing that the East Side location on Kossuth Street could be better used for an industrial park or new housing. However, the 4,500 seat, $16-million fronton opened in June 1976 to packed audiences.

But Friend's involvement with Bridgeport Jai Alai triggered numerous controversies that kept the facility in the news for many years after its opening. Allegations of political payoffs, perjury, and improper bank loans dominated a series of Friend-linked scandals in Connecticut during the 1970s. Friend was acquitted of all charges, but the State Gaming Commission forced him to sell his interest in the fronton. It has proven to be a source of tax revenue to the city, but allegations surrounding Friend added to the growing skepticism about the personalities in Bridgeport's future.

Federal law enforcement officials claimed that a wiretap investigation revealed that Friend and Bridgeport mobster Frank Piccolo sought

Bridgeport Police Officer Ted Meekins has led the fight for increased minority representation in the city police department. In 1970 Meekins formed a chapter of the Guardians, a national organization that specializes in battling for minority police officers' civil rights. Photo by Neil Swanson. Courtesy, Fairfield County Advocate

Facing page: *A decade of lawsuits charging racial discrimination brought greater minority representation to the Bridgeport Police Department. Here new recruits in 1983 commence training before hitting the streets. Photo by Neil Swanson. Courtesy,* Fairfield County Advocate

Above: *With Tedesco's State Street Redevelopment Project came the Lafayette Plaza shopping mall and the garage, shown here in 1965. A source of criticism is the length of the parking garage, which gobbles up several blocks of downtown property. The shopping mall has been a failure, primarily due to the lack of downtown housing to increase the number of city shoppers, who have headed for malls in Trumbull and Stratford. Photo by Frank Decerbo. Courtesy, Post Publishing Company*

Facing page: *The floating Ferryboat Junction Restaurant moored in the Pequonnock River was touted by both the Mandanici and Paoletta administrations as the anchor of downtown entertainment. The boat's owner towed the boat out of the harbor in May 1983 as the restaurant's business bottomed out. In the background is the city's Jai Alai Fronton, another hopeful in the city's revitalization plan. Photo by Frank Decerbo. Courtesy, Post Publishing Company* to purchase the Leonardo da Vinci, one of the largest passenger ships in the world, to transform it into a floating casino. The deal fell through in 1981, according to federal court documents, just weeks before Piccolo was murdered in Bridgeport, and as the ship burned off the coast of Italy. If the incidents of 1980 and 1981 didn't plunge the city's image to rock bottom, they came close: Bridgeport Brass, long one of the city's anchoring industrial companies, announced that high operating expenses and an antiquated building would force its closing; police officer Gerald DiJoseph, checking on a motor vehicle parked in a garage in the city's Hollow neighborhood, was shot to death; women were terrorized by a so-called "bumper rapist" who for several months hit the back ends of women's cars with his auto and then sexually assaulted them; a series of federal indictments socked Mandanici administration officials and uncovered corruption in several city-administered programs, including the city's Comprehensive Employment Training Act and the Rehabilitation Assistance Program, a housing assistance program for low-to-moderate income families. The Parking Authority was investigated for allegedly committing a variety of illegal practices, ranging from city employees receiving kickbacks to authorizing no-show jobs; the mayor himself was notified by federal officials that he

was a possible target of a grand jury investigation, but he was never charged; the manager of Sikorsky Memorial Airport was convicted for lying to a federal grand jury regarding his relationship with mob boss Frank Piccolo.

Bridgeport had several other shocking developments in the summer of 1981 that made the city a reporter's dream, but also crippled the city's image. The sting attempt against Police Superintendent Joe Walsh in August and the shooting death of Frank Piccolo in September continued to put Bridgeport on the front pages of newspapers nationwide. Shortly after the Piccolo murder, Daniel Bifield, a member of the Hell's Angels motorcycle club who federal authorities had described as the "most dangerous man in Connecticut," escaped from the Bridgeport Correctional Center and led the FBI on a six-month manhunt before his capture in Denver, Colorado.

More fallout came with the 1981 mayoral election. Mandanici wore a bullet proof vest after death threats and car firebombings marred the general election campaign. Then one year later, Bridgeporters received the embarrassing news that the new $2.3 million firehouse completed on Central Avenue was actually constructed on private property. The city owned the building, but didn't own the land, and everybody wanted to know how the city could

manage to build a firehouse on private property. Mandanici and his city attorney placed the blame squarely on each other and the matter is still being resolved in the courts.

These kinds of stories contributed to the city becoming the butt of jokes and satire, such as Post Publishing Company writer Jim Clark's crack, "Bridgeport . . . where the circus never left town." It was mirrored in a controversial 1980 song called "Bridgeport," released by local rock group Uncle Chick:

The streets are dirty
and the weather's hot;
if you don't watch out
you're bound to get shot.
There must be some way
to get out of here;
cause you can't drink the water,
can't breathe the air.
Bridgeport, I don't wanna live in Bridgeport
I ain't going back there again.

The song's words were quite extreme from the upbeat 1915 tune, "Bridgeport I've a Longing for You," and the city's centennial song in 1936, "Bridgeport by the Sea." The Chamber of Commerce blasted the rock group for the 1980 song, and some radio stations refused to play the record, yet youthful audiences packed Fairfield County clubs to hear the group play the tune. The controversy and corruption of the Mandanici administration overshadowed the positive aspects of the Mandanici years. The three-term mayor prided himself on the industrial park that created jobs, and on the senior citizen housing projects that provided excellent living conditions for the city's seniors. But the indictments, Mandanici's brash manner, and fights with several Democratic leaders led to his downfall.

Addressing the city's tarnished image became a priority for Leonard Paoletta's 1981 administration. Immediately upon taking office, Paoletta pushed an image campaign called "Up On Bridgeport." The slogan boasted of the city's higher education institutions, health facilities, parks, recreation areas, ethnic diversity, and neighborhoods—all credible attributes for a city image campaign.

Bridgeport received a much-needed shot in the arm in December 1982 when the city pulled a moral victory from a disastrous fire. On December 7 an arsonist slipped into Beardsley Park and set fire to the Police Athletics League's Christmas Village, that for more than twenty-five years had been the site of a Christmas celebration for the city's impoverished children. But the reaction to the shocking fire sparked a massive five-day restoration mission that raised the village from ashes. It became more than a Bridgeport story, growing into one that brought out a collaborative crusade of pride, purpose, and generosity from people all over the world. More than 100 men and women tirelessly worked around the clock in a restoration effort that normally would have taken weeks. People donated thousands of dollars to construct a new building, masons and construction workers donated supplies and time, and others donated food for the workers. Toy companies rushed enough gifts to fill thousands of Santa's toy bags. Nearly 60,000 people visited the village in the days after its reopening. President Ronald Reagan proclaimed on national television, "Yes, Virginia, there is a Santa Claus." Christmas Village turned out to be the best kind of Christmas gift for Bridgeport's image.

Even with the mystique of Christmas Village, "Up On Bridgeport" failed and was dumped after two years because Bridgeport didn't have anything else new to boast about. Once-populated downtown buildings that featured stores, theaters, and industry had become increasingly vacant due to lack of housing to support downtown businesses and competition from suburban shopping centers. Bridgeport's gala downtown shopping days were over.

Toward the end of the "Up On Bridgeport" campaign, the Ferryboat Junction Restaurant,

Sport Hill Climbing Contest, May 30th, 1908, at Bridgeport, Conn. Short Sleeve in Locomobile, Time 1.25.

Above: *The ornate Ritz Ballroom (seen here circa 1925) was opened by Bridgeport dancers George S. McCormick and Joseph R. Barry. Courtesy, Robert Clifford Collection*

Right: *"Connecticut's Leading Night Club," Matt Lucey's Club Howard in the Howard Hotel, was one of many night-clubs and dance halls in Bridgeport several decades ago. Photo by Neil Swanson. Courtesy, Robert Clifford Collection*

Facing page, top: *The Automobile Club of Bridgeport once held a one-mile hill climb up Sport Hill Road. This 1908 post-card shows the winning car, a Locomobile, crossing the finish line. Courtesy, Robert Clifford Collection*

Facing page, right: *The size of the Remington Arms complex on Boston Avenue made this messenger boy on a bicycle a must. Courtesy, Robert Clifford Collection*

Facing page, left: *The small can of caps was produced by the Union Metallic Cartridge Company. Photo by Neil Swanson. Courtesy, Robert Clifford Collection*

Page 201: *As part of the celebration of the city's 150th birth-day, citizens were treated to a fireworks display and an out-door concert. Photo by Neil Swanson. Courtesy, The City of Bridgeport*

This truck, one of a fleet of 200, once delivered pies to thousands of people every day. In 1924, nine tons of pies would leave Bridgeport daily. The Frisbie Pie Company was established in 1872 by William R. Frisbie in a house on Bridgeport's Kossuth Street. Courtesy, Robert Clifford Collection

The Frisbie Pie Company,
Bridgeport, Conn.

*What began as a small family-run bakery in 1872 grew into
the Frisbie Pie Company. This postcard from the early 1920s
shows the bakery that produced nine tons of pies each day.
Courtesy, Robert Clifford Collection*

Above: *This folding fan was a giveaway with illustrations as well as the phone number and address of the funeral home. Photo by Neil Swanson. Courtesy, Robert Clifford Collection*

Facing page: *The Bridgeport Brass Company employed staff artists to paint views of the plant and its workers. The paintings appeared on calendars, magazines, and as large murals to highlight the plant and its products. Courtesy, Historical Collections, Bridgeport Public Library*

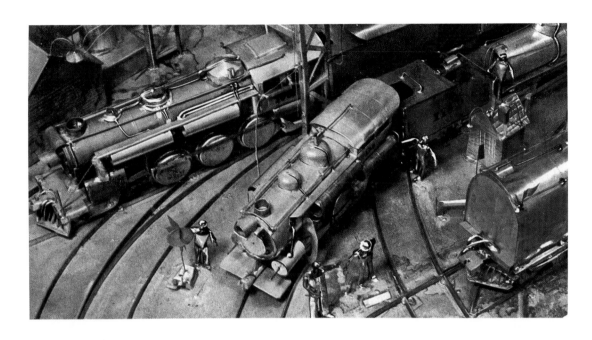

Above and facing page: *These postcards of Pleasure Beach Park best describe the once-great amusement park. The park featured a carousel, miniature train ride, Ferris wheel, roller coaster, and pool. Courtesy, Robert Clifford Collection*

The "Merry-Go-Round" at Steeplechase Isl'd., Bridgeport, Conn.

Dancing Pavilion,
Steeplechase Island, Bridgeport, Conn.

September 7, 1999, Beau Bridges and his wife Wendy join Mayor Joseph Ganim and wife Jennifer for the premiere of the A&E Network's P.T. Barnum special at the new Polka Dot Playhouse on State Street. Bridges won acclaim for his portrayal of the showman. Photo by Kathy Weydig

Above: *A 1950 painting by Ralph Boyer renders the heat of the electric furnace at the Bridgeport Brass Company. Courtesy, Museum of Arts, Science and Industry*

Above: *This worker pouring molten metal is typical of the scenes painted by Ralph Boyer for the Bridgeport Brass Company. Throughout the company's 115-year history, thousands of area workers produced an extensive range of metal goods, from hoopskirt rings to long-distance telephone wires. Courtesy, Museum of Arts, Science and Industry*

Facing page: *Bridgeport Brass Company staff artist Ralph Boyer worked for ten years at the brass mill, recording in oils the daily activities of the workers. Courtesy, Museum of Arts, Science and Industry*

Long Island Sound is well known to sailing enthusiasts along the Eastern and New England seaboard.

The ballpark at Harbor Yark features the Bridgeport Bluefish, the independent Atlantic League team that hs shattered national attendance records for minor league baseball. Photo by Kathy Weydig

*The Ganim family, Mayor Joe, wife Jennifer and children Joe Jr.
and Krista at their home in Black Rock. Photo by J.J. Misencik*

a floating eatery moored in the Pequonnock River that was touted by both the Mandanici and Paoletta administrations as the anchor of the city's revitalization, was secretly towed out of the harbor by its owner, mortally wounding the city's image campaign. The ferryboat restaurant was about the size of a football field and featured a unique Downtown dining style, but had difficulty meeting operating costs. The restaurant slipped out of Bridgeport with the owner owing the city roughly $18,000 in back taxes.

If anything, however, the failure of "Up on Bridgeport" seemed to feed Paoletta's will to accentuate the city's positive aspects. Paoletta and Chamber of Commerce Vice President Neil Sherman effectively used Baldwin Plaza as a showcase for Christmas tree lighting ceremonies, for midday concerts, and as an end point for city parades, which pumped spirit into the city's character. Paoletta insisted that the burst of energy Bridgeport needed would be found in redevelopment of the central business district. Bridgeport had been bypassed by corporate giants while the rest of Fairfield County glowed like a shiny condominium on a beachfront. The city's lackluster image, poor test scores in its school system, and corporations' perception of a high crime rate in the area were some of the reasons businesses stated for not relocating to Bridgeport.

In order to attract corporate offices, Paoletta maintained that the city needed a hotel convention center. With the aid of federal money and banking institutions, the Paoletta administration worked closely with hotel developer Robert Schwartz on a nine-floor, $23 million Hilton Hotel, the first new building Downtown since the construction of Park City Plaza in 1973. Schwartz couldn't turn the hotel into a money maker, so in 1988 he sold it to Ernest Trefz, the McDonald's franchise entrepreneur, and owner of Park City Plaza located directly behind the hotel.

Despite his goodwill and commitment to the task, the financial and public relations headaches of marketing the executive image of a Hilton Hotel in Downtown also haunted Trefz. In 1993, Trefz switched the hotel banner to the Holiday Inn hopeful that the family oriented rates and corporate membership would boost hotel occupancy.

In the mid 1980s, a strong economy and the city's cheaper real estate prices forged other renovation and construction projects including Jack O'Connell's Lafayette Square project and a new corporate headquarters for People's Bank, a 16-story tower that changed the city's skyline and maintained the city's most influential corporate presence.

Under Paoletta's leadership, and the economic boom of the go-go eighties, many Bridgeporters began feeling good about themselves.

This alone, however, does not guarantee a political leader's reelection. Paoletta's firing of Police Superintendent Joseph Walsh consumed the mayor's second term, pitting cop against cop, Paoletta followers against Walsh supporters. Like mayors before and after him, the daily grind of the job took its toll. Handsome and strong-willed, Paoletta literally turned gray from the rigors of the job. He became combative with the press, politicians in his own party and the general public. In order to meet the cost of basic city services, a shrinking tax base and less state and federal funding, Paoletta raised taxes beyond the electorate's breaking points. He was defeated by Democrat Thomas W. Bucci, who served as an assistant city attorney during the Mandanici administration, 25,000 votes to 13,000, an electoral landslide.

Bucci, unlike his predecessors Mandanici and Paoletta, was low key and introspective, providing a unique contrast to the bombast that enveloped politics the 10 previous years. He was the most socially progressive mayor to ever occupy City Hall and intensely loyal to building an administration that reflected the make-up of the community, something that did not endear him to white voters and politicians unwilling to share political power. Bucci placed his share of

Above: *The 400-seat restaurant at Captain's Cove Seaport serves fresh seafood indoors and out. The Seaport was leased by Kaye Williams in 1982 and features a commercial fish house, 400 boat slips, and party boat service. Photo by Neil Swanson*

Facing page: *The fire department never appreciates it, but few can blame these Bridgeport kids for cooling off in the spray on a scorching summer day in the city. Courtesy, Fairfield County Advocate*

In July 1971 this Corsair, one of 6,600 built in Stratford by the Chance Vought Aircraft Corporation, was shipped from El Salvador and presented to Bridgeport and Stratford as a memorial by the Chateau Thierry Detachment Marine Corps League. It rests at the entrance to the Igor Sikorsky Airport. Photo by Neil Swanson

political dinosaurs into positions of influence, but they were being joined by African American and Latinos entering governmental positions for the first time. Bucci encouraged all ethnic and racial groups to become partners in a system of government that developed solutions to mutual problems.

Bucci received good news in 1986 when Congressman Stewart McKinney announced the city had won more than $20 million to overhaul Father Panik Village Housing Project, which the federal Housing and Urban Development declared one of the 10 worst public housing projects in the country. McKinney was just one of several Bridgeport friends who died during the mid to late 80s. Among them was the popular and powerful North End district leader Richard Pinto who was struck by a speeding car while waiting to cross a street in Fairfield.

To Pinto, politics was like sports, a game to share with a friend who needed a job or a client who could count on him for access to his vast political connections. But Pinto also knew how to enjoy life and share his success with friends: A Yankee game in his season box, a feast at Dominicks along Arthur Avenue in the Bronx, an early morning breakfast at his favorite political hangout, the New Colony Diner in the North End, the city's hotbed of political prattle. Old traditions die hard though, especially when two sons are ready to carry the torch—Richard Jr., a public relations executive in New York City and Paul, a property management consultant in greater Bridgeport.

"The number to call is 333-WICC. That's 333-WICC." When talk show legend Erwin "Tiny" Markle spoke those words, studio phones lit up like a Times Square celebration. Markle prodded and pleaded, pestered and painted his audience with wisdom and banter unequaled on the air. More importantly, he urged people to talk about the issues impacting their lives and to talk to each other through the power of his microphone, settling disputes, venting frustration, but coming away with a better understanding than when they

started. Cancer silenced Markle's voice in the early days of 1988.

*   *   *   *   *

They were the most gut-wrenching 10 days in the history of the city. Throughout the Downtown and environs, workers and residents perked up at the sound of the rumble. It was sort of like one of those quirky earthquake tremors or a dynamite blast at a construction site.

It was April 23, 1987. While lunching at a Stratford restaurant shortly after noon, Mayor Bucci received an urgent call. "Get back

Democrat Thomas W. Bucci and his wife, Karen, celebrate his November 5, 1985 victory. Photo by Ed Brinsko.

221

One of many Tedesco administration projects involved placing nearly all city departments under one roof. The former Central High School on Lyon Terrace became the new home for City Hall in the 1960s. City Hall was formerly on State Street. Photo by Corbit Studios. Courtesy, Historical Collections, Bridgeport Public Library

to the city. It's a catastrophe." Bucci raced back to Bridgeport to discover the horror of a massive building collapse. L'Ambiance Plaza, a half-completed rental housing complex on Washington Avenue overlooking the route 25-8 Connector, came apart, burying workers under tons of twisted steel and shattered concrete, the worst construction accident in the history of Connecticut.

Iron and construction rescue volunteers throughout the country frantically and relentlessly searched the ruins for friends and co-workers buried deep beneath the crush. One by one, crane-removed concrete and steel revealed another body. Days into the rescue mission, microphones were dropped between the cracks in the debris searching for signs of life. It was early spring. Raw days, wet nights, an utterly mad life-saving mission.

"Is anybody down there?"

"Did you hear something?"

"I thought I heard something. Maybe."

No reply.

Bucci delivered the painful news to the grief-filled families of the victims at a make-shift support facility in the Kolbe Cathedral High School. Monsignor William Scheyd called upon the families to hold hands in prayer.

A massive collection of eager journalists, camera crews and photographers covered every possible nightmarish angle, raided city hall offices for evidence of blame, checked the background of construction companies and dueled with rescue workers safeguarding access to the disaster area and grieving families.

"Keep those idiots with the cameras away from us," some of the tradesmen would say. A television crew had its power cord cut. An Associated Press photographer had his film ripped away.

Sidebar stories filled newspapers across the country. The outpouring of support by ordinary citizens showed a city with a heart. Psychotherapists helped the families of the victims to cope. Psychics emerged from every direction. "This

person's alive, that one's not," they would say.

City Attorney Lawrence Merly took on the state's powerful insurance companies that were balking at underwriting the city's disaster costs as the struggle to locate the buried workers continued. Speaking before a crew of national journalists, Merly called the insurance companies "barracudas content to allow the workers to rot in the rubble." Merly's rhetoric pried loose an insurance fund of more than $1 million to aid the rescue efforts.

What caused the collapse? Builders had used a construction process called lift slab. Concrete foundations for each floor of the building were poured on the construction site, and then I-beams were jacked up and welded into place. Later, federal investigators made the following determination: the jacking mechanism hoisting the slabs had accidentally slipped.

When it was over, 28 men were dead. A court approved multi-million dollar settlement that included the city, state, developers and insurance companies provided families a small pill for a

April 23, 1987, photographer Wayne Ratzenberger captured this overhead view just minutes after the L'Ambiance Plaza building collapse. Fire, police and emergency medical personnel are at the scene frantically searching the ruins for buried construction workers. Other injured workers are being readied on stretchers for ambulance transfer to city hospitals.

lot of pain. Bucci's clean image, strength during the L'Ambiance disaster (although not directly used as a campaign theme) and relative harmony within the party paved the way for his successful reelection in 1987. But the bomb in the budget was still ticking.

The first signs of municipal financial distress had come under Mayor Hugh Curran when his 1969-70 budget collapsed. He enacted his infamous "mini-tax" to raise enough cash to plug a bleeding budget. Voters revolted, and as punishment they elected Nicholas Panuzio as mayor in 1971, the first Republican mayor since 1923-29.

Though Panuzio was charming and charismatic, it appeared his eager interests centered on using the mayoralty to run for governor (which he tried) or to land a job from the White House (which he achieved). Fearing a difficult reelection campaign in 1973, he curried the favor of the police and fire unions by approving a pension contract that allowed the uniformed employees to retire after 20 years on the job. Despite protests from his Democratic campaign opponent William Mullane, who charged the lucrative contracts would someday break the backs of taxpayers, grateful union workers carried Panuzio to victory. Paying for the "20 and out" pension contract continues to haunt the city's long-suffering taxpayers.

Panuzio's pension contract was just one symptom, however, of the municipal strain. With federal and state funding cutbacks to the cities on the rise, industrial flight eroding the tax base, Bucci was blind to the danger of the fiscal situation he inherited. Defending the need for labor peace, Bucci reversed the acrimonious relationship the unions had with Paoletta by awarding city employees first-term raises that further strained the budget. As the city's budget grew and became more complex, the comptroller's office failed to modernize accounting systems and implement measures like computerization. The city was losing track of its revenues and expenditures.

Further exacerbating the city's budget was the expansion of suburban communities which relied on the city for a variety of services from tax-exempt facilities such as hospitals, court houses, drug treatment centers, sewage and garbage plants. It became a growing burden chiefly brought to light by Bucci's city attorney Lawrence Merly who complained that the city was unfairly forced to provide services to an entire region.

"The roots of the city's fiscal crisis can be traced directly to the large-acre discriminatory zoning in the suburbs which forces the heavy concentration of tax-exempt properties, social institutions and public housing into the city," Merly said over and over. "The way to preserve the comfortable suburban lifestyle is to wall up all the social problems in the city."

Still, the reality of the situation was clear. With the political, judicial and legislative power bases centered on the suburbs, little would change until suburban lawmakers recognized that Bridgeport's problems were affecting their constituencies, namely job loss in the city and crime problems that overflowed into their towns.

In January of 1988, Bucci's confession that he had lost control of city finances set off a community panic. Although most of the municipal bungling was laid at his door, even that which was traced to his predecessors, it didn't matter. The announcement that the city was broke and needed a state bailout occurred on his watch. Business and commerce ground to a halt. A wave of frustration and fear for the city's future froze investment and voters took an immediate turn on a popular mayor. Gov. William O'Neill and the General Assembly imposed a financial review board to oversee city finances.

Intensely protective of his reputation, the humiliating news brought out Bucci's best days as mayor. He reined his political supporters into line, fired the most incompetent, took prudent bargaining positions with unions and brought in a municipal efficiency expert, Jacob Ukeles, to conduct a wide-ranging review of government operations which led to government reforms at all levels including accounting, purchasing and tax collections.

While Bucci braced for another election battle with Paoletta, who was on the comeback trail in 1989, a funny thing happened on the way to the voting booth. Paoletta, endorsed by his party, couldn't get past the Republican primary. An independent community opposition, comprised mostly of outspoken members of the Bridgeport business community, formed an informal group called People For Bridgeport's Future. The group fell upon an energetic political neophyte: Mary Chapar Moran.

A spell-binding speech maker exuding self-confidence overwhelmed Bridgeport voters who promptly forgot to ask Moran about other qualifications for the mayoralty: experience to deal with crises in a volatile urban setting, rational and pragmatic program for governing, dealing with a wide-range of personalities from unionized workers to the governor and a vision for the future. In an atmosphere of fear, desperation and anger, platitudes instead of programs sufficed.

Energetically, Moran rallied a group of enthusiastic volunteers who caught the Republican organization, and Paoletta, napping. When Bridgeport voters woke up the next day they learned that Bucci would be challenged by the first woman nominee of any major political party. Seven weeks later, voters elected Moran the first woman mayor in Bridgeport's history.

No matter how many times the more seasoned Bucci trapped Moran in nonsense and publicly humiliated her for misconceptions about local government, voters were not listening. Bucci was cooked when his budget blew up and nothing would reverse the insurmountable voter anger against him, except history.

Despite her honest attempts to do the right thing and fondness for her community, Moran panicked. Failing to negotiate concessions from city unions and refusing to layoff workers to achieve savings, Moran looked ahead to the

November 1989, Mary Chapar Moran, at left, made history as the first woman mayor of Bridgeport. She is shaking hands with the mayor she defeated, Thomas W. Bucci, a two-term Democrat. Photo by Ed Brinsko

prospects of her reelection campaign: she was a campaigner without a strong record to run on. Her first 18 months in office were punctuated by fights with the financial review board and Governor Lowell P. Weicker Jr. over budget matters. Intrigued by a grandmother heading Connecticut's largest city, the news magazine program 60 Minutes profiled Moran's attempts to govern Bridgeport's social ills. Led by Harry Reasoner, the segment portrayed Bridgeport with all the despair of a Third World country, focusing on the city's crime rate, drug problem and battered inner-city housing. There was nothing pretty about it. The 60 Minutes segment created internal and external havoc. Hundreds of students intending to enroll at the University of Bridgeport bailed out, the business community was outraged and long-suffering Bridgeport citizens saw once more their city barbecued on national television.

Facing another tax increase and unable to frame meaningful arguments deserving of a second term, Moran created an issue she took straight to the voters: Bankruptcy. In June of 1991, she petitioned the federal court to grant the city's right to file bankruptcy. Emphasizing that the city had to break burdensome union contracts and start anew, Moran maintained she was fighting to give voters control of their community from the state Financial Review Board and Weicker. A minority opinion felt it was a good idea: the city was broke and should be considered bankrupt.

Whatever legal implications, opponents to the bankruptcy argued that the financial headaches were enormous. Wall Street, the financial capital of the world just 60 miles away, threw a fit. The two major municipal credit rating agencies pulled the city's bond rating. The bankruptcy decision reverberated throughout the government halls in Hartford and the New England banking community, already suffering from the catastrophic real estate collapse of the 1990 recession.

The New England recession eroded everything in its way, one strength-sapping wave after another, little businesses all the way up to corporate institutions: car dealerships, grocery stores, machine shops and banks. For a while it wasn't a question of whether businesses were headed for the rocks, but an ominous refrain took hold, who would be next? The economy, real estate slump and bad business decisions wiped out city institutions such as Citytrust, Mechanics & Farmers (absorbed by Chase Manhattan Bank of Connecticut) and the BankMart (taken over by Gateway Bank). Other losses included Sears, the Days Hotel and Sprague Meter. As companies tightened their advertising belts, newspapers suffered too. The Bridgeport Light, a community weekly newspaper that had gathered a strong local readership, also hit the rocks. Interestingly, the out-of-work banking executives who generously aimed the word "incompetent" toward City Hall, after Bucci announced the city's fiscal crisis, had suddenly dropped it from their vocabulary. The closings came on the heels of industrial flight during the 1980s including Bridgeport Brass, Carpenter Steel, Bullards and Bryant Electric.

The University of Bridgeport, suffering from a sagging enrollment, was on the verge of closing its doors when an arm of the Unification Church, led by Rev. Sun Myung Moon, took over in 1992. Even Park City Hospital, which served the needs of Bridgeport's inner city residents for 70 years, could not survive as an acute care institution. Park City was merged with the city's oldest hospital, Bridgeport Hospital, in the spring of 1993, to create a specialty hospital on Park Avenue focusing on rehabilitation, psychiatric services and ambulatory surgery.

The oldest literary institution in the city, the Bridgeport Post, took its lumps financially. The paper was purchased during the good times in 1988 by the Canadian-based Thomson newspaper chain for $225 million. New publisher Dudley Thomas, who succeeded the popular and community-generous Elizabeth Pfriem, changed the paper's name to the Connecticut Post in 1992. In an effort to reverse the paper's sagging advertising revenue, Thomas dropped Bridgeport to frame the paper as a regional advertising buy. Claiming he wasn't running away from Bridgeport, Thomas said the name change fit the paper's regional approach to news and advertising, even though the paper showed potent profits carrying the Bridgeport name, before Thomson bought it, in the go-go 1980s.

Moran's bankruptcy decision prevented the city from raising capital in the bond market and school construction projects skidded to a halt. Business leadership and homeowners wondering how it impacted real estate prices asked the most basic question. Who wants to live and do business in a bankrupt city?

Whatever a city's problems, declaration of bankruptcy is a final step toward giving up. All it would take to make Moran Bridgeport's first one-term mayor in nearly 60 years was a Democratic candidate who could organize a reasonably united party and who had a message for the city. What would occur in the years after the 1991 election for mayor was the most remarkable municipal recovery story in the country.

CHAPTER X

The

Comeback

"If you wanted something, you had to work for it."
—George Ganim Sr.

Pondering in his chair in Room 203 of Bridgeport City Hall, there were times when Joseph Peter Ganim thought he should have had his head examined. There he was, 32 years old, a successful young lawyer earning six figures a year, a house on the water in the city's exclusive Black Rock neighborhood, soon to be married to the stunning Jennifer White with children on the horizon. He now was the youngest mayor in the history of Bridgeport fighting for his city's life in federal bankruptcy court. His new salary was $52,000 a year. Lots of luck.

Under normal circumstances, the challenging task of governing the state's largest city is consuming and overwhelming. The difficulties of running the city make most sane people flinch. The best mayors try to surround themselves with experienced advisors and hope for the best within the limitations of their power and authority.

The city Ganim inherited in November of 1991 had hit bottom…financially, psychologically, emotionally.

Huge tax increases and budget deficits were strangling residents and businesses. Soaring crime threatened the livelihood of neighborhoods. The bankruptcy filing that turned Bridgeport into a national symbol of urban decay loomed as the knockout blow that would force Connecticut's largest city over the edge.

As a candidate for mayor, Ganim said all the right things: start with the basics to bring the city back. Fight crime, overhaul government, work with municipal unions to keep spending under control, improve schools, retain and attract business. A sound, basic campaign, but nothing special. In November of 1991 he defeated Moran handily to become the city's 50th chief executive. Six days later he received the oath of office to govern the city his predecessor placed into bankruptcy court. Ganim soon learned that running a campaign and running a city do not compare. Successful campaigns are run on ideas, money and message. Successful cities are run on the force of will to carry out an economic road map, sharp instincts, sound judgement and relationship building. Few thought Ganim was up to the task. But Ganim emerged with something no other mayor in the modern history of the city brought to the office: a temperament uncannily even, very few highs, very few lows and knowing when to make a move. But above all, he was a patient, astute negotiator. This was his greatest strength.

Ganim learned how to negotiate early in life. "Living with four brothers and three sisters gave me a good start," he said. He was born Oct. 21, 1959 in Bridgeport Hospital. His father George Wanis Ganim Sr. was the son of Wanis Joseph Ganim, a Lebanese immigrant who settled in the United States around 1900 at age 18. He did factory work then established his own shoe repair store on Barnum Avenue. Wanis married a fellow Lebanese, Rose Baghdadi in 1914, and they had eight children. Wanis had little formal education, but he read passionately, particularly history, philosophy and literature. He dreamed that at least one of his sons would pursue a career in law, one of his own aspirations. The fruit and vegetable business he opened, which grew from a horse and wagon, to truck delivery business, to an outdoor site at North and Parrot Avenues, would pave the way. All of Wanis' children were required to work in the family business. "My father didn't pay us," George recalled. "He paid our college tuition."

Lebanese immigrant Wanis Ganim, second from left, surrounded by family members at his Bridgeport market that helped groom the work ethic of his son George and his grandchildren. Ganim family photo

November 1991, Mayor Ganim is joined at his inauguration by his parents Josephine and George who delivered the oath of office to his son. Ganim family photo

George earned his law degree from Boston University in 1951. His brother Ray opened a law practice downtown in 1949, which George joined upon graduation. At 16 years of age, Josephine Tarick landed a part time job for George's fledgling law practice. Her father, Dimian Tarick, an oil and coal delivery man, was a Syrian immigrant and her mother, Anna DeBernardi, an Italian immigrant, arrived in Bridgeport from Naples around 1920. Josephine married her boss three years after George hired her. They didn't waste any time raising a family. George and Josephine, like George's parents, produced five sons and three daughters. After his sister Roseanne, Joe was the first born son. Josephine remembered those early years raising a family on Frenchtown Road, eight children in nine years.

"Lots of diapers! Piles and piles of diapers stacked so high you were lucky to make it into the bathroom, that is if the loads and loads of laundry didn't get in the way first," she recalled. "And back then it was all cloth, none of this disposable diaper stuff. Only if you've been a parent can you truly appreciate untangling piles of diapers. Unless, of course, you had piles and piles of dishes to wash...by hand. Diapers and dishes gave us no rest. One of the great days in my life was the day my husband presented me with a portable dishwasher. What relief! Since George didn't want to do the dishes himself he decided to lighten my load. That was a big day in my life."

Breakfast, lunch and dinner headlined a table for 10...every day. In addition to George Sr. and Josephine, there was Roseanne, Joe, George Jr., Laura, Ray, Paul, Mary and Tom. While he practiced law, George Sr. also became active in politics, emerging in 1961 as the Republican mayoral candidate against the entrenched Democratic incumbent, Samuel Tedesco. It wasn't George's year, but little did he know then that he would deliver the oath of office to his son thirty years later.

Young Joe learned about the value of a penny. He, too, was required to work at his grandfather's fruit stand, for a penny here, a penny there. This was his father's philosophy, passed on from Wanis. "If you wanted something, you had to work for it," George Ganim Sr. explained. "You had to earn your way. This was the work ethic that was passed on."

Young Joe also became the poster child for broken bones. According to his mother's baby book, a series of broken bones and injuries required mom's attention over a five-year period.

1971:	pushed into a pole playing football, concussion
Jan. 1972:	broke left hand playing basketball
June 1972:	broke leg riding bike home from church
June 1972:	got cast off of leg and cut whole on bottom of foot on broken glass
Sept. 1973:	fell off horse and broke arm
Nov. 1975:	broke other leg playing football.

To people who knew young Joe, resiliency prevailed. He was only 5'7 and 150 pounds, but that didn't stop him from playing linebacker on the Notre Dame High School football team. The power of larger school kids forced Ganim to pick himself off the turf. He got up again and again. Quitting wasn't a consideration. He studied political science at the University of Connecticut then graduated from the University of Bridgeport School of Law. He immediately joined his father's law firm and succeeded in building a respectable general practice with a specialty in trial law. Delivering closing remarks to juries and settling domestic disputes paid the bills, but they didn't offer the fledgling politician the kind of motivation to stick to a career in law.

He began making the rounds to introduce himself to Bridgeport's Democratic party leadership. At first, Democratic suspicion kept Ganim from making favor with party insiders. His father, after all, was a Republican. Nevertheless, Joe viewed his Democratic affiliation with opportunity. Republicans were eager to embrace him into their party. They needed new blood. If he could meld relationships within the Democratic party and its stronger voter registration base with his Republican family stature this assuredly could make him a more attractive citywide candidate. But first he needed some seasoning as a campaigner. In 1988, at 28 years old, he challenged incumbent State Representative Lee Samowitz in a Democratic primary. Incumbency during this political period was not a safe haven for elected officials who drew the enmity of voters dissatisfied with the city's bleak financial period

and soaring crime rate. Samowitz, to his credit, successfully reminded voters of the money he brought back to Bridgeport from the state capital to aid their cause. He held on in a close race. Ganim's respectable run, however, attracted consideration from party officials lining up with potential challengers to Democratic Mayor Thomas Bucci in 1989.

Bridgeport's Democratic Party was a splintered mess, what veteran Bridgeport newspaper reporter James Callahan described as "a rats nest of infighting, backstabbing and double dealing." As voters expressed frustration with the state of the city, politicians tripped over each other to find a candidate to run against Bucci. Problem was the anti-vote moving against Bucci was so splintered party regulars were unable to coalesce behind one candidate. Bucci faced opposition within his own party from five candidates, some party insiders, some party outsiders. Leading opponents against Bucci had small, but loyal built-in voter bases such as respected State Representatives Jackie Cocco and Robert Keeley and Bucci's former economic development director Charles Tisdale who was the party nominee in 1983. Joe Ganim joined the fray, running an aggressive anti-incumbent and anti-tax campaign. He finished a surprising third in the six-candidate field.

The beating the courageous Bucci endured from his own party and voter frustration helped to ignite the campaign of Mary Moran who galvanized the anti-incumbent sentiment into her victory as Bridgeport's first woman mayor. Ganim didn't go away. In politics, sometimes you win by losing. His respectable losses to Samowitz and Bucci built prestige with party regulars and voters who wanted a mayor unhampered by the strings of party politicians. The message voters sent with Moran's election resonated with Ganim. He would be respectful of the vote-getting ability of the party faithful, but would not sell his political soul to run the city. In exchange for support, it was traditional for Bridgeport Democratic

First Lady in the making, Hillary Clinton, at right, visited Bridgeport during the Presidential campaign of 1992. She made a special appearance at the YMCA for a forum about issues impacting city youth. She is talking to, at left, Bridgeport Alderman John Stafstrom, City Council President Lisa Parziale and Bridgeport Mayor Joseph P. Ganim. Photo by Patrick Coyne.

candidates to cut their deals with party district leaders. District Leader A cuts a deal for parks director, District Leader B cuts a deal to become economic development director. Ganim wanted to be mayor, but not if party politicians were anchored to his governmental decision making. In addition, he had an easy, disarming style that established experience beyond his years. Self-assured, he felt he could get elected without making promises. Besides, becoming mayor of Bridgeport had become either a nasty tooth ache or a political dead end. At $52,000 a year there were not a lot of takers for the job. The new kid on the block Joe Ganim had become the Democratic candidate for mayor.

During the campaign Ganim kept expectations low. He promised nothing he couldn't deliver. "Voters are tired of the same old empty promises," he would say. "If the city's going to come back we must rise above the politics." If a district leader demanded a job for support, Ganim parroted this standard line, "If I win, we'll take a look at it." The politicians, and others who dealt with Ganim, would come to understand the meaning behind this "Well-take-a-look-it" mantra…translation: "I promise nothing."

The Ganim versus Moran showdown was classic blue collar campaigning. In an attempt to highlight the 32-year-old Ganim's youthful inexperience, Moran took to calling Ganim "Joey." She also tried to convince voters that Ganim's partial upbringing in the bucolic neighboring town of Easton disqualified him from being chief executive of Bridgeport. Ganim reminded voters time and again that Moran was disconnected from the myriad of city issues such as public safety and finances. A flashpoint he cited was Moran's taxpayer purchase of a new Buick Park Avenue sedan during the height of the city's fiscal crisis. When the votes were tallied on election night Ganim emerged with a comfortable 5,000 vote plurality.

The day after his victory celebration the mayor-elect set up an impromptu meeting with Governor Lowell Weicker in the governor's office. The contrast between the two men in both size and personality couldn't have been more dramatic. Weicker was an indomitable, bombastic, brooding personality, towering in stature at 6'6", who had served three terms in United States Senate. Ganim, low-key, non-threatening and calm stood about one foot shorter with no public office experience. Just about one year earlier, Weicker jammed a contentious personal income tax through the Connecticut Legislature to repair the state's sagging bottom line, after proclaiming as a candidate for governor that an income tax would be like "adding fuel to the fire." Weicker drew an intense amount of public heat, but the income tax would prove a savior for state finances. Weicker was particularly appalled by Moran's bankruptcy filing. As a child of the state, Bridgeport's fiscal bleeding had a direct impact on the state's finances and bond rating. Weicker wanted something from Ganim, immediate withdrawal of the bankruptcy. Ganim wanted something from Weicker, dramatic state help to close an evil $18 million budget deficit, a projected $250 million budget deficit by the end of 1997 and a credit rating at junk bond status.

Weicker was joined at the meeting by his budget director William Cibes, who also chaired

the Bridgeport Financial Review Board. After a few obligatory congratulations, Weicker wasted no time.

"I want to know if you're going to withdraw the bankruptcy petition?" he asked Ganim. Exhausted from the campaign and operating on little sleep from the night before, Ganim felt like

The indomitable Lowell Weicker, who served as governor of Connecticut from 1990-94, fought furiously against Bridgeport Mayor Mary Moran's bankruptcy filing, then turned his attention to helping the city when Mayor Joseph Ganim withdrew the petition. Photo courtesy of the Connecticut Post.

he had anchors tied to his eyelids. "It was all I could do to stay awake during the meeting," Ganim recalled. Ganim knew he had a major juggling act ahead of him. He couldn't say no to Weicker's request, Ganim needed the governor's support, but the new mayor also did not want to be easy prey. He couldn't be so cooperative as to let Weicker off the hook.

"Well governor," Ganim replied, " I want to do

what's best for Bridgeport and the state, but you have to realize that I just can't snap my fingers and withdraw the bankruptcy petition, there's a legal process that must be followed. Besides, simply withdrawing the bankruptcy petition doesn't eliminate the big financial hole in the future."

Weicker got Ganim's message...let the negotiating begin. "Okay, if you do your part, I'll do mine," Weicker said. Over the course of the next several months Weicker implemented a series of measures to help the ailing city. Concurrently, Ganim began the process of withdrawing the bankruptcy petition and won Weicker's confidence.

With Weicker's help, Ganim successfully retained major employers such as Chase Manhattan Bank of Connecticut, Southern Connecticut Gas Company and Remington Products; moved vigorously to clean up the disgraceful "Mount Trashmore," a 30-foot high, two-block pile of illegal demolition debris from the East End; found a new home for Housatonic Community Technical College at the site of the vacated Hi-Ho Mall; and secured the State Police master barracks for southern Connecticut, more than 100 troopers relocated from Westport to Downtown Bridgeport. Weicker also had the state purchase Beardsley Park and its zoological gardens from the city for $10 million, providing a much-needed infusion of cash. The state also assumed financial responsibility for several other city functions such as operations of the city train station.

While Weicker did his part, Ganim began the job of repairing Bridgeport's finances, infrastructure and beleaguered image. He was sort of like a swan on the water moving along effortlessly, but underneath paddling like mad. Ganim's office and desk had the appearance of war room intelligence. His desk featured piled high stacks of paperwork of the city's most immediate issues. Bankruptcy. Business Flight. Crime. University of Bridgeport.

Working to hold the budget together, Ganim and his labor negotiator Dennis Murphy convinced municipal unions about the desperation of the city's financial condition and achieved roughly $10 million in concessions. They promised job security in exchange for zero pay increases for upwards of 24 months and unpaid furloughs for two weeks. Leading by example, Ganim also returned two weeks of salary to the city. It was a good deal for both sides. Ganim received breathing room for his budget. The city workers kept their jobs.

Ganim negotiated around the clock, whether with unions or trying to save the University of

One of the hallmarks of Ganim's administration has been the leadership of key department heads. At left, City Treasurer Sharon Lemdon, Ganim's executive aide Janet Finch, Chief Administrative Officer Dennis Murphy, Economic Development Director Michael Freimuth, Finance Director Jerome Baron and Police Chief Hector Torres, the first minority to head the police department. Photo by Kristin Burke, Peter Baker Studios.

Bridgeport from closing. His wife, Jennifer, then his steady, recalled the craziness of the situation from Dec. 31, 1991. The University of Bridgeport was on the verge of collapse. Ganim, an alumnus of the UB Law School and member of the Board of Trustees tried furiously to hold the college together. Jennifer, new to all of this, was by his side at the emergency board meeting on New Year's Eve. "It's New Year's Eve and we're at this meeting," she remembered. "Toward the end of

Bridgeport State Senator Alvin Penn has wielded his considerable influence in Hartford to help fund significant development projects such as Harbor Yard and the adjacent sports arena. Photo by Kathy Weydig

the meeting the trustees began to leave the room to change into tuxedos for the evening's festivities. I thought, so this is what being a mayor is all about."

"Many times during those early days I questioned what I had gotten myself into," explained Ganim, reflecting on facing the city's financial hemorrhaging. "It was constant damage control." Slowly, the city began to inch out of the abyss. The around-the-clock hours of reversing red ink made Ganim's eyes bloodshot. Whatever funds his municipal tourniquet saved went back into beefing up the strength of the police department to fight crime.

Ganim reorganized city departments, hired highly credentialed department heads, found innovative ways to raise revenues without dipping into taxpayers pockets such as selling off delinquent tax liens to a private collection firm, negotiated fair union agreements, transitioned welfare recipients from dependency to self-sufficiency, convinced important city businesses to keep their tax dollars and jobs in the city.

Ganim also managed to attend to quality of life issues such as the city's popular library system which had been plagued by dramatic cutbacks. Ganim found the money to increase library hours at all neighborhood branches.

With the help of Police Chief Thomas Sweeney, Bridgeport's first top cop hired through a national search, walking patrols and police precincts provided increased security. Ganim hired more than 100 police officers which eventually led to the sharpest decline in crime in Bridgeport in 25 years. Championed by Ganim's Public Facilities Director John Marsilio, and Clean & Green Director Patrick Coyne, the city launched an unprecedented citywide street paving and beautification program, demolished hundreds of dilapidated buildings and transformed vacant lots into new parks.

Creative department heads such as Marsilio became one of the hallmarks of Ganim's administration and won credibility with voters and the business community. Dennis Murphy, whom Ganim appointed chief administrative officer,

John "Bucky" Marsilio, Bridgeport's Public Facilities Director, has engineered a dramatic citywide signage and beautification campaign that has turned eyesore property into public parks, demolished hundreds of abandoned buildings, paved streets and planted thousands of trees. Photo by Kathy Weydig

When the strain of the job takes its toll, Mayor Ganim finds comfort in chatting with Bridgeport school kids. Ganim has launched a major school improvement initiative to upgrade buildings, provide afterschool programs, and computers in every classroom. Here he signs autographs for students in Bridgeport's West End in 1998. Photo by Robert Jiminez

Jerome Baron, finance director, Michael Freimuth, economic development director, Robert Kochiss, director of Policy and Management and Mark Anastasi, the city attorney, became the nucleus of a management team that won union concessions, balanced budgets and improved services.

Wall Street took notice. The Manhattan-based municipal bond rating agencies that freaked after the bankruptcy filing, rewarded the city's recovery by upgrading Bridgeport bonds to investment grade.

Newspaper articles and headlines told the story, the city and its people were working their way back.

Hartford Courant:
In Bridgeport, Rebound is real

Waterbury Republican:
Bridgeport Rebounds

New Haven Register:
Bridgeport regains its fiscal health

Connecticut Post:
Ganim rescues Bridgeport from the brink of bankruptcy.

In 1993, voters rewarded Ganim with a walloping 80-percent-of-the-vote victory. In 1994, the ambitious young mayor eyed the governor's office after his ally Lowell Weicker decided against reelection. Ganim won the immediate backing of a Connecticut Post editorial. Despite Ganim's early track record, Connecticut's suspicious Democratic party insiders were not ready to embrace the young mayor. This was not new to Ganim who experienced the same skepticism during his early political life in Bridgeport. Ganim ended up as the running mate to state Comptroller William Curry, the party's nominee for governor, who lost in a close election to Republican John Rowland. President Bill Clinton and First Lady Hillary made a fundraising stop at the Bridgeport Holiday Inn on behalf of the Curry/Ganim ticket in October of 1994.

A major issue of the gubernatorial campaign was the expansion of casino gaming in Connecticut beyond the worldy successful Foxwoods casino in the rural town of Ledyard. Bridgeport's untapped waterfront drew the attention of the highest of the high gaming operatives such as Steve Wynn, Donald Trump and the Mashantucket Pequots, operators of Foxwoods, all of whom proposed upwards of billion dollar gaming establishments. Rowland supported gaming expansion in Bridgeport. Curry was against it. Ganim was in the odd position of agreeing with his running mate's opponent. Bridgeport was in need of an economic shot in the arm. To Ganim, the gaming expansion was about jobs, entertainment and tax dollars into the city.

In a non-binding referendum in March of 1995, city voters overwhelmingly approved a legislative vote on the issue. Both Wynn and the Mashantuckets spent millions lobbying the state legislature for approval while Trump did his part to torpedo the gaming bill, in a move to protect his Atlantic City interests from Connecticut cannibalism. Trump's attitude was supremely capitalistic. "If expanded gaming is going to happen in Bridgeport, I want it," he would say. "If I can't have it, I want to kill it." Trump unleashed his lobbyists to stop anyone else from getting in on the action, especially his arch-enemy Wynn. The two gaming moguls have spent many years devising tactics to blow up one another's gaming proposals.

Robert Zeff, owner of the Bridgeport Jai Alai Fronton, had a particular stake in the gaming legislation. He had secured state approval to transform jai alai into a greyhound track with the hope of installing hundreds of slot machines into his parimutuel facility. Zeff was Wynn's local entree, working to approve the gaming bill as furiously as Trump fought it.

Opponents to the gaming bill had significant legislative support, particularly from lower Fairfield County legislators, who cited traffic congestion, health issues and gambling addictions as reason enough to derail the bill. In the end, the new governor could not convince his own Republican legislative base to support gaming in Bridgeport. Despite an impassioned plea on the senate floor from Bridgeport State Senator Alvin Penn, one of the spearheads of the gaming bill, the state senate voted down the bill. Bridgeporters experienced an ugly gaming hangover.

The setback was like a punch to Ganim's gut and it became clearer waterfront revival would require a non-gaming action plan. The defeat, however, challenged Ganim's will to make something happen on his own watch and not Rowland's. Ganim pushed forward with his formula for economic recovery. Attack crime, balance budgets, cut taxes, improve schools and

The diminutive, but mighty, Democratic Town Chairman Mario Testa presides over a restaurant that is packed with politicos, business suits and a loyal neighborhood following that enjoy flavorful food at affordable prices. Testa has provided a successful bridge between Democratic party faithful and Mayor Ganim. Photo courtesy of Mario Testa.

development will come. Others took notice of the city's recovery and Ganim's accomplishments. In the fall of 1996, Newsweek magazine named Ganim one of the "25 Most Dynamic Mayors in America."

Ganim helped to kick start development. An investment group led by former Bridgeport Hydraulic Company chief executive officer Jack McGregor, his wife Mary Jane Foster and Physicians Health Services founder Mickey Herbert convinced city leaders that minor league

Centered by BB, the Bridgeport Bluefish mascot, husband and wife Jack McGregor and Mary Jane Foster convinced city leaders that sports entertainment would infuse life back into the Park City. Their company, Bridgeport Waterfront Investors, has led a private/public partnership featuring baseball and hockey. Photo by Kathy Weydig

baseball would trigger community pride and an economic jolt like nothing in the city in decades. The location for a baseball stadium that intrigued Ganim and his Economic Development Director Michael Freimuth was the vacant Jenkins Valve building in the South End. Located right off Interstate 95, the five-acre parcel was owned by Donald Trump who purchased the industrial warhorse as a prospective site for a gaming facility. When the gaming bill failed to pass the State Senate, Trump lost interest in transforming the land. He also lost interest in paying roughly $300,000 in property taxes. "The assessment on

When it came to gaming in Bridgeport Donald Trump's mantra was clear: "If it happens I want it, if I can't have it I don't want it to happen." Photo courtesy of the Connecticut Post.

this building is crazy," Trump would say. "I've never seen anything like it." Over the years, Ganim and Trump had developed a friendly relationship. One spring day in 1997, Trump fired off a letter to Ganim griping about the injustice of having to pay an extravagant tax bill for an industrial eyesore. Attaching copies of the tax bills to his letter, Trump explained that he wanted to explore a way to turn the building over to the city for a viable use.

Ganim wasn't about to shed any tears for the Manhattan billionaire, but Trump's lamenting triggered a Ganim idea. With Trump's letter in hand the mayor dialed up The Donald and asked him to sign the deed to the property over to the city. Two polished negotiators were at work. Since he knew Trump wanted out of the building, Ganim felt the city was in a greater negotiating position. If Ganim had initiated the offer, The Donald most assuredly would have asked for a price tag well beyond the cost of the taxes. Ganim got his location for the ballpark and Trump walked away from the building.

Backed by the support of Wall Street bond rating agencies and state assistance, Ganim led construction of a $19 million state-of-the art minor league baseball stadium. City Councilmen

The working relationship between Ganim and leadership on the City Council, Bridgeport's legislative body, has led to balanced budgets, tax cuts and brick and mortar projects. Council President John Fabrizi, third from left, is joined by James Holloway, majority leader, Auden Grogins, president pro tem, and Patrick Crossin, chairman of Budgets and Appropriations. Photo by Kristin Burke, Peter Baker Studios.

Michael Marella, William Finch and Patrick Crossin rallied other City Council members to approve taxpayer dollars to build the stadium. Ganim's prescription for the city was paying off and fish food was just what the doctor ordered. The city and the region got hooked on the Bluefish. The South End ball park became alive with full houses of 5,500 per game. First rate minor league ball, family entertainment and attractions for kids in a safe environment. The city had an answer, finally, to the millennium old question: where is there entertainment value in the inner city for kids and families?

The success of Harbor Yard has inspired plans for a massive sports entertainment complex connecting the southern tip of Downtown to the South End. With funding from the state legislature, the city planned to construct a $40 million, 10,000-seat sports arena that will host roughly 150 events each year including minor league hockey, college basketball and concert attractions. The arena was expected to be completed by the fall of year 2000. Jack McGregor and Mary Jane Foster, building on their Bluefish success, were the spearheads of the arena concept.

Across the Harbor, the Conroy Development

Company, led by Alexius Conroy, is pushing forward with plans for a $1 billion development plan to revive the city's Steel Point waterfront. The design calls for outlet stores, marinas, museums, an IMAX theater, restaurants and high speed ferries in what is undoubtedly the most extensive —and ambitious—waterfront revival project in

This is about as close as Mayor Ganim will get to playing professional baseball, but a photo opportunity in the dugout of Harbor Yard, the house Ganim helped build, isn't a bad alternative. Photo by J.J. Misencik

Bridgeport's history.

Bridgeport is now making steady improvement in the Joe Ganim era, recapturing the promise and progress only the highest of eternal optimists could have imagined. The city still has a lot of work to do to overcome decades of inner city neglect from manufacturing job loss. But where once being mayor of Bridgeport was a total dead end, it is now a position highly credentialed. Ganim's impact on the city is the greatest since Socialist Mayor Jasper McLevy and P.T. Barnum before him. Voters further validated Ganim's popularity in 1998 by approving a charter revision for a four-year term for the office of mayor.

Under Ganim's leadership, the city has balanced every budget, cut taxes four years in a row, implemented the largest capital improvement project in school history, reestablished walking patrols and police precincts and won national awards for beautification projects. Mayors from around the country are looking at Bridgeport as a national model for urban renewal.

Bridgeport is no longer just an Average Joe.

Mayor Joseph Ganim, Bridgeport's Doug Flutie, small quarterback...big plays, flanks a model of Bridgeport's sports and entertainment complex that connects the South End with Downtown. Photo by J. J. Misencik.

Cycling enthusiasts have a long history in Bridgeport. Clubs such as the Rambling Wheelmen rode the streets of Bridgeport in the late 1800s, and the streets and parks are full of bikes today during the spring and summer months. The track at Pleasure Beach was an important stop on the bicycle racing tour, as can be seen by the determined look on this young racer's face. Photo by Seeley and Warnock. Courtesy, Historical Collections, Bridgeport Public Library

CHAPTER XI

Partners in Progress

The beginnings of Bridgeport's industrial community followed typical New England and Yankee patterns. Founded to supply the needs of local residents, the first industrial enterprises were linked to agriculture—gristmills, sawmills, tanneries and shipping. Nevertheless, in the first half of the nineteenth century the stage was set for the city's future as a major New England industrial center.

Factory-made and store-bought products overtook local homespun and handcrafted items. The power of steam was quickly recognized. A multifaceted transportation network, an easily accessible location, and a steadily increasing population gave evidence of the business prominence to come.

Thousands of immigrants came to Bridgeport from many foreign nations, including Ireland, Poland, Italy, Germany, Hungary and Russia. They became the area's work force and then a part of the American Dream. Many of these hardworking newcomers assumed a Yankee spirit and founded businesses that became the bedrock of the city's business community.

Throughout the years Bridgeport's business and industry became resilient to changing economic and social conditions. During the Depression no major industries closed, and all but two banks continued their financial services. And when the demands of World War II came to a sudden halt, the city's industry adjusted by following the chamber recommendations for the changeover from defense to consumer-oriented production. Today Bridgeport has an unusually diversified and flexible economy.

In this tradition of resiliency, Bridgeport now prepares for such future changes as a more service-oriented economy while recognizing the continued importance of high-technology production. Present-day entrepreneurs continue the spirit that kept the city successful over the past 150 years.

Throughout Bridgeport's history, however, the human element has been the guiding force. Individuals with the necessary imagination, foresight and business acumen have helped to uphold the city's position as one of the strongest manufacturing and financial regions in New England. The pages that follow are a tribute to the generations of vision, hard work and dedication.

The organizations whose stories are detailed on the following pages illustrate the variety of ways in which individuals and their businesses have contributed to the area's growth and development, and have made Bridgeport one of Connecticut's largest and most successful communities.

PEOPLE'S BANK

In the early 19th Century when cash began to replace the barter system, people needed a place to save their earnings. Yet, in Connecticut, the only banks in existence were commercial—none of them would accept a small savings account. Bridgeport Savings Bank, predecessor to People's Bank, was chartered in 1842. The first headquarters for the fledgling organization was the store of George and Sherwood Sterling, iron merchants, and Sherwood took the helm as president.

The bank's first deposit, of $30, was made on December 24, 1842 in the name of Helen Moore. Moore later became the nation's first woman lighthouse keeper, tending the Fayerweather Lighthouse off Black Rock Harbor until she was 84 years old.

Deposits in the first week of the bank's business totaled $97. It was four months before a withdrawal was made—for $1. Since its first days, the bank has been a catalyst in the city's success, encouraging savings and providing mortgages for immigrants and factory workers that are the backbone of this blue-collar city. Through the years, the bank's existence has often mirrored Bridgeport's—from the heady days of burgeoning industry in the late 19th Century, through the industrial achievements of the early 20th Century, through the stalwart determination of the Great Depression and the bustling factories during World War II. The bank and the city also saw some difficult days together during the economic and real estate crisis of the late 1980s and early 1990s. Today, as Bridgeport's overall business environment is regaining a measure of its historic potential, and the city's quality of life is improving, People's Bank is growing and thriving.

By the mid-19th Century, Bridgeport was already a bustling business, shipping and commercial center, with one of the best natural harbors on Long Island Sound. With the advent of savings banks, communities could access an enormous amount of capital, which the practice of "hoarding" had kept unproductive. The bank's founding fathers encouraged working men to be thrifty and included in their original goals "the extinction of pauperism and advancement of morals."

Deposit funds were mostly invested in real estate loans. One of the bank's early mortgage customers was Phineas T. Barnum, of circus fame. In 1847, the bank loaned

In 1843, the bank paid $12 a year rent for this second floor room (stars in window) near Water and Wall Streets in Bridgeport.

Barnum and his business partner, William H. Noble, $10,000 for a "model" community of homes, complete with an eight-acre park, on Bridgeport's East Side.

Washington Park stands today as one of Bridgeport's symbols of the remarkable vision of those times.

The bank was committed to helping Bridgeport grow, and had the foresight to recognize the importance of having a railroad terminus in the city. Mortgages totaling $13,750 were provided to the Housatonic Railroad Company in 1847. Soon, for the price of $1, residents were able to take an "iron horse" to New York City.

The latter half of the 19th Century saw the bank and the city undergo enormous periods of growth. Turn-of-the-century records show the bank loaned $6,000 to David M. Read for a department store and $40,000 to the Bridgeport Brass Company.

During World War I, the defense

The towering People's Bank building and the architectural grace of the Barnum Museum symbolize Bridgeport's renewal.

industry made Bridgeport a booming city as 50,000 workers flocked to the munitions factories. The bank responded with a "Save Where You Work" program beginning at Remington Arms in 1917. Bank employees were soon accepting payday deposits at more than 100 plants throughout the greater Bridgeport area.

The United States underwent a turbulent period in the early 1920s. Nationwide, banks were plagued with "panic withdrawals" during a 1921 recession, and 10 years later, the Great Depression hit. The management of Bridgeport Savings Bank helped homeowners through this period by amortizing mortgages, and, in many cases, paying delinquent taxes.

On March 7, 1927, Bridgeport Savings bank and People's Savings Bank merged. The new institution had 30 employees and assets of $33 million. In 1942, People's Savings Bank was the first bank in Connecticut to offer Savings Bank Life Insurance. The post-World War II era led to an explosive growth in home ownership. Bridgeport-People's Savings Bank made the first veteran's insured mortgage loan in the state, and went on to become the largest Veterans (VA) and Federal Housing Administration (FHA) mortgage lender in Connecticut. The mid-point of the 20th Century marked a period of expansion for the bank. In the 1950s and 1960s, families moved to the suburbs, and People's followed

its customers. The first People's branch opened in Stratford in 1953 and two years later, a merger with the century-old Southport Savings Bank provided a presence in the greater Fairfield community.

Savings banking in the late 1960s was still a very specialized field. People's, for instance, offered one type of Savings account, and one mortgage —25 years as a fixed rate. Checking accounts were the exclusive province of commercial banks. After years of lobbying efforts, led by Norwick R.G. Goodspeed, who became president of People's in 1967, savings banks were in 1974 granted limited checking powers— effective 1976. In the same year, People's became the first bank in the nation to offer bill paying by phone. By 1999, a call center that handles more than one million calls each month, had evolved.

Perhaps the most dramatic change for People's came during the 1980s. At the bank's urging, the Connecticut legislature passed ground-breaking, mutual holding company legislation in 1985. Three years later, People's became the first bank in the country to convert from a mutual savings bank to a capital stock institution operating within a mutual holding company structure. This gave the bank the capacity to generate capital to finance growth, and provide customers the opportunity to become stockholders, while preserving the "mutual" culture through majority stock ownership by People's Mutual Holdings. People's worked hard with the state legislature to help create People Mutual Holdings and hoped the concept would be met with support and success. It was.

Over the years, People's has raised the capital that allowed the bank to broaden services, while remaining competitive and independent. When the holding company structure was formed in 1988, People's had approximately $6 billion in assets under manage-ment and 72 branches, serving three counties. In 1999, People's is managing more than $12 billion in assets, has 130 branch offices, and is serving every county in Connecticut. People's Bank has reached several important milestones along the way.

• It has become the state's number one residential mortgage lender*

• People's pioneered 7-day supermarket banking in Connecticut and currently leads the nation in supermarket deposits with four times the average deposits of other banks' supermarket branches open the same length of time.

• People's is one of the top 20 credit card issuers in the country.

People's has also greatly expand-ed the services it offers to its cus-tomers. In particular, it has bolstered its commercial, investment, asset management and insurance capabil-ities. People's is the largest indepen-dent bank in Connecticut offering a full range of services to individual, corporate and municipal customers. People's credit cards are issued nationally and in the United Kingdom. A variety of other services are provided through its subsidiaries, including discount brokerage at People's Securities, Inc.; equipment leasing through People's Capital and Leasing Corp.; asset management by Olson Mobeck & Associates, Inc.; and insurance through R.C. Knox and Company, Inc.

This range of financial services is delivered through traditional and supermarket branches, plus regional commercial and trust offices. Brokerage services, through People's Securities, Inc. are available at more than 20 Personal Investment Centers. People's distribution network also includes a 24-hour telephone banking service, participation in a worldwide ATM network, PC and Internet banking and trading, and interactive video banking.

This growth reflects the bank's long-term vision—to be the premier financial services organization in Connecticut. Remaining true to its commitment has served People's well, especially since the commit-ment included community. And it has served Bridgeport well. People's

Decades of experience and community commitment have marked the contributions of People's chief executive officers, past and present, from left Norwick R.G. Goodspeed, current CEO John A. Klein, David E. A. Carson and Samuel Waller Hawley. Copyright 1999 J.J. Misencik

Bridgeport Center, the 16-story People's Bank headquarters, was designed by world-renowned architect Richard Meier.

executives are dedicated members of local boards and educational institutions in the city, and the bank is actively involved in Bridgeport's very visible development momentum—helping to draw business into the city and even offering the office space to attract new companies. Service. Integrity. Vision. The values laid out in 1842 are part of People's Bank today.

Although the needs of financial services customers in the 21st Century are unchartered, in preparation for the new millennium, People's is adding businesses, exploring new delivery channels and technologies, and acquiring and nurturing expertise. It is also growing—in a framework that is integrated and innovative.

In the words of John A. Klein, who will lead the bank in the next century, "When we focus this organization, there is nothing that we can't accomplish." That's the People's culture—a culture that embodies the entrepreneurial spirit of Bridgeport, its home town.

* Source: The Commercial Record.

HOLIDAY INN OF BRIDGEPORT

On Jan. 11, 1993, in a flag raising ceremony attended by Mayor Joseph P. Ganim and Connecticut Attorney General Richard Blumenthal, the hotel formerly known as the Bridgeport Hilton, opened its doors as the Holiday Inn of Bridgeport, forging a new beginning for affordable family and leisure travel accommodations in the Park City.

Under the leadership of owners Ernest and Christian Trefz, the hotel's management and more than 80 employees are more committed than ever to the success of the new Holiday Inn and its continued integration as an important part of the Greater Bridgeport community.

Located at 1070 Main Street, opposite the Fairfield County Courthouse, the hotel serves as a major focus in the downtown area. An active member of the Bridgeport Regional Business Council, the hotel is a popular meeting place for area business organizations, a luncheon gathering spot for the Downtown business community and the site of many banquets, fundraisers and benefit events.

At conversion, the Holiday Inn underwent updating and refurbishment. Lorraine Scelfo, the hotel's director of sales and marketing, expresses its new appeal: "We wish to make each guest's stay a complete success. That's our hospitality promise - and a promise we keep."

The Priority Club is a big plus for guests. This program enables credits to be earned, in the same way frequent flyer miles are credited by the airlines. Guests redeem these credits for travel and merchandise awards and other benefits at the more than 1,600 Holiday Inns world-wide.

Hotel General Manager William J. McGarry says Holiday Inn was founded on family travel. "Now it offers hotels for family fun. We have a more broad-based appeal now, without sacrificing quality."

With 10,000 square feet of meeting rooms, a 5,000 square foot ballroom, its Parc 1070 Restaurant and Lounge, the hotel provides complete, state-of-the-art facilities for Greater Bridgeport's community needs.

The Holiday Inn of Bridgeport serves as headquarters for the Barnum Festival, and hosts the Festival's Ringmaster's Ball, as well as being headquarters for the city's annual St. Patrick's Day Parade.

Lorraine Scelfo expresses great pride in hosting these annual events. "Each year gets better and better. We treat accounts like family and look forward to having them return."

With a renewed focus on the city's harbor and new economic development initiatives, the Holiday Inn of Bridgeport looks forward to serving as an integral part of Bridgeport's Renaissance.

General Manager William McGarry and Director of Sales and Marketing Lorraine Scelfo offer a variety of hotel facilities and services at the Holiday Inn.

UNITED PROPERTIES

Imagine, in Fairfield, a fully leased shopping center featuring a Super Stop & Shop, banking services and discount stores where a worn-out truck terminal existed.

Imagine, just minutes away, an old hot dog stand and bar trans-formed into a shopping plaza brimming with fine foods, a specialty book shop and popular video store.

Imagine antiquated industrial property redeveloped into a state-of-the-art 12-theater movie complex in the Black Rock section of Bridgeport.

There's not a solid achievement that did not first begin in someone's imagination. Alfred Lenoci Sr. understands this. These development successes were spearheaded by the vision of Lenoci Sr. and the partners he assembled, including brother Michael Schinella and sons Alfred Lenoci Jr. and Paul Lenoci.

Hope makes all things possible. Determination turns hope into achievement. In 1968, the Bridgeport native did not have to look very far in anticipation of the region's changing landscape. Greater Bridgeport was expanding, housing developments were mushrooming and the region needed retail and industrial services to complement the demands of change.

A quarter of a century later, the Fairfield-based United Properties had boosted the quality of life for the residents of Greater Bridgeport, expanded towns' tax rolls, and created thousands of jobs, while being a friend to people in need. Partners Alfred Lenoci Sr. and Michael Schinella, Alfred Lenoci Jr. and Paul Lenoci own and manage more than 2-million-square feet of commercial, retail, industrial and residential properties in New Haven and Fairfield counties.

There are risk takers and there are

The owners and partners of United Properties, from left, Alfred Lenoci Jr., Michael Schinella, Alfred Lenoci Sr. and Paul Lenoci. Copyright J.J. Misencik 1993.

security seekers. Lenoci's intuitive understanding of the real estate market led United Properties to a string of redevelopment successes in the late 70s. It started with the purchase of an old truck terminal at 1206 Kings Highway Cutoff in Fairfield. Within a year the terminal was demolished and redeveloped into a new shopping plaza anchored by Stop & Shop.

Success breeds success. Throughout the 80s, turning vision into value became United's trademark with landmark redevelopment projects including the conversion of Clark Metal factory to Fairfield Corporate Center, the old M & K Pharmaceuticals to Home Depot, Fredricks Restaurant/Catering Hall to Staples Plaza and an old hot dog stand and bar into the new Tunxis Hill Plaza.

Like many developers, United Properties prospered from the opportunities of the 80s, but embraced a conservative approach, concentrating on maintaining a diverse portfolio.

The company was careful to mix investments in the commercial, industrial and office markets. The partners stayed true to the most important piece of United Properties' puzzle of success; its tenants. The impressive list of long standing

lessees ranges from retail giants CVS, Stop & Shop and Staples to companies like Metropolitan Life Insurance and John Hancock, to research and development companies including Voltarc Tube and Merchantile Development.

In 1992, United Properties purchased Fairfield Corporate Center, a 67,000-square-foot office building from the FDIC for $3.2 million. The purchase was among the year's largest area deals and was financed by United Properties itself.

Lenoci Sr. has not lost the vision that began his career. His company continues to bring projects to Fairfield County that coincide with its residents' changing needs. United built the 12-theater movie complex in Black Rock for National Amusements, a $12 million project that created 100 jobs for the struggling construction trades and added millions in property taxes to Bridgeport.

United is also responsible for bringing Home Depot, Super Stop & Shop and Bob's Discount Furniture to Bridgeport. The projects are signature United Properties— creating jobs, expanding a town's tax base, maintaining neighborhood character and rallying community support.

BRIDGEPORT REGIONAL BUSINESS COUNCIL

Bridgeport has undergone numerous changes in its 157-year history. It has been a Yankee farming community, a seaport and railway center, a financial center, and the arms and munitions leader of the country during wartime. Bridgeport has been one of Connecticut's smallest towns and now is the state's largest city.

That is not all. Mirroring changes in the rest of the nation and the world, Bridgeport has experienced the growth of technology, which has brought about new ideas in health care, banking, communication, education -- revolutionizing virtually every aspect of "doing business."

Paul Timpanelli, president of The Bridgeport Regional Business Council

Throughout most of those changes -- more than 100 years of them, anyway -- The Bridgeport Regional Business Council and its founding agencies have served the needs of the Bridgeport business community.

Beginning in 1874 with the founding of The Board of Trade, The Business Council's history has been to focus its greatest energy on helping its city prosper. Business is the single greatest determinant of a community's future. No other force begins to approach the ability of the private business sector to accomplish economic prosperity and social good. Business generates a vast array of resources that include, not only the funding to underwrite programs, but the personal talent, the systems, the facilities, the productivity, the goals, the energy and the vision to get them done.

With that philosophy in mind, in 1986, The Bridgeport Regional Business Council was founded. As its predecessors -- The Bridgeport Chamber of Commerce, The Bridgeport Area Chamber of Commerce, The Bridgeport/Industry Council, The Board of Trade -- have done in past years, The Business Council's agenda for the 1990s includes an emphasis on attracting and retaining business to Bridgeport; a program for maximizing the city's potential as an international harbor; creation of a regional economic development commission that will address the business development, transportation and planning needs of the Bridgeport region.

Supporting these goals is the membership, 1,300 individual companies strong, of The Business Council. Those members include the very same manufacturing, construction, banking, service, retail and professional entities that gave

birth to a city and a region rich in resources, diversity and most of all: possibilities.

Programs of The Bridgeport Regional Business Council include meetings, workshops, networking, government relations activity and other traditional chamber of commerce functions such as providing newcomer/new business/travel information. The Business Council's affiliate organizations extend the parent organization's reach into the city's suburban business neighbors (through the Stratford and Trumbull chambers of commerce) and into the city's own small business community through The Bridgeport Chamber of Commerce. The Bridgeport Regional Business Council also works directly with the city to attract state and federal economic development funding and to design a vision for the future.

The Downtown Special Services District and Bridgeport Economic Development Corporation both are administered by Regional Business Council staff.

Few observers would dispute the opinion that Bridgeport stands at the threshold of an era with enormous potential for long-term progress and prosperity. It is, therefore, the mission of The Bridgeport Regional Business Council to maximize that potential.

ALLOY ENGINEERING COMPANY, INC.

"There's no other country but the United States where you can come in as an immigrant and build your own successful company." These are the words of Emmy Nowak, president and chief executive officer of Alloy Engineering Company, Inc. And she speaks from experience.

Hamburg, Germany, was Emmy's home until she was three years old. At that time she and her parents, Erwin and Elfriede Muller Stamm, immigrated to the "land of opportunity," settling in the east end of Bridgeport.

In time, all three members of the Stamm family were employed: Erwin as a tool and die maker earning eighty-eight dollars a month; Elfriede, washing clothes and cleaning homes; and Emmy, at fourteen years of age, waitressing at a Broad Street bakery.

However, nursing was Emmy's first actual occupation. Following graduation from Stratford High School, she received her R.N. from Bridgeport Hospital School of Nursing and became an assistant head nurse in the delivery room. She married Joseph E. Gorgens, who later became an engineer with a local manufacturing firm. She left nursing in 1956, but the role of housewife just didn't suit Emmy. "It doesn't offer enough of a challenge," Emmy recalls telling her husband. In response, he came up with an idea that changed Emmy's life. He suggested that they manufacture thermowells, because no one then, or now for that matter, specialized in producing this metal housing for temperature-sensing elements.

In 1958 the plan was put into action. Emmy would run the new business while her husband continued to work as an engineer. A $20,000 mortgage on their home enabled the couple to purchase surplus equipment dating from the 1940s. And the funds for a 7,000-square-foot brick building on Seaview Avenue came from Emmy's father. The industry was all new to Emmy, and she had a lot to learn; she now had her challenge.

After her marriage ended in divorce in 1961, Emmy decided to continue on her own. "My distributors and customers gave me the needed encouragement, and my employees, the necessary dedication," she recalls proudly.

The employees also helped Emmy when a fire in 1968 did $150,000 worth of damage to the plant. "The employees all said they would continue to work for nothing until we got things in order," she says. Instead, Emmy paid them minimum wage for a few weeks, giving her employees back pay a few months later.

Since then, Alloy Engineering has expanded into a 28,000-square-foot manufacturing plant, with the most recent addition being a 3,000-square-foot employee cafeteria and meeting hall. The firm has the latest equipment including automated systems. Gross sales of over four million dollars were reached in 1985—a broad jump from the $70,000 figure in 1958. Thermowells are sold to original-equipment manufacturers throughout the United States and Canada, with representatives also located in Europe.

Emmy Nowak, president of Alloy Engineering, enters her 28,000-square-foot manufacturing plant.

In 1966 Emmy married Bernard Joseph Nowak, who acts as purchasing agent and secretary of Alloy Engineering Company, Inc. Emmy's son, Richard Gorgens, has followed his mother's lead and has started his own company, Alloy Computer Products, in Massachusetts.

In 1982 Emmy Nowak was named a recipient of the YWCA of Greater Bridgeport's Salute to Women Award for her business acumen and community leadership—an honor she rightly deserves for meeting the challenges of the business world head on.

Emmy Nowak inspects the processing of thermowells.

WILLINGER, SHEPRO, TOWER & BUCCI

There are three kinds of people: those who watch things happen, those who ask what happened and those who make things happen, like the attorneys in the Bridgeport law firm Willinger, Shepro, Tower & Bucci.

Five partners and three associates bring a diverse and wide range of experience and knowledge to this team of professionals. Whether institutional or individual, each client receives the seasoned attention of a primary attorney while the firm works as a cohesive unit toward the single goal of client satisfaction.

"We embrace a team-quality approach in an increasingly complex legal system," said partner Charles J. Willinger Jr. "Our clients rely on us because we rely on the efforts of a team of professionals who know their way around and take pride in putting the client first."

The firm, which practices law throughout the state of Connecticut, specializes in the areas of commercial and residential real estate development on behalf of institutional and private clients, the negotiation and closing of secured and unsecured transactions, financing, bankruptcy, land use, landlord/tenant matters, leasing, foreclosures, loan workouts and collections for institutional clients and all phases of civil litigation including trials in all state and federal courts.

Clients include People's Bank, Dime Savings Bank of New York, Gateway Bank, UST Bank/Corporation, as well as many other thrift and lending institutions in the areas of commercial and residential loan transactions, loan workouts, foreclosures and associated litigation. The firm also has an active civil trial practice concentrating in the prosecution and defense of all types of commercial litigation and appellate cases.

Charles J. Willinger Jr. was born in Bridgeport and graduated from Fairfield University and the University of Miami where he received his law degree. A respected specialist in land use, his areas of concentration include real estate, financing transactions, loan restructures and corporate law, and appearances before all state and local land use regulatory boards including planning and zoning commissions, coastal area management, inland wetland agencies, Department of Environmental Protection and Department of Transportation.

Daniel Shepro received his law degree from Boston University and has served as a Superior Court trial referee since 1988. A member of the Connecticut and American Bar associations, Connecticut Trial Lawyers Association and the American Trial Lawyers Association, his expertise includes trials and appeals in all courts, loan restructures, bankruptcy, creditor's rights and corporate law.

Stephen E. Tower, born in Bridgeport, earned his law degree from Columbia University. A member of the Board of Tax Review for the Town of Fairfield, his specialties include real estate, foreclosures, mortgages, loan restructures, bankruptcy, creditor's rights, financing transactions and corporate law.

Thomas W. Bucci, who served as mayor of Bridgeport from 1985-89, received his law degree from the University of Connecticut. His area of expertise includes trial and appellate practice in all courts, loan restructures, bankruptcy, creditor's rights, corporate law and labor law. He has successfully appeared before the U.S. Supreme Court.

Anne Marie Kent was born in Bridgeport and graduated from the Bridgeport School of Law. Recipient of the Outstanding Legal Scholarship Award in 1981, her expertise centers on land use planning, including representation before state and municipal agencies and regulatory boards, commercial litigation and appeals and appearances before state and federal trial and appellate courts.

Associates Russell D. Liskov, Hyla F. Crane and Bradd Robbins concentrate on trials and appeals in all courts, loan restructures, bankruptcy, creditor's rights, family law, real estate transactions, development and leasing, foreclosures and related litigation, real estate development, commercial lending, leasing and related transactions.

The firm is approved closing attorneys for: Chicago Title Insurance Company; Security Title Insurance Company; Lawyers Title Insurance Corp; First American Title Insurance Company; Stewart Title Guaranty Company; and the vast majority of Fairfield and New Haven County lending institutions.

At Willinger, Shepro, Tower & Bucci, each client can be confident of representation by not only the best and the brightest -- but the best of the brightest.

From atop the People's Bank building overlooking Long Island Sound, from left, law partners Anne Marie Kent, Charles J. Willinger Jr., Thomas W. Bucci, Stephen E. Tower and Daniel Shepro. Photo by Wayne Ratzenberger.

KASPER GROUP

In 1920, 18-year-old Bridgeporter Joseph T. Kasper, Sr. was already active in the fields of surveying and engineering. He decided to take the next logical step -- starting his own business. He saw Bridgeport's potential as well as a need in the private sector for an engineering and surveying firm.

Kasper's faith was rewarded. There were many improvements and much progress to be made in Bridgeport, and the firm grew along with the city. Kasper Group, Inc. has grown into a full-service, multi-disciplined firm with a staff of 60, offering engineering, landscaping architecture and surveying services to public and private clients throughout Connecticut, New York and New Jersey.

The main office on Fairfield Avenue is supplemented by locations in Bethel and Wethersfield, Connecticut. The services of Kasper Group, Inc. under its separate divisions, landscape architecture, transportation, surveying, mechanical and electrical, civil/structural, environmental, and construction management, are many and cover a broad spectrum.

Services include designs for major corporations, renovations to private and public buildings and bridges, site-improvement design, design for electrical and mechanical systems, master and site planning for private and public use, and designs for highway and transportation facilities.

Kasper Group's project list is just as impressive. In Bridgeport alone, projects include a civic center study, urban-renewal projects, the Ox Brook flood-control project, the East Side Elementary School, YWCA and YMCA renovations, coastal plan for Bridgeport, renovation of the municipal parking garage and bus terminal, upgrading of the East Side and West Side wastewater treatment plants and Waterfront Park on the Pequonnock River.

The firm has also designed the

Gateway to the Sound project, which includes esplanade improvements such as general landscaping, signage, and intersection renovations on Park Avenue from Fairfield Avenue to Long Island Sound. The firm recently completed the new Aquaculture Technical School in Black Rock and is now working with the Bridgeport Housing Authority on the renovations of P.T. Barnum Apartments and with Sacred Heart University on its campus Master Plan.

Much of the firm's growth in the past several decades is due to Joseph T. Kasper, Jr., who joined his father in 1952 after graduating from Michigan State University. He became president in 1976. Active in many civic and cultural programs in Greater Bridgeport, Kasper served as Barnum Festival Ringmaster in 1989.

Two Kasper Group projects: at left the Aquaculture Technical School and above renovations to P.T. Barnum Apartments.

ST. VINCENT'S MEDICAL CENTER

Most people know St. Vincent's today as the modern 391-bed Medical Center, while others may also remember the original hospital with its familiar cupola and the reassuring presence of the Daughters of Charity.

Yet St. Vincent's is also St. Vincent's Health Services, a diversified healthcare organization restructured in 1987 to provide medical and health-related services.The transition from hospital to medical center to health service system reflects the growth and change in society and healthcare needs. But it has also challenged traditional notions of a community hospital.

What is the role of a community hospital as it tries to bridge the gap between rich and poor, suburb and city, primary care and high tech medicine?

St. Vincent's moved toward an answer at the end of the 1980s by creating a "Mission Focus" and Mission Committee under the direction of Mary Patricia Finneran, Chairman of the Board of Directors. The effort began with the writing of a mission statement and the process of mission orientation for all employees.

The goal was to define and reaffirm the mission in a new era. The task brought many employees a history lesson dating back to the 17th century when St. Vincent DePaul began the work of the Daughters of Charity. But mission effectiveness was much more than an exercise in looking back on the historic care for the poor, it also required looking ahead and sharing a vision for the year 2001 as a member of the Daughters of Charity National Health System, the nation's largest private not for profit hospital system.

A deeper commitment to the community would inevitably fol-

On September 28, 1917, Corbit Studio caught these St. Vincent's physicians (in white) and the proud St. Vincent's Hospital Ambulance driver Aubrey E. Burlison in front of Bridgeport High School (now City Hall). It was customary for physicians to ride in ambulances during that era. The city's very first motor-driven ambulance was a Locomobile, made in Bridgeport.

low the process of redefining mission. The challenge of reaching out to the poor and medically under-served was renewed as the number of poor, homeless, and uninsured in the Bridgeport area grew.

In keeping with this mission awareness, St. Vincent's has expanded its outreach to the community with initiatives such as the "Hollow" Neighborhood Health Center, the Merton House Clinic, the Kolbe-Cathedral High School Teen Health Center, the Parish Nurse Program, the Special Needs Center and other collaborative efforts in the community beginning in the middle of the 1980s.

St. Vincent's Hospital became a reality in 1903 because of the vision of a Bridgeport Catholic

priest, the encouragement of local physicians and the commitment of the Daughters of Charity of St. Vincent DePaul, the largest order of religious women in the world. The three-floor hospital consisted of seventy-five beds and was staffed by twenty-four doctors. In addition, a School of Nursing was opened, beginning the institution's long-standing commitment to education.

Over the next three decades extensive additions were made to accommodate the consistently growing number of patients. At the same time, with the help of modern diagnostic and medical equipment, physicians successfully completed a number of life-saving surgeries, impossible only a few years earlier. Most hospitals add wings or floors as they grow. Instead, in 1976 St. Vincent's built a new, 440,000-square-foot building behind its original facility. This ten-story medical center accommodates 400 beds and a space age matrix of technology. The new facility's name was changed to St. Vincent's Medical Center in order to reflect the comprehensive services available to patients.In the years that followed St. Vincent's became one of the first hospitals in the state to utilize full-body CT scanning and also to develop a department of diagnostic radiology.

It also became the regional open-heart center for Fairfield County. And, utilizing a tripartite approach of radiation therapy, surgery and oncology (the area's first cancer unit), physicians were able to do more than ever to help cancer patients. In the 1980s, Short Stay Center accounted for over 40 percent of all surgeries performed at St. Vincent's. Expanded programs in cardiology, physical therapy and neurosciences were typical of growth experienced in the early 1980s.

New additions include a renovated Emergency Department and Psychiatric Day Treatment Center. By the end of the 1980s, St Vincent's had also established a roof-top heliport for air-ambulance service, opened a $1.5 million Cardiac Catheterization Laboratory and installed Magnetic Resonance Imaging (MRI), contributing to its growing reputation as a diagnostic and treatment center. The sophisticated technology and excellence of its physicians have also brought St. Vincent's closer to the cutting edge of medicine through participation in national research projects.

Today, St. Vincent's is affiliated with New York Medical College and the Yale University School of Medicine for teaching programs in surgery, internal medicine and other disciplines. Annually over sixty physicians in residency and fellowship programs are trained in numerous subspecialty fields at St. Vincent's, one of the 300 major affiliated teaching hospitals in the United States.

The institution also provides training for radiology technicians, as well as programs in medical, respiratory and ultrasound technology and nuclear medicine.

In 1992, the School of Nursing graduated its last nursing class and was officially accredited as the St. Vincent's College of Nursing, making St. Vincent's a place of higher learning.

The St. Vincent's of today retains its vital link with the past, yet it has emerged as a major cardiac and cancer care center, and a partner with the community to bring quality care and preventive services to the region.

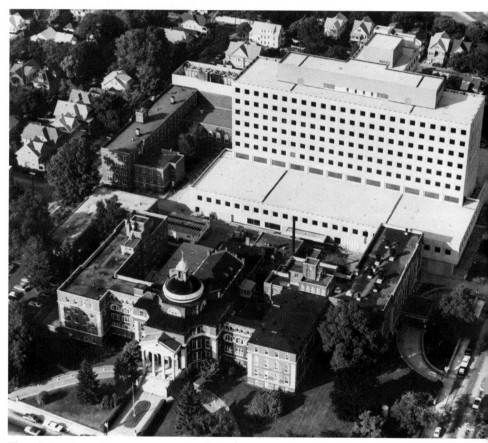

Though St. Vincent's occupies the same "Hawley Farm" site of its founding, the historic domed Hospital of 1903 has been replaced by the 10-level St. Vincent's Medical Center opened in 1976. In 1987, St. Vincent's changed again, but this time the transition was to a new organizational structure, St. Vincent's Health Services. The reorganization created a full service health care organization including the Medical Center, Immediate Care facilities, a College of Nursing, the Special Needs Center and other health-related programs.

Patrons

The following companies have made a valuable commitment to the quality of this publication. Harbor Communications gratefully acknowledges their participation in *Only In Bridgeport 2000: An Illustrated History of the Park City—*

Bridgeport Regional Business Council
People's Bank
Bridgeport Holiday Inn
United Properties
Alloy Engineering
Willinger, Shepro, Tower & Bucci
Kasper Group
St. Vincent's Medical Center

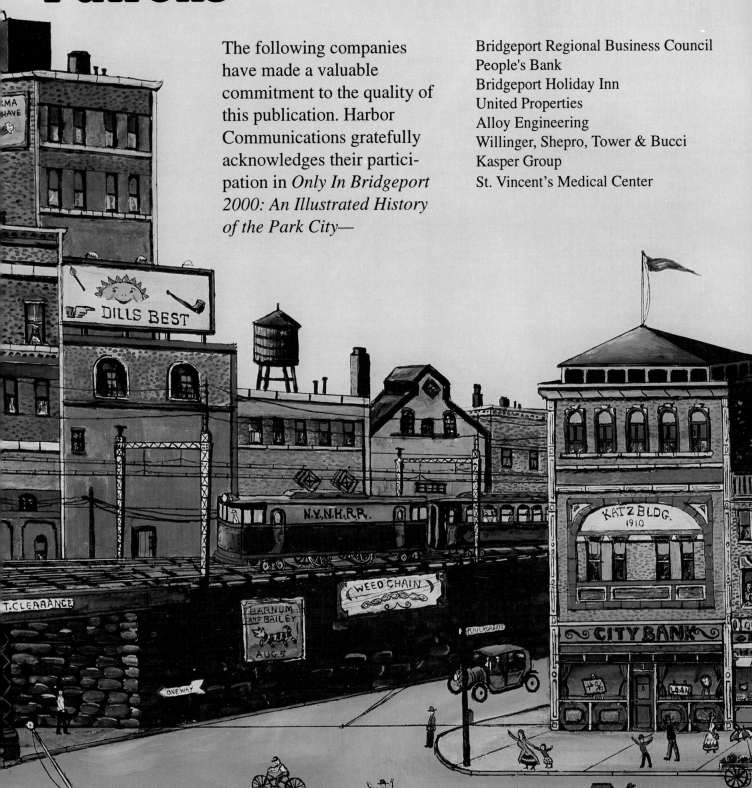

ISBN 0-89781-169-0

Bibliography

Barnum, Phineas T. *Struggles and Triumphs; or Forty Years' Recollections of P.T. Barnum.* Hartford: J.B. Burr, 1869.

Brilvitch, Charles W. *Landmark Architecture of Bridgeport, Connecticut: One Hundred Fifty Buildings Illustrating the Architectural Development of the City, 1663-1902.* Bridgeport: 1975. Typescript.

Brilvitch, Charles W. *Washington Park: A Guide to its Victorian Treasures.* Bridgeport: Upper East Side Neighborhood Housing Services, 1980.

Chance Vought Aircraft Corporation. *Wings for the Navy: A History of Chance Vought Aircraft.* Stratford, Connecticut: 1943.

Collier, Christopher. *The Pride of Bridgeport: Men and Machines in the Nineteenth Century.* Bridgeport: The Museum of Art, Science and Industry, 1979.

Connecticut National Bank. *Bridgeport's First Bank: The Story of Connecticut National Bank, 1806-1956.* Bridgeport: 1956.

Crispino, James A. *The Assimilation of Ethnic Groups: the Italian Case.* Staten Island, New York: Center for Migration Studies, 1980.

Curtiss, Lucy S. *Two Hundred Fifty Years: The Story of the United Congregational Church of Bridgeport, 1695-1945.* Bridgeport: 1945.

Danenberg, Elsie Nicholas. *The Story of Bridgeport.* Bridgeport: Bridgeport Centennial, 1936.

Desmond, Alice Curtis. *Barnum Presents General Tom Thumb.* New York: Macmillan, 1954.

Golovin, Anne Castrodale. *Bridgeport's Gothic Ornament: The Harral-Wheeler House.* Washington: Smithsonian Institution Press, 1972.

Guillette, Mary E. *American Indians in Connecticut, Past to Present. A Report Prepared for the Connecticut Indian Affairs Council.* Hartford: Connecticut Department of Environmental Protection, 1979.

Harris, Neil. *Humbug: The Art of P.T. Barnum.* Boston: Little, Brown, 1973.

Howell, Richard. *Tales from Bohemia Land.* Bridgeport: Bridgeport Herald Publishers, 1928.

Janick, Herbert F., Jr. *A Diverse People: Connecticut, 1914 to the Present.* Chester, Connecticut: Pequot Press, 1975.

Jones, Dick, ed. *Black Rock: a Bicentennial Picture Book: a Visual History of the Old Seaport of Bridgeport, Connecticut, 1644 to 1976.* Bridgeport: Black Rock Civic and Business Men's Club, 1976.

Koenig, Samuel. *Immigrant Settlements in Connecticut.* Hartford, Connecticut: Connecticut State Department of Education, 1938.

Municipal Register of the City of Bridgeport, Connecticut. Bridgeport: Controller, 1873-1961.

O'Dwyer, William J., and Randolph, Stella. *History by Contract: the Beginning of Motorized Aviation, August 14, 1901, Gustave Whitehead. Fairfield, Connecticut.* Leutershausen, West Germany: Fritz Majer and Son, 1978.

Olmstead, Alan. *Olmstead Papers on Jasper McLevy.* 1944. Historical Collections, Bridgeport Public Library.

Orcutt, Samuel. *The History of the Old Town of Stratford and the City of Bridgeport, Connecticut.* New Haven: Tuttle, Morehouse and Taylor, 1886.

Palmquist, David W. *Bridgeport: A Pictorial History.* Virginia Beach: The Donning Company, 1981. Revised edition, 1985.

Pearce, Arthur W. *The Future Out of the Past: An Illustrated History of the Warner Brothers Company on its 90th Anniversary.* Bridgeport: 1964.

Saxon, A.H. *Selected Letters of P.T. Barnum.* New York: Columbia University Press, 1983.

Stave, Bruce M. "The Great Depression and Urban Political Continuity: Bridgeport Chooses Socialism." In *Socialism and the Cities,* edited by Bruce M. Stave, pp. 157-183. Port Washington, New York: Kennikat Press, 1975.

Waldo, George C., ed. *History of Bridgeport and Vicinity.* New York: S.J. Clarke, 1917.

Others sources include numerous interviews and newspaper and magazine clippings, newspaper microfilm, maps, atlases, Bridgeport municipal records, pamphlets, and other materials available in the Historical Collections of the Bridgeport Public Library.

Index